The Torch Is Passed

The TORCH IS PASSED

The Kennedy Brothers & American Liberalism

by David Burner &
Thomas R. West

c.1

Atheneum · New York · 1984

Library of Congress Cataloging in
Publication Data

Burner, David,
  The torch is passed.

  Includes bibliographical references and
index.
    1. Kennedy, John F. (John Fitzgerald),
1917–1963.   2. Kennedy, Robert F.,
1925–1968.   3. Kennedy, Edward Moore,
1932–   .   4. Liberalism—United
States—History—20th century.   5. United
States—Politics and government—
1945–   .   I. West, Thomas R.
(Thomas Reed), 1936–   .   II. Title.
E842.1.B87   1984   973.922′092′2
83-45506
ISBN 0-689-11438-9

*Copyright © 1984 by David Burner
and Thomas R. West
All rights reserved
Published simultaneously in Canada by
McClelland and Stewart Ltd.
Composition by Yankee Typesetters, Inc.,
Concord, New Hampshire
Printed and bound by Fairfield Graphics,
Fairfield, Pennsylvania
Designed by Mary Ahern
First Edition*

To
Robert T. London, M.D.

ACKNOWLEDGMENTS

THIS BOOK IS BASED ON THE JOHN F. KENNEDY PRESIDENTIAL ARCHIVES (including the hundreds of manuscript pages of White House tapes opened in 1983) and several dozen manuscript collections elsewhere, along with the vast secondary material on the Kennedys. But it is not primarily a scholarly study. It is intended to recall a recent political period, to reflect on it, to suggest what among the ideas of the period may be useful today. In an epilogue Thomas R. West considers some of the strengths and shortcomings of midcentury and more recent liberalism. The rest of the book is a critical history of the Kennedy era by David Burner and was given final form by the two authors as they debated the meaning of recent liberalism.

The authors wish jointly to acknowledge the very helpful criticisms of Robert Marcus and William Leuchtenburg, the first-rate editing of Susan Leon of Atheneum and the generous reading of Tom Stewart of that firm, early criticisms and encouragement from Donna Martin, and aid from these members of the Kennedy administration: McGeorge Bundy, Dean Rusk, and Arthur Schlesinger, Jr. For criticisms received David Burner would like to thank Jack Barnard, Michael Barnhart, Robin Berger, Robert Burner, Sandra Burner, Neil Cowan, Mark Hessler, Janice Litwin, Jim Moore (for particular help on the Edward Kennedy chapter), Pat Palermo, and many able students and librarians. Many thanks from Mr. Burner also to the efficient and patient staffs of the acquisitions and circulation departments of the SUNY at Stony Brook library, to all of the Stony Brook history department support staff, and to archivists at the John F. Kennedy Presidential Library, including William Johnson, William Moss, and particularly Ron Whelan. Tom West wishes to thank his colleagues Max Bloomfield, Thomas Henderson, Nelson Lichtenstein, Jon Wakelyn, and John Zeender; for continuing help, Jim Mooney; for particular suggestions, David Field; and for criticisms, Wesley DeMarco, Lowell Dyson, Eileen Guerrin, Patricia Guerrin, Nancy Joyce, Monica Kennedy, Stephanie Laughlin, Thomas Lavrakas, Ron Pagnucco, and Frank Wilhoit.

David Burner
St. James, New York

CONTENTS

The Torch Is Passed

The Torch Is Passed

1

Introduction: The Kennedy Public

THE EARLIEST STUDIES OF JOHN KENNEDY WERE A MEMORIAL TO him. Liberals came to believe that they had found their President. The fascination with Kennedy has continued, and not alone among liberals but within a public that in the twentieth November after his assassination watched docudrama after documentary about the mourned leader's career. But meanwhile had come the Vietnam years and, along with them and perhaps apart from them, an embarrassment at all the uncritical adulation and the entrancement by the Kennedy rhetoric. President Kennedy had never been a liberal, critics said; he had been drawn to the romance of war; he as much as any other President had ensnared us in Vietnam; he had celebrated energy and action for their own dangerous sake. Another story about John Kennedy and his brothers can be related without repentance. It tells of the progression of the Kennedy brothers from the shrewd conservatism of their upbringing to a liberal politics. And it analyzes the intellectual fracturing of the liberalism that came to power with them, as its premises spawned their own contradictions.

In addition to being a political family contributing to mainline politics and indirectly to more radical movements of the

3

sixties, the Kennedys have been an American family, like other Americans unaccustomed to clear ideology or to fundamental questions about economic arrangements or social customs. The upbringing that the elder Joseph Kennedy provided, a schooling in the values of wealth and competition, could have placed John, Robert, and Edward, along with their elder brother Joseph, Jr., within the right wing of American politics. But John, beginning his career as a congressman of no definable persuasion, ended as an ally of the civil rights movement and as a catalyst to a political and cultural left he would not have understood. Robert's angry moral energies, once committed to Joseph McCarthy's Communist-hunting subcommittee and then to the pursuit of labor racketeering, later battled for social and economic progressivism and peace. Edward has been for many years a leader among liberal Democrats. There is not in this the logic of a political philosophy that becomes transformed as it elaborates its first implications. The logic is rather of circumstances: the circumstances, for example, that connected John Kennedy in his presidential years with liberal academicians. Explaining the development of the Kennedy politics, therefore, requires as much biographical and political detail as critical analysis, and the second chapter of this book will be a selective narrative of the family and of John's prepresidential career.

While the Kennedys were increasingly identifying themselves with liberalism, liberals themselves were going through a vigorous but agonized development. They found a moment of aspiration in the early sixties and then split into disputing liberal and radical camps. Cold war liberalism confronted the antiwar movement; welfare-state policies faced an attack on the central state from the left; technocratic liberalism encountered in the civil rights activists and then in the peace demonstrators a politics of immediacy and moral witness. In this moral dialectic Americans were for a time more articulate and argumentative about fundamental questions than is common in this country.

There is, of course, no abstract "liberalism" any more than there is an abstract "nation" or "virtue." Liberalism has always existed in the particular words and acts of its practitioners. The story of the Kennedys and of the politics that surged around them illuminates the contradictions within recent liberalism, contradictions that give energy to the politics they also confuse. The fortunes of the Kennedys illustrate more about recent times than does, for instance, the career of an impeccably liberal Hubert Humphrey. In his youth Humphrey had made his commitment to Democratic party progressivism. He lived his commitment with such simple loyalty that few of the instabilities within American liberalism revealed themselves in his politics until well into the Vietnam years, when his faithful adherence to the anti-Communist militancy of an earlier liberalism brought him up against the antiwar movement. But the Kennedys contributed to the political ferment: John through his image, Robert through a measurable shift in his convictions, and Edward through his service in sustaining into another era the Kennedy liberalism that emerged. Attending the story of the Kennedys themselves and their political career, therefore, will be a continuing analysis of the larger political and cultural disputes of their era, especially those that reflect on the unresolved intellectual quandaries of twentieth-century American liberalism.

The word "liberalism" stretches very far. Classically designating nothing more specific than the range of modern political movements that have favored constitutions, parliaments, and intellectual pluralism, the word has also referred more particularly both to the harsh rationalist free-market economic doctrines of the early nineteenth century and to the welfare measures that in this country now soften the effect of the market on institutions. Here liberalism will mean about what American newspapers and politicians have meant by it for half a century: the politics of the welfare state combined with a Wilsonian sense of mission abroad and a sponsorship of civil rights and liberties at home. That definition in itself pulls the word almost to the breaking point. In the United States the near absence at midcentury of any socialist movement that would clearly define liberalism as a centrist ideology has allowed the term to reach still farther, to signify virtually anything to the left of what is somewhat inadequately called conservatism. So liberals, having no democratic socialism to differ with and viewed by the American right virtually as creatures of Moscow anyway, included in their ranks some people who in the sixties were prepared to move truly to the left, denouncing liberalism as half-hearted or as reaction in disguise. Others continued to call themselves liberals while seeking a more advanced welfare state or a dismantling of American cold war institutions. The terminology is difficult, and this book will be using "liberal," "left," and the frankly evaluative "progressive" as carefully as possible.

A similar care is intended here in employing the labels "conservative" and "right." In this country the terms are sometimes interchangeable. But in tone they conflict. Conservatism connotes a loyalty to the past and a solicitous respect for whatever is most workable or most unjustly endangered in the present. President Dwight Eisenhower manifested this during the 1950s in his refusal to be rushed into an expansion of the military. A leftist or a revolutionary, and certainly a liberal, can have a conservative's loyalties and a conservative's affection for a national or cultural heritage. The term "the right" carries no such connotations. It does not even necessarily suggest a regard for the past or a distaste for change; it connotes hostility, defense of privilege (including the privileges of a racial or an ethnic majority), an impulse to exclude the outsider and crush political opponents. We may at times in this book refer to certain spokesmen for the right as conservatives; we shall try to avoid the mistake of labeling all conservatives as rightists.

The cold war clarified during the Truman and Eisenhower years the distinctions of ideology and temperament between liberals and conservatives and more particularly between liberals and the right. The cold war put to Americans fundamental questions of how the nation was collectively to think, to feel, to behave as it encountered a world of unprecedented dangers and demands. For some years the debate on foreign policy even embraced the vocabulary of the argument over the welfare state. Liberals defended programs of foreign aid that the right dismissed as a surrender of American wealth comparable to its redistribution at home, and they sought diplomatic and military engagements against communism that politicians to the right considered one more manifestation of the liberal compulsion to solve everybody's problems.

From the early years of the confrontation between the victorious Allies of World War II, cold warriors such as George F. Kennan and Secretary of State Dean Acheson proposed major commitments of American will and resources abroad. For a time many on the right favored isolation from the troubles of Europe. Then before long they were demanding a fiercer engagement with the Communists than the Truman administration was prepared for. What sustained anticommunism of this sort were the visceral satisfactions of Redbaiting or dreaming about putting the Communists to sudden flight, as by an attack on China during the Korean War. Liberals generally preferred self-restraint and the measured strategies of containment. Their idea of policy had an exact expression in one of their earliest triumphs: the Berlin airlift of 1948–49, precisely centered between extremes of retreat and military overreaction, as skilled in its technical accomplishment by air and ground crews as in its administrative direction. Liberals implicitly asked the whole nation to conduct itself in that steady way in the face of first the conventional and then the nuclear stalemate. This could put a strain on the American temperament. The hinterland, the sociologist David Riesman once admonished the Kennedy people, is too emotional to tolerate the limited operations that elitists contemplate. Riesman was probably underestimating the hinterland, but right-wingers, at any rate, had for years offered it instant gratification. Against this background of debate, Kennedy seemed the very image of the cold warrior technician intelligence, and the test ban treaty appeared the perfection of liberal good sense, as the response to the Berlin and missile crises of his presidency appeared the perfection of liberal resolve.

The vindication of cold war liberalism was short-lived, for that liberalism carried a latent instability. In arguing their case against the impatient right, Kennedy liberals had become increasingly committed to a logic that denied the presence of a monolithic international communism and broke the world into its multiplicity of regions, cultures, political arrangements, and local needs. That brought into question the whole point of a cold war that from its inception had posited a fairly well unified Communist opponent. By the end of the 1960s cold war liberalism was so mired in complexity, so insistent on the distinctiveness of each local situation that it had neither a rhetoric nor an explanation capable of justifying its own war in Vietnam. John Kennedy himself would not live to preside over a policy finally twisted and broken with self-contradiction, as it pursued in Vietnam a conflict for which it could not allow itself a satisfyingly belligerent and chauvinistic rationale.

The flaws in the thinking of the cold war strategists are easy to define. In their rediscovery of high political emotion, liberals later would learn to condemn past administrations for bringing to desperately human facts little more than the calculations of a computerized intelligence. But the temperament of the Kennedy strategists had its special strengths of nerve and patience, and it was precisely the quickness to perceive complications, the analytical dislike of ideological formulas that finally carried many liberals beyond the cold war. John Kennedy was both in person and in time a figure central to that paradox.

In 1961, however, Americans were questioning neither the cold war nor the technology that sustained our posture within it. And as Kennedy, in his hard New England accent, spoke to the nation over television, its most advanced medium, he seemed more than any other American President to represent the crisp competence and relentless energies of his age. Perhaps he would be able to reawaken the country's inventiveness, rejuvenate its ability to compete, make it as restlessly innovative as twentieth-century technology itself. He relished the clean virtues of modern technology and expertise, this commander of a PT boat, this reader of Ian Fleming novels, with their light, precise gadgetry out of the century to which the laconic intelligence of the hero exactly responds and with their plots that imagine not a simple conflict between the West and a monolithic Communist bloc but a multiplicity of interests and intrigues. American liberals especially, not yet having undergone the Vietnam experience, were able to believe that the twentieth-century scientific and technical mind is an ally of political progressivism, sharing its curiosity and its urge to shape an imperfect world toward perfection. An expression of their confidence was the Peace Corps, which presumed an alliance between compassion and technical skill.

In the course of Kennedy's presidency many liberals, taking it for granted that a statesman so attractive, educated, and articulate was one of their kind, put their trust in the technocratic intellect typified by Kennedy's secretary of defense, Robert McNamara. But they were simultaneously trying to understand a kind of event that put commonsense reason and strategy to shame, as civil rights demonstrators lived freedom in an instant that defied the normal terms of the political process. The Kennedy administration gave little evidence of understanding that freedom. After the demonstrations Americans could believe in magic. Much of the cultural history of the years that Kennedy's presidency unsuspectingly opened describes a pursuit of magic, of immediate revelatory experience. Actually the twentieth-century imagination, nurtured by modern technology, is in some ways prepared for this, prepared to expect distance to vanish over television or matter to vanish into energy. And the endlessly discussed style of the Kennedy presidency, so shallow, or at least so shallow beside the claims that were once made for it, so tenuous in connections even with the real person of the President himself, had a part in evoking the sense that the times were magic, that experience could at any second leap beyond its old content. But the Kennedy style did not offer a resolution of the tension between the two minds, and by the end of the decade technocratic liberalism was in open warfare with a politics of immediacy and emotion.

Much of the malaise today among liberals measures the loss of faith in technocratic methods and precision, a faith that can be so naïve and yet can demand so intense an application of skill and learning to the conquest of poverty, disease, and tyranny. Technology itself, as the horror of its application to Vietnam came to light, and as worry over the American environment increased, was to become among liberals an object of distrust. Ecologists, advocates of disarmament, opponents of industrial nuclear power—all suggest that in the steel and plastic of twentieth-century civilization lurks a force that wars upon the living earth. Ecologists are hostile to the John Kennedy recent critics have revealed to them. Yet in mentality the ecology activists are closer than they think to the forces they oppose. They compose and construct nature, analyzing it into balances, and plan architecturally to preserve and enhance these balances. The passage from Kennedy liberalism to an ecological radicalism that is both its opposite and its continuation is one of the more important stories of recent political ideology.

Along with the technocratic liberalism of the early sixties went a more strictly political progressivism that, in the years of the Kennedy presidency and beyond, continued the traditions of the New Deal. Liberals, relieved during the Republican years of the 1950s to see the institutions of the New and the Fair Deals merely preserved, were now stirring themselves to build fresh coalitions that would carry through more advanced reforms. And here the technocratic liberalism that stood for sociological studies of poverty and statistical investigations of housing sought alliance with forces in the civil rights movement, on the campuses, and elsewhere that sometimes had a different understanding of social reformation.

The two brothers who followed the President in sustaining a Kennedy liberalism that John Kennedy had never, perhaps, quite perceived have had a central place in this political work.

And yet this progressivism had a more precarious political base than at first seemed apparent. Once, in the 1930s, liberals had thought that there existed an American citizenry of farmers, · laborers, the middle classes, and the poor—the poor to be perceived, in effect, not as a separate culture but as farmers without land and workers without jobs—that could be expected to gather, like a big quarrelsome family, within whatever political household promised to extend political and economic democracy. That belief made some sense in the Great Depression, when the New Deal pieced together a program various enough to offer something to just about every class in major trouble. The first important shock to that liberal conception of American democracy came perhaps with the Red-hunting of the early fifties, when an old tension between civil liberties and popular sentiment again revealed itself. It was shock enough, at any rate, to send some intellectuals out of the camp of confident progressivism and into a more skeptical examination of democratic politics. But even a decade later, with a strongly Democratic constituency of organized labor, a growing bloc of black Americans, and a government that appeared to be seriously attacking the nation's poverty, liberals could look to a revival of New Deal democracy. Then within the black community nationalism and separatism became strident. Labor, recoiling from what in the counterculture and the antiwar movement appeared to be a self-indulgent attack on the moral grounds of the Republic, turned rightward in defense of patriotism and traditional mores. Liberals discovered that most of the very poor do not vote. The liberals, in sum, lost the sense of political community that had sustained earlier progressive politics.

Splintering from the older liberalism, and fracturing within itself, was the freedom movement, which had stretched from the Montgomery bus boycott of the mid-fifties to Selma a decade later. Even at its strongest it had been more complex and fragile than it seemed, a coalition of black southerners fighting conditions they had known all their lives, of young white northerners going south to test themselves against conditions they had known not at all except in the nightmares their consciences presented to them, of southern white liberals who had at last found a resolution to their doubts, of folk singers whose freedom songs on a college campus could both move and sentimentalize a young consciousness. The freedom movement imparted something of its spirit later in the decade to the counterculture, which could at once expand and trivialize the idea of spontaneous experience and freedom. There were communes in which you did not realize your freedom through a rational act of courage; you smoked or swallowed it. In a love-in, community did not construct itself for the task of a march and maintain its order in the face of hostile mobs; it floated together in a city park on an afternoon. Yet the counterculture, like the civil rights movement, contributed to liberating the American imagination into the knowledge of immediate freedom, experience, and community.

Technocracy, party politics, and the politics of witness have argued their way through the years following John Kennedy's presidency. Not long after the end of that presidency the public that he had symbolized was flying apart. Robert Kennedy, meanwhile, was making consciously the leftward journey that John Kennedy had appeared to make or perhaps had made half-sleepwalking. Robert could not have held to the whole of his brother's political public or its body of beliefs. Both by 1968 were in pieces. Robert Kennedy, then, had to be the leader of a faction. Yet if he did not command so amorphous a portion of the electorate, the segment that he did represent seemed possessed of the reach toward the future that John Kennedy had appeared to personify. John Kennedy unwittingly created the Kennedy politics; Robert Kennedy understood what had been created and was articulate about it. Later Edward Kennedy would have the advantage and the burden of taking up a Kennedy liberalism that had fully discovered itself just as it was disintegrating.

It was good to live in the early 1960s, when the tension between virtue and power seemed resolved, when technical intel-

lect appeared ranged on the side of social benevolence, when
civil rights workers in remote southern towns began to gain
the sympathy of the government, when youthful energy and self-
cultivation did not yet mean the therapies of selfishness, when
prosperity was on the side of all kinds of goals beyond the
pleasures of the prosperous. The nation has lost that moment,
and perhaps we are the wiser. Liberalism in that confident time
was too smoothly sure that it could handle all the instruments
of power, and it had temporarily lost its curiosity about the
dangers and moral ambiguity of power itself. But soon politics
was taking much of its vigor from the energies that dissipated as
they passed from that overconfident, somewhat tinsely Kennedy
liberalism into the left movements of the late sixties, energies
that now struggle to find an articulate progressive ideology.

This nation finds its strength not only in the traditional,
the ritualistic, the local, as other and perhaps richer cultures do,
but also in deliberate acts of making or willing, which can include the remaking of character or the making of a public. The
essence of American innocence is less a lack of experience than
the willingness to make each experience the basis not of skepticism but of belief. The United States is a work of technology; it
put itself together with railroads and trucks and computers. The
adage "This country will be a great place when we get it finished" says something about the worth as well as the naïveté of
American civilization. The making of a politics, the shaping of
a coalition like that which gathered itself around the Kennedy
family, are part of the process by which the country invents
itself.

2

Strive and Succeed

THE YOUNG POLITICIAN WHO CAPTURED THE PUBLIC IMAGINATION in the early 1960s owed his air of energy and purpose to an upbringing that had embodied the ambitions of a particular Irish-American family. Generations of appetite and competitiveness expressed themselves in a presidency that seemed forever eager to do or witness something grander: confront the Soviets, evoke a national purpose, get to the moon. John Kennedy's father had not been so ambitious; he merely wanted a Kennedy to be President. That would be the final triumph for an Irish-American Catholic, the vindication of a heritage, and at the same time an escape from its burdens.

Between 1845 and 1850, as much of its potato crop lay rotting in the ground, Ireland buried a million victims of the famine. Patrick Joseph Kennedy's County Wexford escaped much of the suffering, but eager for adventure and success, he joined the one million migrants who crossed the Atlantic to the New World during and just after these troubled years. Near the wharves in Boston Harbor he continued his trade of cooper and married Bridget Murphy, who bore him a son, Patrick, and three daughters. The elder Patrick died, probably of consumption, in his thirties.[1]

The new land offered relief from much more than the po-

tato famine. The Old World had subjected Ireland as well as
the rest of the British Isles and much of the European continent
to landlords, this class that intellectual conservatives so favored.
In Ireland the landlords were able in the midst of the famine to
export grain while the people of the land starved. And there was
the newer Manchester school of laissez-faire economists, who
spoke for the ambitions of the manufacturing classes and the
industrial cities, economists who wanted to discard old charitable institutions and regulations, isolate each individual as a
competitor, and let the market decide who could eat and how
much. These economists despised the old thickheaded landhold-
ing classes that sat on the country's natural wealth and could not
put it to innovative use. But the Manchester school would never
have expropriated the landholders, for it held private property
to be inviolate. And the laissez-faire ideology worked to restrain
the amount of relief that the British government might provide
to the famine-struck Irish. Let economic forces have their way,
its proponents commanded; do not corrupt the starving by feed-
ing them.

Most of the Irish were probably unaware of the newer
laissez-faire economics. But the character of their social life was
profoundly at odds with the spirit of its universe of coldly separate, self-interested individuals. While the Irish valued strong
individuality, they lived and acted in community. They had
long bargained at the local level for the favors of the central
government. Their church and the Catholic Association movement, as well as their secret societies that plotted against British
rule, required loyalty, discipline, and commonality of purpose.
The immigrants to American cities continued in their communal
ways, clustering in neighborhoods, sharing the rituals of their
church, gathering in saloons, and joining political clubs. The
Irish immigrants to Boston, like those in other American cities,
knew that a practical politics could raise their fortunes.

In our century an economics affirming competitiveness and
the private as opposed to the public responsibilities of property
goes by the label of conservatism. But Boston's antebellum

communal Irish, as Oscar Handlin presents them in *Boston's Immigrants*, were more genuinely conservative in their loyalty to the network of traditions and institutions—above all else, the institution of the Roman Catholic Church—that surrounded them. They were hostile to the reformist impulses that they encountered in their adopted region: the antislavery movement, women's rights, the common schools. And the Irish were to retain into the twentieth century that tendency to adhere to what at the moment presents itself as conservative. By then conservatism had come to mean at its best a respect for the institutions of family and neighborhood and church and at its worst Red-baiting and racism.[2]

Political talk was a great diversion among the nineteenth-century Irish poor, and the corner saloon promised not only talk but an occasional brawl and perhaps a political job. Here the first American-born Patrick Kennedy, a friendly, mustachioed saloonkeeper who did favors for his customers, entered politics. His saloon, like many others, was a political club, and its informal welfare politics dispensed small funds to the politically grateful needy.

Pat Kennedy, who gave out free beer to voters and used such devices as repeaters at the polls, rose quickly to become a ward boss. Later he was a member of both the Massachusetts lower house and the state senate, and he seconded Grover Cleveland's nomination at the 1888 Democratic Convention. He ended his career not as an elected official but as a liquor wholesaler, a banker, and one of Boston's most powerful backstage politicians, known by some as the Mayor of East Boston. His wife, Mary Hickey Kennedy, who came from a family more established than his, gave birth in 1888 to Joseph Patrick Kennedy, father of President John Kennedy. The parents cultivated their many children with good music and high principles; Joe's sister Loretta has described her father as an idealist and her mother as a visionary.[3]

Joe Kennedy, heir to this wealth and influence, did not need to make money but did so from an early age. Captain of his parochial school's baseball team, the Assumptions, he sold newspapers to pay for flashy uniforms, and these attracted crowds and admission fees while he also passed the hat. The Assumptions invariably defeated the Playfairs. At the age of eleven Joe worked as a ticket taker on an excursion boat. A close friend of these years could remember his industry and his greeting: "How can we make some money?"[4]

After seventh grade the genial, gregarious Joe transferred to the Boston Latin School in preparation for Harvard. Self-assured but so poor a student that he took an extra year to earn his diploma, he played baseball and football, managed the basketball team, and became class president. The school yearbook predicted that he would make his fortune "in a very roundabout way." At Harvard Joe switched from an economics to a music major. Afterward he usually concealed his taste for good music lest he be thought effete. His "great love for classical music," remarks a biographer, "marred his otherwise perfectly philistinian façade." In later years he rarely read a book, but liked to play baroque music during business negotiations. During college Joe earned some $5,000 by operating a sightseeing bus line and lived well as a member of the Delta Upsilon fraternity. Yet the Irish Catholic Kennedy was not invited to join the most prestigious campus clubs. He had decided, of course, to become a young millionaire, a goal he would reach in his mid-thirties.

Banking seemed a good route for Joe Kennedy's climb to the top. After graduating from Harvard, he worked briefly at his father's East Boston Columbia Trust Company and then in 1912 became an assistant bank examiner for the state, again through his father's influence. "If you're going to get money," explained Kennedy at the time, "you have to find out where it is." As an examiner he was able to discover the strengths and weaknesses of particular institutions. Within two years Joe Kennedy at the age of twenty-five had through the use of borrowed money saved Columbia Trust from a merger and negotiated himself into its presidency. National news stories portrayed him as the country's youngest bank president. The post developed his political interests since he had to watch legislation affecting investments.[5]

In his private as well as in his financial life Kennedy set out after the best prize. In 1914 William Cardinal O'Connell officiated at his marriage to Rose Fitzgerald. Rose, whose ancestors, like Joe's, had come from County Wexford, was the oldest daughter of Boston's mayor, John F. "Honey Fitz" Fitzgerald. Fitz's political tactics included diatribes against the Back Bay Brahmins and opponents who "ate steak on Friday." The mayor created innumerable jobs like "city dermatologist" for his cronies and took sizable amounts of graft as well as building many new schools in the Irish slums. He would croon "Sweet Adeline" on the slightest notice. Once when struck by a truck, he would not let the ambulance take him to a hospital until he had sat up and sung "Sweet Adeline" to assure his public that he was all right. Honey Fitz, like other ethnic politicians of the period, gave to city politics a warmth and kindness that correct and reforming statesmen would not have supplied. He was removed from Congress in 1919 on charges of voting fraud.[6]

Fitz's political styles and his political success were inseparable from his Irish ethnicity. Yet like Joseph Kennedy, who was later to receive in the ambassadorship to Great Britain the most Anglo of Anglo-American appointments, the Fitzgeralds were moving away from their immigrant background. Honey Fitz had gone to the Boston Latin School, a school for the offspring of the city's Brahmin elite, and until forced to withdraw for financial reasons, he had attended Harvard Medical School. Rose was trained as a daughter of the upper classes. After placing third in a large high school class and being voted the prettiest senior, she had spent a year at finishing school in Blumenthal in Germany, becoming proficient in both German and French, and after her return had attended Manhattanville College. She organized a social and charitable club, the Ace of Clubs, taught catechism classes in the North End slums, took courses in language and art at Boston University, studied the piano at the New England Conservatory of Music, and participated in a little theater group. At the age of twenty she was appointed to the Boston Public Library's book selection committee; she was its youngest member. Rose had a political apprenticeship, serving as a hostess at her father's functions. Wealth did not spoil her. She had an aristocrat's capacity for self-control and for an unrevealing public demeanor; it was perhaps religious stoicism that allowed her to endure the many years of Joe's philanderings.[7]

Rose's husband ran his bank like a good politician, understanding the usefulness of personal relations with his customers. As one favor led to another, he became treasurer of Old Colony Realty, which promised the new Irish middle class suburban sites protected "against the encroachment of undesirable elements." Joe's connection with Mayor Fitzgerald got him the strange dowry of a directorship of the Collateral Loan Company, a city-run pawnshop, and he proceeded to expose some embezzlements. Here was an instance of the streak of rectitude that coexisted with his opportunism—an expression of the same austerity that characterized his personal life. In those days he did not drink, smoke, or gamble; perhaps he was working to escape a stereotype of the Irish that was current among old-stock Americans.[8]

In 1917, after some delay because of prejudice toward him, Kennedy was elected a trustee of the state's largest utility, Massachusetts Electric, where he served with Charles Francis Adams and the stockbroker Galen Stone. During the war he drove himself hard and developed an ulcer as assistant general manager of Bethlehem Steel's shipyards at Quincy for an annual salary of $20,000. He broke many production records, building thirty-six destroyers in two years. On one occasion Kennedy clashed with Assistant Secretary of the Navy Franklin D. Roosevelt. The shipbuilder refused to deliver two ships to Argentina, which had not paid for them. FDR towed the boats away with four navy tugs manned with armed sailors.

After learning the stock business thoroughly, Kennedy in search of greater opportunity moved his family in 1926 by private railway car to suburban Riverdale, New York, and three years later to a $250,000 house in Bronxville, New York, a community known for its ethnic restrictions. The Kennedys spent time at vacation houses in Palm Beach, Florida, and Hyannis Port on Cape Cod. New England could be grudging in its hospitality to Irish Catholics. Kennedy's daughters were absent from the Cape season's list of debutantes, and he was refused entrance to a Nantucket country club. In the 1930s a Boston newspaper called Kennedy an "Irish American." He growled, "I was born here. My children were born here. What the hell do I have to do to be an American?" Would he ever be able fully to triumph over the perceptions that, when he was growing up, had dictated that Boston papers have two society sections, one for the Irish and the other for Americans of older stock?

In the late 1920s Joe Kennedy spent thirty-two furious months in Hollywood, a speculator's paradise. Earlier he had owned a chain of New England movie theaters and, one source has it, learned that "Hollywood could wring you dry. He wanted to get where the wringing was done." It was a time of frenetic prosperity, not of orderly business operation, for the movie industry. To suit the sixty million Americans who attended the movies each week, Kennedy ground out forgettable low-budget Tom Mix westerns and snappy melodramas like *A Poor Girl's Romance* and *Red Hot Roofs*. His most prominent achievement was to engage the acting, and apparently the affections, of Gloria Swanson, the "Queen of Hollywood." He cast her in *The Queen Kelly*, directed by Erich von Stroheim, a movie about a harlot nun that Kennedy would not release (von Stroheim shows a sequence from it in his role of butler-projectionist in the 1950 film *Sunset Boulevard*, which cast Miss Swanson as an aging movie star). It was Miss Swanson's money, not Kennedy's, that was lost—and his, not hers, that multiplied with her first talkie, *The Trespasser*. Joe maintained her in Beverly Hills and gave her presents. In time she learned he was charging both the presents and the dwelling to her business account. The end of their collaboration, according to Miss Swanson, came abruptly when she questioned his judgment. After profiting from the merger of several corporations, Kennedy sold out before the stock market crash, having become a millionaire many times over before returning to New York in 1930. Corporations, he noted, were for the benefit of the corporate management, not the stockholders.[9]

Rose, meanwhile, kept card files on the nine offspring, took them on trips to historical sites, got them to church almost daily, and pinned to her dress or their pillowcases numerous reminder notes concerning their welfare. "Money doesn't give you any license to relax," she said, though domestic servants aided in the children's upbringing. She instructed them in an upper-class code of social responsibility and service. Rose drilled them in such points as the proper use of *I* and *me*, and on their way to dinner they were required to read news stories she had tacked on a bulletin board so that they could have family political discussions. Her ambitions for them may not have been far different from her husband's; she has confided that she wanted to rear her sons to greatness. The long workdays of her husband and the largeness of their brood prevented him from having close touch with them. One story tells of his pulling Joe, Jr., his first-born, on a sled; deep in thought about a financial matter, he returned home only with the sled. The family rushed out to rescue the boy, gurgling in a sidewalk snowbank. Once, to stabilize the price of Yellow Cab Company stock, the elder Kennedy remained in a New York City hotel room for several weeks.

Although Joe wrote in 1936, "I have no political ambitions for myself or for my children," they were to be his revenge on the Boston upper crust. He fed them on ambition—not to make money, which they already had, but to become a dynasty. He taught them to look on the future as a project. The Kennedy family compound at Hyannis Port, on a bluff overlooking Nantucket Sound, was a good training ground. With its early bedtimes and vigorous calisthenics at dawn, it suggested a rigorous summer camp. Joe, for example, was quick to scold a child who smiled too readily or got along on charm alone. "Remember," he would say, "a smile and a dime can only get you a ride on a streetcar."

Kennedy forced the boys into competitions, such as the wealthy WASP's sport of sailing, that were supposed to develop character. On Nantucket Sound he followed the boys in a separate boat, telling them their mistakes over a bullhorn. It was winning—*doing one's best* referred to winning—not simply sportsmanship, that he was after. Joe, Jr., once used an oversize sail to win a race, and a Kennedy boy could be a graceless loser. "Don't play unless you can be captain" and "Second place is failure" are injunctions attributed to the father. He explained that *Victura*, the name he had chosen for his first sailboat, meant "something about winning." After a day of sailing on the bay the children had to be seated for dinner five minutes before the father entered the room. He would then deliver a critique of their maneuvers and perhaps force a slacker to eat in the kitchen. On rainy days the father and children would sometimes sit down to a favored game of Monopoly.[10]

Intellect also had to be toughened. One exercise was for each brother after lunch to take the part of a Founding Father and argue points on the basis of *The Federalist Papers*. The elder Kennedy welcomed disagreement from his children. "The truth," comments one visitor, "is that they couldn't possibly be around the old man without being interested in damn near everything. Some [of his notions] are sound, some are preposterous. But everything he says tends to be interesting."[11]

The Kennedy children were receiving a training not only in competition but in the ways of the patrician classes. It has flavored the political progressivism of the Kennedys with a manner that, except for Robert's, deviates from the earnest moralism some liberals prefer. The most recent generation of Kennedys, the grandchildren of Rose and Joseph, are capable of combining highly visible night-clubbing with programmatic daytime work in liberal causes. Demands for achievement of the sort that Joseph Kennedy made, of course, were not peculiar to the Kennedy family; it is a message that many American children receive, perhaps more indirectly, from their parents. It is to be found, for example, in the immigrant experience. While the elder Kennedy was at more than a generation's remove from that experience, he was devoted with a passion to a major goal within immigrant groups, which is to break fully out of the ghetto into an established American society and culture—the society of the Anglo-American upper classes.

An education that teaches the virtues of achievement is legitimate. But it can involve differing notions of achievement. It can look to excellence, or simply to winning, or to both; as well as raising achievers, it can raise bullies or misfits. Joseph Kennedy probably had a respect for excellence, but his rage was for winning and for acceptance within the upper classes. A friend traveling with him recalls his complaint that she was not introducing him to "the very best people." He sent his sons to Choate and Harvard as he chose Palm Beach for his winter home; they were the best places to be. Joe's and Rose's forebears had lived in a world of repeat voters and casual graft. It was an education in survival and triumph that Kennedy passed on to his sons; whatever the disciplined and abstemious Joe may have told them about the traditional virtues, he ignored many of them. His Catholicism was of a hard American kind that reconciled Christianity with ambition and competitiveness. The sons, who went mostly to Protestant schools while the daughters attended Catholic ones, received from their parents a schooling in motivation and effort; otherwise they could not have achieved as they would. They also had their parents' love. When Jack was sick with scarlet fever in 1920, his father prayed for him in church and promised to give half his small fortune to charity if the boy was spared. According to Rose Kennedy, her husband did exactly that; in fact, he gave about $4,000, half of his liquid capital.[12]

The existence of a mentally retarded Kennedy child, Rosemary, might have suggested that winning, on the world's terms, as a way of life was an illusion. But Joe Kennedy maintained that illusion. As late as 1959 a member of the family read and approved Joseph Dineen's *The Kennedy Family*, which noted of Rosemary simply that she preferred a secluded life. James MacGregor Burns once remarked that she was helping nuns take care of retarded children. When Joe told the truth to a reporter in 1960, it was with an apologetic air: "I used to think it was something to hide, something not to talk about."[13]

For all his hardness, there was about Joseph Kennedy something of F. Scott Fitzgerald's Jay Gatsby. Dreams could be willed, he seemed to think, or rather, anyone who observed his public progress and then the careers of his sons could think so. There are "plastic hours," Irving Howe has written of the 1960s, when the world seems ready to assume new forms. And that era was to have as its first President the scion of a family that for many years had made events plastic to its touch.

In business, success followed success. A familiar anecdote tells that a shoeshine boy gave Joseph Kennedy accurate tips during the summer of 1929; claiming that a market a shoeshine boy could predict was no market for him, he liquidated his securities. "Only a fool holds out for top dollar," he observed. Then, during the steep descent into 1932, Kennedy—described as "a whole den of bears"—made more by selling stocks short than he had by selling out in 1929. The market's decline discouraged the return of confidence in the economy, and President Herbert Hoover, whom Democrats in the coming decade would excoriate as the politician of the rich, remarked that Kennedy and other prominent Democratic shortsellers like Bernard Baruch and John J. Raskob were unpatriotic for enriching themselves at the expense of the country.

Kennedy was now looking beyond the stock market to national politics. He visited Franklin D. Roosevelt in 1930 at the governor's mansion in Albany, New York; soon Kennedy decided to support Roosevelt for President and to campaign for him— "for my own security and for the security of our kids." Kennedy had decided that the country needed reform; he worried about "how ugly and menacing hungry men may become." For the 1932 primary campaign Kennedy agreed to raise money and pull Roman Catholic support away from Alfred E. Smith. He did well at both tasks, also lending the campaign $50,000, which was never repaid. He traveled with Roosevelt on many campaign tours. But by his own account his main contribution was to persuade William Randolph Hearst, fearful of Al Smith or an internationalist candidate, to order the California delegates to move to Roosevelt and break the convention deadlock. The privilege of obtaining the American franchise on Gordon's gin and several Scotch whiskies may have been a reward for his services; "medicinal" licenses issued in Washington allowed him to stock up in time for repeal, and a trip to Great Britain with James Roosevelt enabled him to secure franchises.[14]

But Kennedy wanted, and got, more than personal enrichment. In a speech prepared by Kennedy which Roosevelt delivered at Columbus, Ohio, during the presidential campaign, the candidate laid out the blueprint for what would become the Securities and Exchange Commission. In 1934 he became chairman of that commission, of which he had been one of the principal architects. The job offered the prestige of public service, something he might some day cash in on either for himself or for his sons. "It takes a thief to catch a thief," said Roosevelt, who liked Kennedy and recognized in him qualities he valued. Lacking fixed ideas about how to improve the ailing economy, both men regarded problems as practical matters to be resolved as common sense dictated. Their friendships and their appointments were often based on personal affinity rather than on ideology. Kennedy, for instance, though commonly regarded as a conservative, brought William O. Douglas to the SEC and offered Adlai Stevenson an important post. Later he supported FDR's court-packing scheme, something no true conservative could easily do, and thought enough of the Marxist Harold Laski, who had been eased out of Harvard after supporting the Boston police strike of 1919, to send sons Joe, Jr., and John to him as students. At his new job Kennedy worked all day and then far into the night at his thirty-three room $500,000 Maryland estate on the Potomac River, the interior design of which combined French, English, Jacobean, Roman, early American, and Hollywood styles; the subcellar contained a movie theater for about 100 guests. The gold-plated faucets and sterling silver toilet seats offended liberal guests, while Joe simply enjoyed the architecture he termed "bouillabaisse"—as FDR might have. Joe called it the Hindenburg Palace.[15]

Kennedy's best-known innovation at the SEC was to prohibit short sales from being consummated at a price lower than the last one on the ticker. His administration of the commission, however, went on the conservative premise that intelligent regulation or self-regulation of business would forestall radical attacks on capitalism; in 1935 corporate underwriting quadrupled, which enabled him to claim on resigning from the commission that government supervision served enlightened self-interest.[16]

In 1936 Kennedy brought out *I'm for Roosevelt*, ghost-written by Arthur Krock of the *New York Times*, calling for businessmen to exercise self-discipline for their own protection. The book contended, as would historians of a later day, that businessmen should be grateful for Roosevelt's rescue of capitalism. "It was useful," Kennedy observed, "to have a Roosevelt who had the confidence of the masses" and "could keep them from attempting more radical things than the New Deal." At a 1937 reunion he lectured his surly Harvard classmates that with the sit-down strikes business was "reaping the whirlwind of a quarter century of mishandling of labor relations." If he lacked the sensibilities of a liberal, he had apparently acquired with his wealth some sense of stewardship. Robert Kennedy is recorded as reporting, with candor, that his upbringing did not teach him to be sensitive to the race issue, adding that he could remember being told of his responsibilities to the hungry.[17]

Kennedy's support of the New Deal is consonant with his background and career, for however ruthless an individualist he was, however detached from family and friends, he was always a part of the Democratic political community, and the financial world in which he moved was also one of systems and connections. The New Deal understood connections; it was an attempt to preserve and strengthen the national political and social community that was a condition for the survival of the nation's economic institutions.

Joe Kennedy returned to government service for nearly a year beginning in March 1937. As chairman of the Maritime Commission, designed to revive the ailing shipbuilding industry, he squeezed out some of the smaller shipping lines but was able to discover a means of financing sufficient to replace outmoded vessels. After one meeting he grumbled that none of the shipowners could write a check for $1 million. Because he favored laws for compulsory arbitration of labor disputes, the National Maritime Union labeled him a "union-wrecker." Kennedy worked prodigiously in the service of a grateful President at "the toughest job I ever handled in my life."

Then came Kennedy's grand opportunity: the ambassadorship to Great Britain. He badly wanted the job, which was among the most prestigious within the old American Anglophile aristocracy. The office would make him the social superior of Boston's "best people"; it was an achievement by which one generation of Kennedys could extend the reach of the next. The appointment of a Catholic Irishman as the nation's representative to Britain was not novel—Cleveland had chosen one for the highest diplomatic post there—but it was a headline event. The selection could strengthen FDR's position in his Irish constituency and among isolationist Catholics. It is possible that Roosevelt along with other Americans had some thought of the relentlessly Anglophile Walter Hines Page, the ambassador during the world war, and feared a repetition of the diplomacy that had then drawn our fortunes so closely to Great Britain's. Besides, the appointment of a person of Irish descent to the principal post in Britain would have appealed to a President—confident, of course, of his own upper-class credentials—who would relish the irony of the appointment. When FDR's son James suggested the selection, the President "laughed so hard he almost toppled from his wheelchair." So Kennedy early in 1938 became ambassador.

The ambassador, once labeled in the popular press as Jolly
Joe Kennedy, called the queen a "cute trick" and cut down the
practice of introducing American debutantes to British royalty.
He put his feet on his desk during his first press conference, remarking, "You can't expect me to develop into a statesman
overnight." In time he developed a close relationship with Prime
Minister Neville Chamberlain and with the Cliveden circle of
appeasers who supported the Munich Conference of 1938. "I
have four boys," Kennedy had said two years before, "and I
don't want them killed in a foreign war." And like former businessman Herbert Hoover and former Chancellor of the Ex-
chequer Chamberlain, he feared for capitalism, believing that
war destroys capital and could bring postwar collectivism. Kennedy encouraged Roosevelt to support Munich. The President,
more and more concerned about the situation in Europe and increasingly troubled by a growing conflict between the State Department and Kennedy, began to bypass the ambassador in communications with the British. A speech Kennedy had planned to
deliver in Scotland contained the sentence "I can't for the life of
me understand why anybody would want to go to war to save the
Czechs." The ambassador, impressed by the flier Charles Lind-
bergh's oral reports to him about Nazi air superiority, helped
bring their message to the attention of Prime Minister Chamberlain prior to Munich. In October 1938 Kennedy declared in a
Trafalgar Day address before the Navy League, "The democracies and dictators should cooperate for the common good, rather
than emphasize self-apparent differences." While the speech
"seemed to be unpopular with the Jews etc.," Jack wrote his
father from Harvard, it "was considered to be very good by everyone who wasn't bitterly anti-fascist." When Roosevelt suggested
lifting the ban on arms shipments to Spain, Kennedy had
joined the Roman Catholic hierarchy's effective protest against
a policy that would aid the leftists. The United States was not
looking for a confrontation with fascism; our abstention from
any support for the Spanish Loyalists is evidence enough of that.
But neither was Washington prepared to have its representatives

speak amiably of the Fascist powers, and in any event the government may have feared that the slightest encouragement to the dictatorships would further threaten a peace that it preferred to intervention.[18]

In these years Kennedy earned a reputation for being an anti-Semite. The German ambassador to Great Britain, Herbert von Dirksen, reported that Kennedy told him, "I'm for Hitler." He warned that the campaign against Jews was unnecessarily stirring up trouble but observed that "very strong anti-Semite tendencies existed in the United States and that a large portion of the population had an understanding of the German attitude toward the Jews." Dirksen remarked, "From his whole personality, I believe he would get on well with the Führer." It is possible, of course, that Dirksen purposely or wishfully misconstrued Kennedy's remarks. The meetings with Dirksen may simply have aimed to improve German-American relations in pursuit of Kennedy's repeated hope of getting "the dictators and democracies together to work out ways and means to avert economic disaster." In the 1930s he urged his Hollywood Jewish acquaintances to cease making films offensive to the dictators. In early 1939 Father Charles Coughlin's anti-Semitic, pro-German *Social Justice* ran a cover picture of the Kennedy family and named Joseph Kennedy "Man of the Week."[19]

Kennedy was a long time coming to support any plan for the mass evacuation of Jews from Germany; he believed such a project to be too risky when war might break out at the slightest provocation. This was also Chamberlain's position. But the whole anti-Fascist world was slow in coming to this simple act of humanity and did not begin to do enough. Kennedy was actually one of the earlier officials to take action. He started conversations with the British to evolve a plan to transport tens of thousands of Jews from Germany and Central Europe to North and South America and Africa. Initial Polish noncooperation, then the reluctance of most nations to increase their immigration quotas, and finally war ended their talks but not before they had rescued sizable numbers of Jews.

Kennedy, against the President's wishes, returned to the United States on October 27, 1940, considering resignation and repudiation of FDR. Perhaps it was Rose who dissuaded him; she argued for loyalty to an administration that had given such recognition to a Roman Catholic. Clare Boothe Luce remembers Kennedy's remark that Roosevelt had pledged to support Joe, Jr., for governor of Massachusetts in 1942; certainly disloyalty in 1940 might injure the political future of his son. The President had Kennedy brought directly from his plane to the White House and exerted all his charm. His promise to the nation, "Your boys are not going to be sent into any foreign wars," together with a lull in the fighting, steadied Joe's resolve, and two days later he gave a moving radio speech urging the President's reelection: "Our children and your children are more important than anything else in the world." Joseph in these days even went so far as to endorse lend-lease, which made the United States a virtual confederate of the Allies. He warned, however, about the power that the plan gave the President, and he had already informed Roosevelt that he intended to resign.[20]

In June 1941 Kennedy was quoted as saying that Hitler was "the greatest genius of the century" and that Britain was done for within sixty days. He worried about what he called "the growing Jewish influence in the press and in Washington demanding continuance of the war." In part Kennedy was expressing the prejudices of his time; perhaps, too, as in the conversation with Dirksen, he was adapting himself to the audience of the moment in a style FDR himself had perfected. Still, Kennedy had an overriding fear of communism, believing the long-run danger to be not Germany but Russia, and he hoped the two would face off in battle.[21]

After an indiscreet interview with a Boston reporter immediately following the presidential election, Kennedy did resign his post. His references to the king's stuttering, Winston Churchill's heavy drinking, and the queen's manner as resembling that of a dowdy housewife were small indiscretions compared to his remarks about the "death of democracy" in Britain.

Roosevelt received many letters warning against the appointment of Kennedy to a wartime post: he was variously denounced as "indiscreet," "vituperative," and "defeatist." When Roosevelt died in 1945 after having kept Kennedy at considerable distance during the war, the former ambassador was to remark that while there was "real sorrow" for two or three days, "there is also no doubt that it was a great thing for the country." For a time Joe had wondered whether the presidency itself might be within his own reach; he had been listed fifth in a poll of likely presidential candidates should Roosevelt not run in 1940. Now he had quit political life, and whatever future there was for his ambitions lay in his sons; he would continue to shape them to his purpose.[22]

The first of the sons was Joe, Jr. As if in training for success, he drank little and ate moderately; at Henri Soulé's Le Pavillon, later owned in part by his father, he dined on milk and well-done beef. At least until after World War II the elder Kennedy, too, had or affected habits of austerity. When he pointedly told Winston Churchill that he had sworn off drinking and smoking for the duration of the war, Churchill shot back: "My God, you make me feel as if I should go around in sackcloth and ashes." The elder Joseph assessed Churchill as "a remarkable man, or as remarkable as any man can be, who's loaded with brandy by ten o'clock in the morning."

"Someday I'll be President," Joe, Jr., said, and he took elocution lessons. Perhaps this grand goal was a way of competing with his amazingly successful father, or possibly it was merely a sense that as his father's eldest son he would take on by primogeniture the senior Kennedy's projects. Edward remembers his brother's daring him into higher and higher dives from Eden Roc on the Riviera until his father put a stop to it. A classmate at Choate has described Joe as the kind of boy who "couldn't pass a hat without squashing it or leave an unprotected shin unkicked." Jack was to recall in a eulogy his "hot temper" and his "sardonic half smile as though he were kidding you." At Choate and at Harvard Joe specialized in athletics and women. Football was his

particular domain. A knee torn at Harvard practice required surgery, for a time Joe's arm was in a plaster cast, and a blow to
the head gave him a concussion. In Europe he missed the world's
bobsled record by two seconds.[23]

Joe's Catholicism was rigorous, apparently without the
skepticism that informed his brother Jack's faith. He prayed
nightly at his bedside and got a headache visiting the Anti-
Religious Museum in Moscow. His senior thesis, "Intervention
in Spain," narrates the history of the Hands Off Spain Committee, a student group of which he was a member that favored
Francisco Franco. After graduation he went to England to study
at the London School of Economics with Harold Laski. The
elder Kennedy apparently believed that there was value in ac-
quainting the young man with dangerous ideas, and he now
wished to equip his sons for intellectual competition as he had
trained them for athletic contests. He also wanted his son to
find out what, as he expressed it, "the have-nots are thinking and
planning" since he would "have some money someday." Laski's
influence, if any, was evidently transitory. On a trip to Spain
during the Civil War, when he was nearly the only American in
Madrid at a time of great danger there, Joe, Jr., revealed a continuing sympathy for Franco that was common among Catholics.
He also approved of the Munich Pact and in a 1938 letter to a
friend spoke of the Germans as a "marvelous people," whom it
would be "tough . . . to keep . . . from getting what they
want." Laski later said that he had taught "plenty of students
. . . abler than Joe, not a few immensely abler," and remembered especially "his relentless teasing to be President of the
United States." As a delegate to the 1940 Democratic Convention Joe supported the nomination not of Roosevelt but of James
Farley.[24]

The aggressive and ambitious Joe, Jr., must have been a
major presence in the early life of John Kennedy, the next oldest
brother, born on May 29, 1917. "Jack hates to lose at anything,"
his sister Eunice has commented. "That's the one thing he gets
really emotional about." Some of his competitiveness may have

come from conflict with his older brother. Joe's "pugnacious personality," according to Jack, later "smoothed out but it was a problem in my boyhood." One day young Jack and Joe raced around their Boston city block from different directions and collided in a game of chicken; Joe was unhurt, but Jack required twenty-eight stitches. In the Choate days Jack wrote his father about a hazing administered to his brother: "All the sixth formers had a swat or two. Did the sixth formers kick him. O Man he was all blisters, they almost paddled the life out of him. What I wouldn't have given to be a sixth former." Joe regularly bested his weaker brother in fights and on several occasions stole Jack's dates. Afflicted with back trouble from birth, with asthma, scarlet fever, swellings of the throat that regularly sent him to hospitals in ambulances, and the gamut of childhood diseases, Jack was introspective—an "introvert" in his youth, according to his father—devouring romances, such as Sir Walter Scott's Waverley novels, and biographies of colorful and successful people. Alone with his books and thoughts, with physical frailty to overcome, Jack was well conditioned for a will and ambition more inward, less an expression of sheer animal exuberance, than the aggressiveness of his older brother. And the endurance of childhood frailty could explain both the courage with which even an unfriendly observer could later credit Jack Kennedy and the respect for valor and skill that would make him a devotee of elite military units.[25]

As a young boy Jack told his mother, "If you study too much, you're liable to go crazy," and he got by on cuteness, asking, for instance, which was his father's sweet tooth. At Choate his grades were mediocre, and he traded votes to win the designation "Most likely to succeed." He belonged to a clique so disruptive that the headmaster once denounced its members in chapel and suspended them. Jack's pranks, though, were innocent enough, on the order of taking all the pillows from a dormitory and cramming them into a friend's room. The young student did not seem promising. But Ralph Horton, an accomplice in misbehavior, remembers an English teacher's telling Jack that he had a flair for writing. His friend, Horton reports, was sharp on giving answers to questions as he listened to the radio program "Information Please." Horton's explanation for that facility testifies to Jack's preoccupation with self-improvement along the lines of what his father worked to inculcate. Jack, who once spoke of the difficulty of concentrating, put himself through a regimen in which, after reading an article, he would mentally scan, analyze, and criticize it. At Choate he drove himself to recall mountains of information and began to read the *New York Times* daily, with special attention to diplomatic news.[26]

After part of a year at Princeton Jack entered a hospital for treatment of his asthma and his weak back, further injured by participation in sports; for recuperation he worked at an Arizona ranch before some unsuccessful starts in London at studying with Laski. Next came Harvard. Though weighing only 150 pounds, Jack played football there, where he chose athletes as friends. Once he kept on playing after cracking a leg bone in a collision with an equipment wagon on the sidelines; another time he ruptured a spinal disk in a scrimmage. Football at this time formed the elite corps of Harvard's social life. Jack's academic record included a D+ from William Langer, the famous historian of Europe, but improved as he matured.

At the end of his freshman year Jack toured Europe and raised only vague questions about Generalissimo Franco's Falangists, who he thought would strengthen Spain. Beginning the following year, he made additional visits to his parents in London and served on the embassy staff. It was one of the gravest periods of recent European history and probably quickened his appetite for a public career. During the last half of his junior year he was in London writing his thesis. Before returning to Harvard for his senior year, he had the formidable job in Scotland of reassuring American tourists returning home after the Germans had torpedoed the British liner *Athenia* in the North Atlantic.

Jack's father, who seemed up to the very last moment to have wanted to appease Hitler, may have been more ambivalent on the subject than some of his public statements would indicate. Before our entry into the war he was urging his son not to let Chamberlain off too easily in the senior thesis Jack was about to publish, which in its thesis form carried the manuscript title "Appeasement at Munich Is the Inevitable Result of the Failure of England to Rearm and the Effect of Public Opinion on This." But even after the war the elder Kennedy could defend Munich. A handwritten section of some memoirs that were being prepared for him a few years after the end of the hostilities argues for an understanding of Munich and Chamberlain as seeking peace in a desperate time. The manuscript's explanation of the ambassador's troubles on the Jewish question would have pulled him in deeper. Among those who had been able to countenance war with Germany, it announces, were a number of Jewish publicists. "They should not be condemned for such an objective. After all, the lives and fortunes of their compatriots were being destroyed by Hitler. Compromise could hardly cure that situation; only the destruction of Nazism could do so. . . . The tactics of this group may some day be analyzed. But they did not hesitate to resort to slander and falsehood to achieve their aims. . . . I received my share of it."[27]

Why England Slept, the reworking of Jack's thesis, published in 1940, differs sharply in tone. Chamberlain turned to appeasement, the book argues, to buy the time Great Britain needed for military preparation. (Actually Hitler, using his totalitarian powers of organization and able after Munich to draw on the resources of the Sudetenland, would be far stronger than the British in 1939.) Jack observes that Chamberlain, having "an essentially 'business' mentality . . . , could not understand how any problems could possibly be solved by war." *Why England Slept* carefully lays out a number of reasons for Britain's predicament. Its major thesis is that democracies, having a capacity for longer endurance of crisis than do repressive states, tend in the absence of clear emergency to encourage interest groups to pursue their private aims, which in the 1930s clashed with rearmament. The book praises Churchill and calls for a renewal of British national energies and unity, the kind of appeal that John was to make to his fellow Americans in the 1960 campaign. The ideas had formed at a time when the expansionism of the Fascist powers could no longer be overlooked. Yet the book is not clearly interventionist either. Instead, it argues that the United States should stay out of the conflict and rearm; the argument can be taken to mean either that we should get ready to go in or that we should concentrate on staying out. Dismissed by Laski as "very immature," on a level with the work of fifty other seniors at a good university, *Why England Slept* is in fact a good book written by a bright young man whose father's money insured that it would see publication. Or rather, written in draft by a bright young man. The dissertation itself was Kennedy's own work, brought in segments to his professor Bruce Hopper and refined in response to Hopper's criticisms. But it appears that the study had a major rewriting by Arthur Krock, the ambassador's speech writer Harvey Klammer, or both.

Jack Kennedy, about whom so much is known, nonetheless eludes a critical observer who looks at him as student, as senator, and as President. How intelligent was he? What political questions did he at any moment of his life care about? Books psychoanalyze him and the rest of his family in detail and answer, "he cared about power." Power in itself is an abstraction. What specific forms of power appealed to him? His performance at Harvard and before provides an early enigmatic occasion for gauging his ambitions.[28]

Some of Kennedy's professors commented on him unenthusiastically, and the received impression is of a student little interested in ideas. Yet after several semesters he had earned a B+ average at Harvard and made the dean's list, thereby becoming eligible to graduate with honors. The influential political scientist Arthur Holcombe, who gave him Bs, was to observe: "He had no interest in causes, his approach was that of a young scientist in a laboratory." Hopper noted: "He is surprisingly able, when he gets down to work." Hopper called attention to the "felicity of phrase and graceful presentation" in John's senior thesis, which won a magna cum laude against Joe's cum laude.

Why England Slept takes a broad theme and looks inquisitively upon the character of a whole society. And a couple of years later Kennedy wrote a letter carefully and knowledgeably discussing the politics and economics of Stresemann and Bruening. That the letter was not intended for publication does not necessarily mean that it was the product of a reflective young intellectual. Here, as in a report on Palestine written to his father in 1939, Kennedy perhaps was simply performing the gestures of scholarship and intellectual curiosity, having acquired them as he may have wished also to acquire the gestures of the British upper classes. But the letter does not accord smoothly with that image of mediocrity that predominates in the serious literature about him. And if there is a recurring picture of him from friends, it is that he could be a stimulating person to be with. "Very argumentative in a nice way," one close acquaintance has written. "He questioned everything. He had a great intellectual curiosity and the best sense of humor of any of the Kennedys." One of his many girl friends has complained, "He listened to *every* radio news broadcast." In Moscow American Ambassador Charles Bohlen became acquainted with Kennedy and found him "an extremely personable, attractive, and bright young man."[29]

After he was graduated from Harvard, Jack went to Stanford to earn a master's degree in economics, finance, and business administration. His original inclination to study law was lessened when Joe returned to Harvard to pursue that career. Jack left Palo Alto after ten weeks and began a tour of Latin America. In the meantime, Joe, who before Pearl Harbor had opposed conscription, left his second year at law school to join the dangerous navy air corps. Jack also decided to enlist. But his back was in such bad shape that both the army and the navy rejected him. A stiff exercise program and a political push from his father won him entry into the navy as an ensign, a commissioned rank.

Jack's first work in the fall of 1941 preceding Pearl Harbor was in the Office of Naval Intelligence in Washington. He there began a sexual liaison with a beautiful married journalist, Inga Arvad. He told her that he wished the quiet life of a teacher and writer of American history at a boys' preparatory school. The affair is astonishing because he was an intelligence officer and as Miss Europe she had been Hitler's personal guest at the Berlin Olympic Games of 1936—"a perfect example of Nordic beauty," *der Führer* called the blue-eyed blonde, to whom he granted a private interview. Inga had also received from Hermann Göring an award for winning a beauty contest in Berlin. FDR himself had asked J. Edgar Hoover to watch her closely. Hoover did. Or at least he had Jack and Inga's conversations recorded, evidently while they were having sexual intercourse in South Carolina. Jack's father—another intimate of this friendly woman, her son reports—averted his son's being cashiered from the navy and had him transferred out of Washington and, in mid-1942, to Northwestern University to take a course in seamanship. Jack learned in ninety days how to be a seagoing officer. He was appointed an instructor but had his father use influence to get him into action. By way of a Florida training post he was sent to the South Pacific to command a PT boat.[30]

Many of the fast, light boats were piloted by an elite drawn from upper-class families experienced in yachts and sailing. The boats had earned enthusiastic publicity when they were used for the daring evacuation of General Douglas MacArthur, his wife, and his son from Corregidor. MacArthur, convinced that by this act the PTs would win the war, propagandized for a large force, as did the best seller *They Were Expendable*, serialized in *Reader's Digest* during 1942. Yet the PTs sank few Japanese craft and sank some American ships by error. If they had any benefit, it was to strengthen morale at home.

Lacking the physical qualifications even to be a Sea Scout, Jack allowed himself to occupy a post where his bad back could disable him at a dangerous moment. In Pacific training he repeatedly piloted his boat recklessly, once risking his crew by braking too late and slamming into a dock in a game with another boat that tested which would brake first. On the night of August 1, 1943, in the Solomon Islands, the night before he became a hero, Kennedy's ship had been separated from its sister vessels during a confused encounter with a fast-moving Japanese convoy, which Jack and other boat commanders missed an opportunity to attack. The PT was the most maneuverable of navy vessels, and some expert opinion argues that only negligence on the part of its comander could have put *PT 109* into a position in which a Japanese destroyer sliced it in half. Perhaps that is an unfair allegation since it had been pitch-dark, but Kennedy himself later was to remark, "That whole story was more fucked-up than [the Bay of Pigs]." The plywood boat carrying thousands of gallons of gasoline was a floating bomb; in its explosion at 2:12 A.M. on August 2 two men died immediately. The boat lacked a life raft, which was standard equipment. The radioman was away from his post. In his own official report Kennedy blamed himself for running only one of his three engines in gear. General Mac-Arthur is reported to have said that Jack should have been court-martialed; senior naval personnel at his Florida training base were open in their condemnation. But Jack's towing of a badly burned crew member across miles of sea and his persistent efforts to save his crew were authentically heroic. For the incident he received the Purple Heart and a citation.[31]

Soon after his rescue Jack took command of another PT boat. On one occasion he found himself without enough gas to return to port after an expedition to evacuate an island. The gasoline supply crew had assured him that he would not be called into action that night and refused his requests to refuel. Once again Jack found himself at the center of controversy. The heavily armed *PT 59* attacked Japanese barges close to shore; the extra guns and crew slowed it down and made the forays very dangerous. According to one shipmate, "It got so that the crew didn't like to go out with him because he took so many chances." Then he devised a plan for daylight attacks with over-size guns against the Japanese on the nearby Warrior or Choiseul River. It was a reckless plan. Kennedy's boat would have been an easy target for shore batteries, and turning the eighty-foot craft around in midstream would have been dangerous. The idea caused more than one senior officer to question his judgment, and eventually Jack himself became disillusioned with the PTs and came home to have his back looked after.

Kennedy's career in the Pacific demonstrated courage, and to his own crews he was indisputably a hero. His wartime performance belonged to a lifetime of courage that took differing forms. Its deepest expression was the endurance of severe illness from childhood onward, so that during his presidency he was frequently in pain and when not before the public relied on crutches; but that endurance was undramatic and brought no military citations.

Meanwhile, Joe, Jr., in the navy had continued to be the roughneck and good Catholic of his earlier days. As president of his Florida base's Holy Name Society he would douse his mates with cold water to awaken them for early-morning mass, playfully chiding for anti-Semitism a priest who objected that he was using this treatment on Jews as well. In his early days of military training in Florida Joe himself evidently disliked authority. After a series of demerits he was assigned hours of marching and kept to the base on weekends.

After Jack's adventure Joe, according to a family friend, brooded in rage, "clenching and unclenching his fists" upon hearing toasts at Hyannis Port praising the Pacific hero who now outranked him. At his post in Britain, Joe volunteered both himself and his crew for extra flying missions over the English Channel, missions that have been described as "hours and hours of dull monotony sprinkled with a few moments of stark horror." Relentless in search of glory, Joe risked his plane against orders in flights close to the German-held island of Guernsey off Brest and near a German E-boat that was within the shield of antiaircraft fire. There could be strategy in this; a heroic record would be of particular use in postwar American politics in putting behind him his warnings that it would be better to accept Hitler's domination of Europe than to join the British.

Finally, the impatient Joe was offered the perfect moment. For the destruction of the strategically deadly and psychologi-

cally dangerous German V-1 rocket sites in France, impregnable
to conventional attack, someone hit on the ingenious idea of
creating a giant bomb in the form of an aircraft drone, its fuse to
be set by volunteers who would parachute just before approaching the English Channel. A former flier at Firstfield Base has
reported that the plan, named Aphrodite, was not untested.
The army had already sent six missions within the joint venture. None had succeeded, and one pilot had been killed, two
badly injured. Joe Kennedy, Jr., volunteered to lead the first
navy mission, and on a dismal summer's day after the Normandy invasion, black ammunition handlers loaded the plane
with eleven tons of explosives, probably the largest charge ever
put together up to that time. Takeoff for the B-24 aircraft,
painted white and named *Snowbird*, was 1752 hours Greenwich
civil time on August 8, 1944. Noting a dangerous defect in the
firing system, an electronics officer warned Joe not to go, but
Kennedy ignored him. The engines seemed sluggish as he slowly
maneuvered down the muddy runway, and the wheels left the
ground dangerously late. Minutes later the plane exploded over
Newdelight Wood with two high-order blasts one second apart;
the pilot following in a secondary mother plane has described
"the biggest explosion I ever saw until the pictures of the atom
bomb." It was the greatest airborne explosion over England during the war. Elliott Roosevelt, part of the air escort, was blinded
for a short time by the flash. Joe, Jr., won a posthumous Navy
Cross, and his father's friend Secretary of the Navy James V.
Forrestal ordered that a new 2,200-ton destroyer be named
Joseph P. Kennedy, Jr.; Robert Kennedy, fresh out of Harvard
Naval ROTC, was to serve on it briefly. Some months afterward
it was discovered that the intended target had been abandoned
for some time before the planned attack.[32]

For most of a year after Joe's death his father spent much
of each day alone, listening to his beloved classical music. He
had reared Joe to stretch to goals the father could not attain.
Young Joe's "worldly success was so assured and inevitable," his
brother Jack wrote beautifully in a family tribute, *As We Re-*

member Joe, "that his death seems to have cut into the natural order of things." The privately printed book also claims that Joe *"was"* successful, that his mission over "Europe" saved a great many lives.[33]

The war brought other grief to the Kennedys. The exuberant Kathleen ("Kick") had become popular in London, which was a fitting revenge for the blackballing of the family by a New England country club. In 1944 she married the wealthy Anglican William Cavendish, the Marquess of Hartington, despite parental disapproval on both sides and that of Bobby and Eunice, all on religious grounds, along with some outrage within the Catholic public. The young couple finally received the blessing of the groom's parents but not the bride's, who failed to attend the May ceremony and sent no word, although the elder Kennedy later wired a conciliatory message. Only Joe, Jr., was present. In August 1944 Kathleen, now reconciled with her family in the United States, received word that her husband had been killed leading an infantry charge in Normandy. According to the author Pearl Buck, Kathleen wrote to a friend: "God has taken care of the religious problem in His own way." She died in a plane crash in 1948.[34]

In the midst of its losses the family enjoyed worldly success. During and after the war Joe Kennedy speculated in real estate. His biggest coup, the purchase of Chicago's Merchandise Mart, earned him perhaps $60 million over the next decade and soon the attentiveness of Mayor Richard Daley. In Manhattan Kennedy presciently chose his sites: chiefly tracts of land from Forty-second to Fifty-ninth streets, east of Sixth Avenue. He watched their value double again and again. When tenants had their rents raised sharply, his lawyers argued that others technically owned the properties. Later he made a killing by stubbornly holding back a building needed for Lincoln Center. Oil and gas investments came next, and he considered buying the Brooklyn Dodgers for Jack but feared a third world war that would dampen the spirits even of Dodger supporters. By 1960 Joe Kennedy was worth between $200 and $400 million. Trust funds begun for his sons in the 1920s were now worth well over $10 million each. His son John had been a millionaire by the age of twelve. After the oil tycoons, Joe Kennedy was the richest self-made man in America.

In the postwar world he did not aim for political visibility. The views that he did express are of a kind that is loosely termed isolationist. By the late 1930s isolationism, with its ancestry in early twentieth-century progressivism, had been in the process of becoming a conservative's persuasion. And even in the early post-war years, when the enemy was communism, numbers of conservatives remained isolationist, if somewhat ambivalently so. They could look on the Truman administration's interventions for the protection of Western Europe against the Soviet Union as one more instance of a liberal's compulsion to waste American energies in the service of everyone on earth, and they could warn that further American involvement in Europe might infect us with what they saw as European decadence. Having held out against confrontations between the democracies and Nazi Germany, the elder Kennedy now opposed an overextension of our commitments to resist communism abroad. Arthur M. Schlesinger, Jr., making in *The Vital Center* what was in 1949 a liberal's argument, writes of an "important segment of business opinion" that "still hesitates to undertake a foreign policy of the magnitude necessary to prop up a free world against totalitarianism lest it add a few dollars to the tax rate," and Schlesinger presents Joseph Kennedy as an example of the isolationist spokesman for business. In a talk at the University of Virginia arranged by his son Robert, then a law student there, Kennedy criticized American meddling in the world. He denounced the Truman Doctrine, arguing that the policies of the Democrats had won us no dependable friends and had spread American might too thinly. Communism left to itself would breed internal dissension; Kennedy predicted the split between Communist China and the Soviet Union.[35]

Joseph Kennedy's isolationism did not sound quite like that of a right-winger or, at any rate, the sort of reactionary whom liberals have in mind, sympathetic to repressive anti-Communist regimes. "What business is it of ours to support French colonial policy in Indo-China or to achieve Mr. Syngman Rhee's concepts of democracy in Korea?" the speaker asked his Charlottesville, Virginia, audience. A news release prepared for him after a trip to Europe and dated May 20, 1951, reports his complaint: "We have . . . failed utterly to understand that there is a strong liberal feeling throughout Europe that is a valuable asset in the fight against Communism. By terming this as a Communist movement, we are only convincing the people over there that we are driving them into a war." One of the contentions of the postwar Kennedy was that an independent nation had a right to choose communism; the failures of that system would in time make it give way to democratic capitalism. About a decade separated Joseph Kennedy's opinions from his son John's policies for combating Communist insurgency and facing down Soviet expansion.[36]

Joseph Kennedy was still making public pronouncements, but from the end of the war onward he could work quietly to insure the further progress of a family that was becoming nationally prominent. He would soon see one of his sons fully established in politics; Robert, meanwhile, was preparing for a career in government service, and Edward was attending Harvard. In his later years the elder Kennedy became more and more a private person, knowing that his outspokenness could damage the political fortunes of his progeny. As John was receiving the 1960 Democratic nomination for presidential candidate, his father was having dinner with Henry Luce, during which Joe, with some experience at the business of purchasing offices, suggested that his guest buy a congressional seat for Luce's son. At Palm Beach and Hyannis Port, the senior Kennedys accommodated various in-laws in their large but close family. Joe lived until 1969; Rose Kennedy would be ninety-four years old in 1984.

The elder Joseph Kennedy quoted Francis Bacon's pronouncement that the progenitor of a family dynasty possesses qualities of good and evil. As John Adams had confided to his diary in 1802: "Am I planning the illustration of my family or the welfare of my country?" The qualities of mind and emotion that distinguished the picaresque Joseph Kennedy and his sons— an ability to succeed that drew both on talent and on sheer determination to be successful, a willful daring that had its roughest embodiment in the younger Joe—could have expressed themselves in some right-wing ideology of competition consonant with the father's career in business. One of Jack Kennedy's college friends reports, "We had a real shouting match about the Wagner Labor Act because he felt it was leaning much too far towards labor. I was saying, 'Come on, Jack, that's what your father thinks. You're just spouting what your father says!' Jack was *fils papa*, his father's son." From his earliest days in politics into the 1950s John Kennedy was something of a rightist, especially on questions of communism, and Robert Kennedy was a lawyer of Joseph McCarthy's Red-hunting Senate subcommittee. Yet the ambition and energies of the Kennedy brothers eventually found their outlet in liberalism. The forces of social change had the initiative in turning the Kennedy brothers toward liberalism. But there is a historical appropriateness in the liberalism of the Kennedys.

While the Kennedy family did not boast the aristocratic heritage and its immunity to financial chicanery that the Roosevelts could enjoy, it had its own assured communal milieu: strong connections within and among generations and, for much of the nineteenth century, the larger communities of Irish Catholicism and of urban and ethnic politics, with roots in the Irish traditions. These communities were not of a Burkean sort, traditional and unchanging. They created themselves out of action and had no identity or place except an American one that encouraged changing identities. The elder Joseph Kennedy never committed himself totally, and with no possibility of retreat, to the ruthless privacy of his career in business but went back to the Democratic political community. And he prepared his sons for public careers, in which success would be measured by popular acceptance. American liberals through their welfare measures have aimed at the establishment of economic community, a co-operative social order. In this, liberalism has been more intuitively conservative than the individualist philosophy that in this country goes falsely by the name of conservatism. And at the same time liberals have thought to achieve community not by that sinking into ancient routines and institutions that European conservatism championed but by positive acts of politics and legislation and administration—acts that invite the kinds of energies the Kennedy family has expressed for generations.

The elder Joseph Kennedy came to the New Deal through Democratic politics and, according to his account, his conviction that capitalism needed social reform for its own protection. It was not until the presidency of John Kennedy, and not really until its last days, that progressivism and the Kennedys were to enter into full alliance.

Some Kennedy had to be President, and Jack now took his brother Joe's place. "I told him Joe was dead," his father wrote later, "and that it was his responsibility." The father, according to Jack, "wanted his eldest son in politics. 'Wanted' isn't the right word. He demanded it. You know my father."

To increase the family name's visibility in the Bay State, Joe Kennedy served in 1945 as chairman of a commission to study the establishment of a Massachusetts department of commerce. He sold his Haig & Haig Scotch franchise at this time, perhaps out of fear that it might embarrass his sons' careers. Jack, seeking to keep himself before the public in preparation for the midterm election of 1946, served as a reporter for the Hearst papers. After working on an article arguing that the great powers should limit armaments instead of rearming, he covered the founding of the United Nations. He followed the British political campaign, publicly predicting that the election would be close but not that Churchill would lose. He later told newsman Peter Lisagor that he had written a story forecasting a victory for Labour but, confronted by his bosses, furious at so absurd a notion, had reworked his analysis to predict the Conservative triumph they expected; now he regretted that he had not stood by his original story. In his brief postwar news career he also reported on the Potsdam Conference. His editors, having billed him as "the PT hero who would explain the G.I. viewpoint," found his prose stilted.[37]

In 1946 Joe put Jack into the race for the congressional seat that Boston's Mayor James Michael Curley had once held. (Curley would soon be incarcerated in Danbury prison.) The Kennedys, though living elsewhere, had remained Boston's leading Irish family. Curley quipped that Jack, possessing the names of Fitzgerald and Kennedy, could forgo campaigning and proceed directly to Washington. But it was not as easy as that. The elder Kennedy had in effect planted his son in Boston politics, putting him into a harsh soil of working-class families, of city wards with their established leaders and rights of succession. The Kennedy and the Fitzgerald families had once belonged to that politics, but the shy young patrician Jack had to learn fast and to campaign hard, despite his reticence and his bad back, using his war record to make his Harvard manner more acceptable.[38]

Kennedy referred to himself as a fighting conservative; what he meant by the phrase was about as clear as a great deal of his rhetoric. He could also perform the political gestures of a liberal. Friendly biographers tell us of his horror at finding a gas stove and a toilet occupying the same bleak room in a Cambridge slum; the eleventh district, stretching to East Boston and almost wholly Roman Catholic, was the poorest in the state. Jack had a set speech beginning with a description of the sinking of *PT 109*, focusing on the heroism of some member of his crew. The expressed point of the little talk—a point reappearing in the 1960 presidential campaign—was the need for the electorate to make patriotic sacrifices in peacetime as it had in war. The candidate concentrated on bread-and-butter issues: housing and jobs.

The rhetoric of sacrifice went with the politics of self-interest. Navy and college friends of Jack, as well as all the Kennedys, including Rose, did their part. Amateurs were out front, but behind them worked the pols in one of the earliest campaigns

orchestrated by an advertising agency—that was the idea of the
elder Kennedy, who in Hollywood had been acquainted with the
techniques of public relations. Donating large sums to popular
Catholic charities, Joe Kennedy helped set up the Joseph P.
Kennedy, Jr., Chapter of the Veterans of Foreign Wars. He was
also responsible for running a second Joseph Russo in the Democratic primary to cut into the vote of a popular city councilman
of that name. Other primary candidates received thousands of
dollars from Joe to stay in the race or leave it, as occasion warranted—a common practice in Boston then. Always in the background, a biographer of Joe Kennedy notes, "was the smell of
Kennedy money, the sense of Kennedy power . . . the hope of
Kennedy reward." Joe had John Hersey's *New Yorker PT* 109
story reprinted in abridged form in *Reader's Digest*; every family
in the district got a copy before election day. Kenneth O'Donnell, Kennedy's political associate for many years, remarks that
the candidate, not given to the schmaltz of the old politics, did
not go to wakes except for those of friends. O'Donnell's comments are those of a loyal friend, but a certain distance and reserve in fact continued to mark Kennedy's behavior in a career
that encourages at least a façade of warmth. A Kennedy style
was entering Massachusetts politics, at variance with the ethnic
political ways of the Commonwealth's past. Kennedy won his
first election by a wide margin. He was twenty-nine years old.[39]

What did the victorious candidate believe in? Why, apart
from his family's and his own ambitious for a public career, had
he set out for Washington? Certainly the first letter that he
wrote for his constituents does not tell much. The report, which
was never distributed, complains of the poorly lighted House
chamber, the bad acoustics, and rude members who read newspapers or talked during speeches. For many years following, no
one consistent core of ideas was to reveal itself. Yet even at moments of his career deemed barren of definable intellectual commitments, there appeared in the politician Kennedy, as there had
appeared in the student, hints of a curiosity that would look beyond the conventions in which he daily trafficked. A year before

his entry into Congress he had been in Britain during a general election, and the economist Barbara Ward has remembered that he "was fascinated by the political process . . . and you would see already that this young lieutenant . . . was political to his fingertips." In 1947 or 1948, by her recollection, she met Kennedy on the *Queen Mary*, yellow with the malaria he had contracted in the service—was he completely well a day in his life?— but eager with questions about the social program of the Labour party, especially socialized medicine, and showing the same "extraordinary intellectual vividness." The emergence over time of a set of beliefs, or perhaps the gradual imprinting upon his mind of a set of national conditions, was to be many years away.[40]

The young congressman, reacting to the Soviet presence in Eastern Europe, did have at least one conviction, which he shared with much of his Catholic constituency: communism was a menace that had fooled or corrupted the American government. A 1948 headline in the *Boston Globe* reads: KENNEDY SAYS ROOSEVELT SOLD POLAND TO REDS. "At the Yalta Conference a sick Roosevelt, with the advice of General [George] Marshall," Kennedy said a year later (appropriately at Salem, Massachusetts), "gave the Kurile Islands as well as control of various strategic ports to the Soviet Union." Blame for the loss of China rested "squarely on the White House and the Department of State." The congressman denounced the Johns Hopkins Orientalist Owen Lattimore, who would later come under attack from Senator Joseph McCarthy for having advised the State Department to reconcile itself to Communist rule in China. Speaking at a Harvard seminar in 1950, Kennedy announced his liking for McCarthy, his support of the highly restrictive McCarran-Walter Immigration and Nationality bill, his disdain of the Fair Deal and the Truman administration, his pleasure at Richard Nixon's victory over the liberal senator Helen Gahagan Douglas in that year's contest in California, and his desire to get "the foreigners off our backs." He initially opposed the firing of General Douglas MacArthur. He was friendly to Nixon and McCarthy, and to George Smathers, whose vicious senatorial campaign defeated the liberal Claude Pepper in Florida. He opposed most expenditures for foreign aid, speaking on the floor of the House against aid to "Hottentots." He was almost alone in opposing tax cuts in 1947 and 1948, preferring a stronger air force. He also favored vast civil defense measures, as he would after the Berlin crisis of 1961.[41]

Kennedy's position on social and economic issues was in the center or to the right. He still disliked the Wagner Act of 1935, and at one point he called the Taft-Hartley bill a "fairly reasonable measure." He derided liberal "do-gooders" and voted against aid to the Navaho and Hopi Indians, money for public libraries in areas without any, funds for hospital construction, federal support for rural electrification coperatives, and a bill prohibiting discrimination in employment. But he favored an extension of Social Security benefits, a minimum wage law, and a national health program that would not "enslave" the medical profession. Acting for the United States Junior Chamber of Commerce, a group of industrialists friendly to his father once chose him one of ten outstanding young men of the year.[42]

But as Kennedy was rising to political prominence, illness once more stalked him. En route to the Soviet Union in September 1947 to study labor and education, Kennedy was stricken with Addison's disease, and he was given about a year to live. The illness weakens adrenal flow and increases susceptibility to secondary disease. But oral cortisone dramatically improved Kennedy's condition. It was a classic case. Kennedy's back surgery, undergone despite a history of Addison's, was reported in the November 1955 journal of the American Medical Association, *Archives of Surgery*. Dr. Janet Travell, his physician, found after the operation that he had a hole in his back that kept getting infected. He was very anemic, she ascertained, and he had acute allergies. She also discovered that the whole left side of his body was smaller than his right. In her oral history prepared for the Kennedy Library, Dr. Travell says candidly that while he did have Addison's disease, as it was then defined, to anticipate any criticisms about his capacity to hold office she signed a statement in the late 1950s that he did not; she explains that by a technicality she was correct. What was the effect on Kennedy of illness that might strike him down in his mid-forties? Surely his health affected his attendance in the House of Representatives. His increasingly frequent one-night stands with women—a "smorgasbord," one friend has recalled—may also have been a result. A serious illness may have set him on a tight schedule for success for the Senate and the presidency. And with the threat of death, fatalism and confidence may come more easily. A woman Kennedy dated has remembered him as insistent that he did not have much time, driven to grab everything he wanted, including her.[43]

Could the young congressman have foreseen anything of the double future for which circumstances were already directly preparing him: the increasingly successful political career and the pain of illness, which in his most private thoughts may have constituted, more than worldly ambition and more than some political philosophy, the motive for his relentless political effort and seeking? He seemed to become easily bored with the House. As early as 1948 he was anticipating a senatorial race, accepting few speaking engagements in his own congressional district but many throughout the rest of the state. A member of what commentators have called the Tuesday–Thursday Club—those were the days of the week when most House votes were taken and otherwise absent members appeared—he often devoted four full days to campaigning in Massachusetts. He was after the Senate seat of Henry Cabot Lodge, Jr., which would be available in 1952.

"We're going to sell Jack like soap flakes," said the Kennedy patriarch. Money drenched Kennedy campaign headquarters; advertising was a barrage. The Kennedys repeated their strategy of charitable contributions, awarding them out of its Joseph P. Kennedy, Jr., Foundation, of which John was president. In 1951, for example, $5,000 went to the Italian-American Charitable Society. Of another ethnic charity "Dad" wrote to Jack in March

1952: "We might send them a check for $1000 only because it is this year." A political hack wrote in 1951: "In connection with . . . our interest in Jack, it occurs . . . that it might be of mutual benefit if the Kennedy Foundation could . . . aid the [Negro] project. . . . You realize, of course, that we could make quite an event of the support of the Foundation, but it would have to be timed carefully." Jack Kennedy wrote disarmingly to a California correspondent as the 1952 campaign approached: "The Foundation has been concentrating its donations . . . in the Massachusetts area." Joe lent a half million dollars to the McCarthyite publisher of the *Boston Post*. "You know we had to buy that fucking paper, or I'd have been licked," he is reputed to have told a Harvard classmate.[44]

Jack later insisted: "It wasn't the Kennedy name and the Kennedy money that won that election. I beat Lodge because I hustled for three years. I worked for what I got. *I* worked for it." Doubtless true. And perhaps any discomfort that Kennedy ever felt over his family's money-soaked campaigns indicates a greater sensitivity than the American people as a whole may feel. A campaign manager has observed that Kennedys can spend as much as they want on campaigns because the public knows they have the money for it. Never having worried very much about why wealth is distributed as it is, Americans do not ordinarily resent the extravagance of the wealthy. It is the welfare checks of the poor that more commonly anger them.

Robert Kennedy served as campaign manager and provided much of the energy for the 1952 Senate contest, coercing some politicos, bullying others, and compiling a lengthy study that claimed to demonstrate that Lodge had been soft on communism. The Kennedy tactic of flooding the campaign at every point with every resource dictated even the gathering of names to put John on the ballot. Only 2,500 names were needed; the candidate garnered more than 262,000, and each petitioner received a letter of thanks. Joe urged his Catholic Republican friend Senator Joseph McCarthy not to visit the state on behalf of Lodge. The Wisconsin senator would nonetheless have come into Massachusetts had Lodge agreed to appear with him and endorse his work. Part of the strategy was to attack Lodge for spending too little time on domestic issues, and the *Boston Post* denounced him as a "Truman Socialistic New Dealer." The candidate also played host at lots of tea parties attended by lots of Kennedys; members of the Kennedy family saturated the state, shaking some two million hands. To a Jewish audience Jack observed, "Remember, I'm running for the Senate, not my father." Once again the Hersey *PT 109* article went out, this time to "every dwelling in Massachusetts" and was carefully placed on bus seats and in cabs. On the title page was the banner headline JOHN FUL-FILLS DREAM OF BROTHER JOE WHO MET DEATH IN THE SKY OVER THE ENGLISH CHANNEL. The Kennedy camp tried to phone every Massachusetts voter at least twice. Archbishop Richard Cushing's public weekday baptism of Bobby and Ethel's baby just before the election typifies the prominence the family enjoyed. Jack won by some 70,000 votes.

In 1953 Jack Kennedy, one of Washington's most debonair bachelors, married Jacqueline Bouvier, daughter of John V. Bouvier III, a financier, and Mrs. Hugh D. Auchincloss of Newport and New York. The looks, graces, and lineage of the wife went with much of what the Kennedy family had been cultivating. The upbringing of the bride had included attendance at Miss Porter's School, which emphasized manners, but she had also tried a career in journalism. Stories about her indicate a good deal beyond a wedding cake figure. She translated several French articles for John, including materials on Indochina. When Joe Kennedy complained that Palm Beach had lost its "old zipperoo," she chided him: "You ought to write a series of grandfather stories for children like 'The Duck with Moxie' or 'The Donkey Who Couldn't Fight His Way Out of a Telephone Booth.'" To the question of where the Democrats should hold their 1960 convention, she answered "Acapulco." Yet it was her surface, her attractiveness and social finish, that lent itself to the later public perception of the Kennedy style. And apparently she relished presenting just that surface to the public and to herself.

Jack once returned a Jaguar she had given him, and in 1961, to his disgust, she spent $50,000 on clothing.[45]

As a senator, John Kennedy engaged in little of the rhetoric that had once denounced the government gifts to the Soviet Union and Lodge's softness on communism. Travel to Europe and the Far East in 1951 evidently broadened his views and his awareness of what he termed the "fires of nationalism." That same year he said on "Meet the Press" that the executive branch had for the most part cleared out its subversives. He was also privately criticizing the Red-hunting craze. Later he voted against McCarthy's wishes on federal appointments. He once told William Benton of Connecticut, defeated in a bid for reelection to the Senate after opposing McCarthy, that Benton should have been included in *Profiles in Courage*. Yet he did not otherwise join the liberals in their eventually successful resistance to Red-baiting. His own Massachusetts Irish Catholic constituency of 75,000—once having contained many supporters of the pro-Nazi and anti-Semitic Father Charles Coughlin and until 1944 having as its cardinal the reactionary William O'Connell—was intensely anti-Communist and predominantly favorable to McCarthy. Jack's brother Robert was a counsel for McCarthy's permanent investigatory subcommittee. Though voting early in 1953 with most senators to approve the nomination of McCarthy's foe James B. Conant, recently president of Harvard, to be ambassador to West Germany, Jack Kennedy told the Senate that he could never have favored Conant as commissioner of education. A speech that had been prepared for delivery at St. Paul, Minnesota, on November 15, 1953, at a testimonial dinner for Senator Hubert Humphrey and Representative Eugene McCarthy did put a distance between Kennedy and the tactics of Joseph McCarthy: "I want you to note that I said . . . Representative, not Senator, McCarthy. Indeed, I think what this country needs is more of this type of . . . McCarthyism." But the next year Kennedy, having just undergone two serious back operations, was the only one of the ninety-six senators who neither voted directly on the censure of Joe McCarthy nor used the device of pairing with a senator of opposite persuasion so that he could recuperate and still have an effect on the vote.[46]

Asserting that his friend would surely have voted for the censure, for no Democrat voted against it, Kenneth O'Donnell argues that Kennedy had been sick too long to keep up with the question. But it is clear that he had been thinking about it. His adviser Theodore Sorensen, who for that matter was empowered to deliver Kennedy's vote, reports persuading Kennedy not to vote or pair since censure would violate McCarthy's procedural rights. Kennedy did not even announce his position on the censure. He had indeed prepared a speech justifying on legal grounds a vote to censure, but pointedly remarking, "Many times I have voted with Senator McCarthy, for the full appropriation of funds for this Committee, for his amendment to reduce our assistance to nations trading with Communists, and on other matters. I have not sought to end his investigations of Communist subversion." The undelivered speech took a thin, safe line: opposing the tactics of McCarthy's subordinates, claiming that no international damage had resulted from McCarthy's work, and avoiding the all-important question of McCarthy's methods. Kennedy after the censure cosponsored a Senate resolution affirming the necessity for a rigorous investigation of communism.

As another Irish Catholic with a war record Kennedy could have been a good opponent of McCarthy, but the junior senator from Wisconsin was close to the family, not only to the elder Kennedy, who contributed to his campaigns, but to Jack, Eunice, her husband-to-be Sargent Shriver, and Patricia, whom he dated. Jack liked McCarthy, who, when he was not on the attack, had a way that could mellow even a political enemy. Early in 1954 Jack interrupted a speaker at the hundredth anniversary of Harvard's Spee Club who had remarked how glad he was that Harvard College had produced neither an Alger Hiss nor a Joe McCarthy. "How dare you couple the name of a great American patriot with that of a traitor?" Kennedy demanded. The friendship of Kennedys, rarely given to the full, could be wholehearted. "I might say," wrote Jack as late as 1958 to a constituent, "that I do not think that action by the Senate necessarily implies condemnation of the late Senator McCarthy."[47]

Kennedy himself, in fact, as a member of the lower House had once scooped two better-known anti-Communists, McCarthy and Nixon. With signal help from his staff and from fellow congressman Richard Kersten he accomplished the first dramatic postwar encounter between the Congress and the American Communist Party. On the Education and Labor Committee of the Eightieth Congress, he diligently pursued the Communist Harold Christoffel of the United Auto Workers, showing that his quarry had committed perjury before the committee. Christoffel was convicted. Kennedy claimed that Christoffel should not be able to appeal the decision, but the Supreme Court overturned it. In 1954 Kennedy joined other Democrats in supporting the Communist Control Act, which outlawed the party. Adlai Stevenson and Hubert Humphrey also supported the act, Humphrey proposing an amendment denying to the Communist party almost any rights at all. That is a measure of the public mentality of a generation that had witnessed in nazism the force and danger of revolutionary ideology and believed with reason that the American Communist party had given its loyalty to a hostile foreign power. But other Americans, among them J. Edgar Hoover and Eisenhower's attorney general, Herbert Brownell, opposed the act on constitutional procedural grounds. Nothing in Kennedy's career up to this time suggests a temperament capable of questioning popular anticommunism or the measures that expressed it. Certainly his constituency would have wanted it no other way.[48]

During his recuperation from back surgery Jack worked on materials that were to be published as *Profiles in Courage*, a narration of incidents from the public lives of senators who had dared take unpopular or politically risky stands for the sake of principle. The production of the book is a telling incident in the packaging of politicians. It is a convention among twentieth-century public figures to have written for them in their own names books that serve as public presentations of them as reflective commentators. Kennedy did write in draft the equivalent of a chapter or two, but the book is largely the work of the faithful Ted Sorensen, whose father had been campaign manager for George Norris, one of the senators profiled. Sorensen had suggested the idea. He has modestly remarked, "I prepared the materials on which the book is based." Kennedy acknowledged to Drew Pearson that the publisher had paid $6,000 to Sorensen, whom James MacGregor Burns has understood to say flat-out that he had written the book. He cannot be accused of writing all of it: James Landis remembers contributing to the chapter on Daniel Webster. There is a certain boldness about Sorensen; he drafted an apology for Pearson to publish after the columnist had questioned Kennedy's authorship.[49]

Profiles in Courage, whoever its authors, is a highly readable book. One of its most suitable audiences would be high school students who could learn from it some American history, along with instruction in civic morality. It is worth having been written and published; it is undoubtedly more literate and richer in theme than much of what politicians have ghostwritten for them. It is, of course, a book about political courage rather than an exercise in courage on the part of John Kennedy. To talk of the virtues of defying a constituency will not offend a constituency. It is, if anything, flattering to the electorate; only an actual defiance will get a politician in trouble.

Profiles, its putative author a certified war hero, locates the courage of its subjects not in war, which some of them had experienced, but in the intellectual and moral struggles of politics. So courage, as the book presents it, can be private, undramatic, the endurance of loss of a career or the scorn of the public. And *Profiles* offers some impressive examples, among them Republican Senator Edmund G. Ross of Kansas, who defied his state and party to vote against convicting President Andrew Johnson —a vote cast in isolation, with no admiring audience to applaud the heroism. Yet there is something about the courage explored in *Profiles* that makes it at times more automatic, less an act of self-conquest than it might be. Nineteenth-century statesmen were supposed to tell their publics and themselves that their principles counted to them for more than conventional success, and surely many of them meant it, meant it so surely that the gestures of intractable rectitude could come with little confusion and pain. Among the profiled heroes is John Quincy Adams, one of the most intellectually powerful and granitically moral Americans of the century; the book describes, for instance, his support of Jefferson's embargo, much to the anger of the fellow New England Federalists. But Adams knew himself absolutely as an Adams, an embodiment of Principle, and he had the approval of his father, the second President of the Republic, another towering figure. How difficult was it for him simply to act like an Adams? Very difficult perhaps, but all that *Profiles* can give is his undisturbed surface. *Profiles* makes a good point about courage: that its motive is not an abstract concept of the public good but self-love and self-respect.

Hindsight suggests some ways in which *Profiles in Courage* and the rest of John Kennedy's career can illuminate each other. The depiction of courage that is nearly synonymous with self-control under stress hints at the style that the Kennedy administration would try to bring to foreign policy. That the courage in question stood in every case against some kind of popular feeling is also relevant to the Kennedy phenomenon. Kennedy's advisers worked hard to package their man to the public taste, and he seldom consciously took a position unpopular with his constituency, though he did so once or twice. Yet while it has been said that he made you feel he was your best friend, there remained about him a certain aloofness, and his administration was to favor technical expertise over the warmer arts of popular politics. Several of the heroes in *Profiles* had their moments of bravery in defense of compromise against what the book portrays as militant extremism. That quest of the carefully constructed solution, not fully gratifying to the passions of any faction, has its affinities to the technician mentality and to the steady sobriety that the book detects in courage. *Profiles* is also a commentary on the moral priorities of Kennedy and his advisers at this time. Much of the compromising that the book approves of was for reconciling North and South before the Civil War by a shelving of the slavery issue or for reconciling the sections after the war at the expense of the freedmen. In referring to Reconstruction as "a black nightmare the South never could forget," the author or authors were merely falling back on what in the mid-fifties was still the received popular mythology about Reconstruction. But for decades careful scholarship had been learning to perceive that period as one of progress for racial justice. It would not be until the civil rights movement of the early 1960s, with its vision beyond anything the authorship of *Profiles* or the rest of the nation at midcentury had arrived at, that the more sophisticated historiography of Reconstruction could be communicated even to the educated public.

Whether *Profiles in Courage* is Pulitzer Prize material, Arthur Krock as a member of the Pulitzer committee made sure that it obtained one. In 1955 it pushed out, among other contenders, Burns's magnificent *Roosevelt: The Lion and the Fox.* Sorensen's presence in a book that bears Kennedy's name does not in itself raise any very clear moral issue. Even scholars paraphrase widely, and they incorporate into their own books materials that their colleagues have sketched out for them. Editors rescue abysmal material, sometimes receiving no thanks in a book's acknowledgments. Politicians and other prominent figures whose reputations do not rest on scholarship have books ghostwritten for them, and the practice is rarely questioned. As for Kennedy's acceptance of a Pulitzer Prize for such a work, about all that can be said is that he was a twentieth-century politician, readying himself to be packaged and media-sent. Wherever he centered his integrity, it was not in the code of a writer or scholar; otherwise he would not have had anyone write a book for him. To confess to the real origins of *Profiles*, become a public spectacle in payment for his honesty, and weaken his career lay outside the field of possibilities that a careerist of his sort could have seriously imagined. Published in the era of Joe Mc-

Carthy's censure, *Profiles in Courage* gave rise to the frequent comment that Kennedy should have shown less profile and more courage.[50]

Kennedy's record on civil rights in his senatorial years reflects not much more curiosity about the issue than does *Profiles in Courage*. He courted segregationists like Senator Herman Talmadge and Governor Marvin Griffin. On the four critical civil rights votes in the Senate of his day, he sided with the South twice and with liberals twice. In contrast with his Massachusetts colleague Leverett Saltonstall, he supported Title III of the 1957 Civil Rights Act, which would have given the attorney general broad powers to seek federal injunctions against violators of civil rights, including the right to vote. Title III failed to pass. But earlier, ostensibly for procedural reasons, Kennedy had voted in a peculiar coalition to keep the bill as a whole from bypassing the Senate Judiciary Committee, where, conservatives hoped, it could be defeated. He also voted for an amendment, which narrowly passed, requiring jury trials for accused violators of the prospective law. The enforcement of civil rights in the South would be in what was then the dubious keeping of local juries. Many northern intellectuals, including numerous members of law school faculties, favored the jury trial as a constitutional safeguard; James Landis of Harvard, who advised Kennedy to vote yes, told him, "This is a problem that the South has to gradually come to." Kennedy wrote to one southerner, "the legislation . . . will be effected by *Southern* courts, and juries considering civil rights cases will be *Southern* juries."[51]

Vice President Nixon, presiding over the Senate, where he made procedural rulings against southerners, called the day of the jury trial amendment "one of the saddest days in the history of the Senate because it was a vote against the right to vote." Nixon, by contrast with Kennedy, was an honorary member of the NAACP in the 1950s, he once cast a tie-breaking vote to end a Senate filibuster against civil rights legislation, and he received praise from Eleanor Roosevelt for working on behalf of civil rights.

Kennedy had good reason for caution. His most important constituency had been the South in the 1956 vice presidential voting—his first reach beyond the Senate—and he tried to hold on to it as long as he could. He had become a candidate not long after acquiring prominence through publishing *Profiles in Courage*. A run for the vice presidency in 1956 appealed to him quite simply because it was a challenge and because Sorensen advised that it would be an acceptable route to the presidency for a Roman Catholic. Kennedy allowed Ted Sorensen, who was by then almost in himself Jack's national political machine, to leak the Bailey memorandum, named for the Connecticut state Democratic chairman, arguing that a Catholic candidate would strengthen rather than harm a national ticket. Eisenhower, the memorandum observed, had won dangerously strong Catholic support in 1952. The leak was a brilliant way of turning a possible Kennedy liability into an asset. At the 1956 Chicago convention Kennedy appeared before the delegates on the first night, narrating a film of the recent history of the party. Later he gave the principal nominating speech for Adlai Stevenson; Sorensen had been its author. Southern backing made Kennedy an important challenger in the open convention fight for the vice presidential spot. Lyndon Johnson, like other politicos, resented the rich young independent as an upstart. Yet the Texan called him "the fighting sailor who wears the scars of battle." Kennedy lost to Tennessee Senator Estes Kefauver, a racial liberal with a better record on agricultural price supports than Kennedy who, unlike Kennedy, had been willing to engage in a tearful appeal to Humphrey for assistance. Kennedy's assessment of Kefauver as "the kind of person who kept looking over your shoulder for someone more important as he talked with you" is less an accurate portrayal of Kefauver than an illustration of Kennedy's distaste for the manners of politics. The remark, like Kennedy's comment that labor leader James Hoffa had "no discrimination or taste," hints of the disdain of the wellborn for people who have not been able to attain their position with money and easy grace.[52]

Kennedy was fortunate not to gain the vice presidential nomination. The Democrats were going to lose, and a Catholic on the ticket might have been blamed. As it was, the run for the vice presidency further established Kennedy as a national political figure. Stevenson's decision to open the vice presidential nomination instead of picking his running mate had brought to the convention an excitement that could attach to Kennedy, and he was attractive as he appeared before the delegates in graceful acceptance of the outcome. Kennedy, Stevenson wrote him, had left the convention "a much bigger man than you arrived. If there was a hero, it was you." It was, as Burns puts it, a moment of triumphant defeat.[53]

3

The Candidate
Discovers
the Liberals

TWENTIETH-CENTURY AMERICAN LIBERALS ELUDE ANY COMPLETE
definition. Their central commitment is to putting every available instrument—law, administration, social science, pure science,
technology—to the improvement of life, and since Americans
of almost any political persuasion can answer to that description, liberals are distinguishable only by degree. They want a
faster pace of egalitarian change than conservatives desire. They
do not take to the philosophical certainties of sectarian left
groups, and their militant antagonism to totalitarian movements
and regimes has strengthened their unwillingness to couch their
arguments in metallic ideological vocabularies. For much of the
century they seemed to trust more than others to the methodo-
logical precision and the dispassionate mind of modern science
and sociology. One way of identifying American liberalism, then,
is to locate it in professions and social groups in which that trust
is strongest, groups that since the late nineteenth century have

been applying scientific, technical, and professional methods to the investigation and solution of social problems.

Prominent in this respect are academicians and media professionals. That does not necessarily mean that most journalists and professors are liberal; it means that journalistic inquiry in muckraking or other forms, the labors of sociologists and economists, and literary or similar academic criticisms of culture can turn their practitioners into reformist commentators on the world they investigate. Critical analysis, of course, can also make for ironic detachment, sometimes in paradoxical conjunction with a desire to act upon the world. Professors and journalists are usually detached from power, even when the detachment is not deliberate, and they may long for some agent of power they can attach themselves to. They want this for the worst of reasons —a frustrated appetite to dominate—and for the best—a desire for the spread of prosperity, justice, and enlightenment.

Liberal professionals, therefore, seek even as they fear a kind of public figure who is in many ways their opposite; they look for the aggressive activist, the leader. Sometimes they are drawn to a labor unionist, to a politician who speaks for the urban poor, to anyone they are convinced must be more authentic than they, for liberals can be despairingly conscious of being privileged and unworthy of their social and economic good fortune. But at other times they are attracted by a patrician, possessed of education and tastes like theirs but confident and easy in the uses of power: a Theodore Roosevelt, Franklin D. Roosevelt, or John F. Kennedy. And the patrician may be attracted to the liberal professional, recognizing the common ground of education and profiting from sharper ideas, clearer writing, more sophisticated social analysis than a busy politician can achieve.

The late 1950s were a propitious time for Kennedy and the liberal professionals to find each other. Liberal scholarship and social criticism were again on the attack, widely listened to in their assaults on what was then perceived, even among American suburbanites, to be the mediocrity of the culture of suburbia. And at a time when the poor were not very noticeable except to one another, the culture of suburbia was thought to be the culture of the nation. When just a few years later Newton Minow, President Kennedy's chairman of the Federal Communications Commission, called television a vast wasteland and tried to get the commission to require better programming, he was acting in the spirit of the liberal social criticism of the times. Liberal journalism was also combative, not only against the culture that distressed social critics but against the inactivity of the national government and other American institutions. John Kennedy apparently belonged to that small company of Americans who actually read *New York Times* editorials. Liberals, in politics as well as in the professions, were insisting above all else on the need for the nation to awaken lethargic energies and to begin a period of growth in its economy—to finance an increase in its military and foreign aid, its education and culture. Nothing could have better suited the style, rhetoric, or taste that is remembered of Kennedy in his presidential years.

Today Americans see not liberalism but conservatism as the political camp more single-mindedly committed to the growth of the economy. But in the 1950s when the Soviet industrial growth rate was larger than ours, the belief in growth as a primary national objective was unchallenged. Rockefeller Panel reports during the late fifties called repeatedly for it. After the 1960 elections President Eisenhower's Commission on National Goals released its report, *Goals for Americans*. Besides urging an increase in military spending, which the philosophy of growth envisioned along with economic expansion, the document argued for a policy of foreign aid that would stimulate growth in Latin America and Africa and for spending that would quicken the domestic economy.

It was actually the liberals who spoke most insistently for growth. Liberalism still belonged to the tradition that presumed an affinity between social reform and the forces of science and technology, and it had not been many years since the New Deal era, when artists made poetry, in words or films or murals, of an American people expressing themselves in the works of modern industry. More particularly, a commitment to an activist government made midcentury liberals fit champions of federally planned and stimulated growth. No ecology movement had yet come to turn a portion of liberals suspicious of industrial development. Conservationists, predecessors of present-day ecologists, stood in the proud lineage of early twentieth-century progressivism, when conservation had meant the ordered protection and careful deployment of the continent's resources at the service of productivity. An ethos of growth was to inform the thinking, for example, of Walt W. Rostow, a liberal adviser in the early days of the Kennedy administration. His *Stages of Economic Growth: A Non-Communist Manifesto*, published in 1960, proposes that the West aid poorer countries through stages of economic maturation that will end by providing a general well-being communism cannot match. The nation, Rostow says, should look on the Soviet Union as a business rival.

A commitment to bigness, a conviction that economic growth is a precondition for a good life, an unashamed dedication to large national objectives abroad distinguished the liberalism of the times from the radicalism that was later to call for a technology and an economics of smaller scale, prudently managed. While no major political faction opposed growth or bigness, a reflective conservatism came closest to doing so. In 1952 the *Atlantic* carried an article by Arthur M. Schlesinger, Jr., one of the most trenchant early spokesmen for cold war liberalism, attacking for their narrowness the foreign policy goals of Senator Robert A. Taft, then seeking the Republican presidential nomination. A responding article by a conservative professor makes a careful case for Taft's modest military and diplomatic objectives that, with some rephrasing, would read like the work of a liberal of the 1980s.[1]

After the Soviet launching of *Sputnik I* in 1957 Kennedy was among the first public figures to enter a troubled national discussion about the failure of our school system to produce a similar achievement. His party made a major issue of the necessity for education in science. But the question of *Sputnik* as

Americans addressed it reflected at least peripherally their continuing general preoccupation with the national character. Did our lag in this one scientific endeavor indicate that our school system encouraged softness and indolence? Critics had been complaining for some years about a conformity, in the workplace and in the suburbs, that represented our moral timidity of imagination. Here the anxiety directly concerned the national character, and the notion that we were a conformist people, that our work was unleavened by curiosity and daring provided an explanation of why our science and technology had not taken our country into space. In retrospect the discussion is revealing not so much for whatever actual defects in American civilization it may have illuminated as for its own implicit American assumption about the rejuvenation of national character: that a people should forever work to define their imperfections and correct them.

As publicists discussed the intangible needs of American society, the economy offered its own argument for a change in political direction. By the end of the fifties it had reached the state of sluggishness and considerable unemployment recurrent in modern economies that have solved the worst problems of major depressions. Big companies competed sedately for marginal increases in their portions of the market or purchased their smaller competitors, for the most part avoiding price wars and enjoying a protected, comfortable, and highly profitable existence. While the economy was making many Americans remarkably prosperous, it put Republicans at a disadvantage within a portion of the electorate. A politically important segment of the work force now belonged to large labor unions that throughout the decade had exacted wage increases for their memberships as company profits rose. But by 1958 the threat or the fact of unemployment affected many union members as well as less protected workers. Conservatives further antagonized labor by bringing before several state legislatures right to work bills outlawing arrangements between management and labor that required membership in a union as a condition for employment.[2]

Beneath those economic classes having access to the political process dwelt the poor. The poverty that remained in American society was less brutal and less widespread than the deprivations suffered by Americans earlier in the century. The real, if rocky, prosperity of the day, supplemented by the modest welfare programs of the New and the Fair Deals, which continued under Eisenhower, provided some barriers against extreme suffering. The poor, as Michael Harrington observes in a book John Kennedy read, *The Other America*, had become in large measure "invisible": isolated in migrant camps or inner cities the middle class had abandoned; confined in lonely tenement rooms or in hospitals; appearing on the streets in mass-produced clothes that hid the poverty of the wearers. Within a few years poverty was to become highly visible in American politics. But at the time John Kennedy was making his campaign for the presidency, it had a small place, if that, in the rhetoric of politics. The election year of 1960 was a time not of anger or of deep distress but of political restlessness, for which the public style of John Kennedy was well fitted.

That academic liberals should have presented themselves as the partisans of energetic domestic programs is to be expected; they had been so since the early New Deal. That they should have joined with conservatives in a lament over the decline in national character, a demand for an education productive of tougher minds and higher ambitions, sets them apart from more recent liberals. The academic liberals of the late fifties had not been exposed to the personalist doctrines that have led their recent counterparts to surrender the concern for character to conservatives and fundamentalist preachers. More startling is the urgent, relentless preoccupation of the liberals of the Eisenhower era with the country's need for an advance in weaponry. No Reagan Republican, pleading for the MX missile, can compete with those midcentury liberals in their anger at the state of the American defense system. In this, too, they were the party of energy and growth.

In a press conference on January 26, 1960, William McGaffin of the *Chicago Daily News* asked President Eisenhower why, "in view of the international prestige at stake," we were not acting more strenuously to catch up with Russia in space. Begin that question again, demanded the President. McGaffin responded, "I said, in view of the international prestige at stake." "Is it?" replied Eisenhower, and the reporter asked if the President did not think it was. "Not particularly, no," answered the chief executive who was one of the nation's great military heroes. It is a conservative's answer, conservative in his refusal to be rushed by the latest occasion for worry and excitement, conservative in his determination to distinguish what is of enduring importance from what is not. It also reveals what it was in Eisenhower that during the 1950s and early 1960s, before the most recent reappraisals of him, made liberals and intellectuals so cruelly contemptuous. The man had no ideas, no vision, at least not if ideas are judged by the amount of motion they are intended to generate.[3]

The President, who instead of increasing defense spending after *Sputnik*, cut it, spoke like a later-day campaigner for the nuclear freeze when he argued for his defense budget: "A deterrent has no added power, once it has become completely adequate for compelling the respect of any potential enemy." Liberals could have agreed with the letter of that dictum, which technically is something of a tautology. But its implication, which is that the country could settle for an economical deterrent force and need not go restlessly seeking bigger weapons, could not have won their assent. In the later years of the Eisenhower administration liberals were reacting to projections that seemed to indicate an actual or future Soviet superiority over us in nuclear weaponry, the "missile gap" of the 1960 presidential campaign. The Gaither Report for 1957 warned of it, as did General James Gavin's *War and Peace in the Space Age.*

A "feeling of emergency grips the people of the free world," announced the *New York Times* in the autumn of 1957, and "our people will not hesitate to make whatever sacrifices are needed." The *Times* in those days wanted a presidential leadership that could affirm that we were in a "race for survival." The paper did not merely desire to close the missile gap; it sought a crash program that could "assure our superiority in missiles." Nelson Rockefeller, the most prominent spokesman for the liberal wing of the Republican party and, after his New York State gubernatorial victory of 1958, one of the most influential politicians in the country, wanted a massive program of fallout shelters for the state and called for resumption of nuclear testing, which had been halted in 1958. The Rockefeller Brothers Fund Report of 1958, prepared under the direction of Henry Kissinger, then identifiable as a liberal, observes that a nuclear stand-off does not consist of two static opposing weapon systems but is dynamic and requires us to improve our deterrent force as technology advances the opponent's force. The report's claim for a civil defense program, foreshadowing the first months of the Kennedy presidency in its emphasis on will, argues that deterrence depends not only on power but on a willingness to use it, which a civil defense policy promising survival could strengthen within a nation. Joseph Alsop, a Democratic liberal and speaking for a militancy that would later get him known as a right-winger, was among the journalists convinced of the missile gap. After the election of Kennedy the discussion of a missile gap continued for only a brief time. Richard Rovere, the liberal author of a devastating retrospective of Joseph McCarthy, wrote in the *New Yorker* for January 21, 1961, that the missile gap would probably be permanent. The *New Republic*, by reputation about as leftist as any prominent journal could get in an American politics that had virtually banished the far left from sight, on January 30 blamed Eisenhower for the missile gap. But the conservative *U.S. News & World Report* in the preceding week had given figures indicating that the gap did not exist.[4]

While the liberals were the more insistent on an increase in nuclear weaponry, it was the Eisenhower administration, speaking particularly through Secretary of State John Foster Dulles, that had been more prepared to center the country's defense in these weapons. Its rationale had been that with a sufficient nuclear force we could face down Soviet aggression without the use of conventional troops. The trouble with this doctrine was that without an adequate conventional military to supplement its nuclear bombs, the country would have no flexibility in its response to a Soviet or local Communist thrust abroad. To threaten a nuclear strike in retaliation for a Communist-inspired insurgency or coup might not be credible; the Soviet leadership could reasonably assume that we would not invite a nuclear counterstrike against us to save a few hundred square miles far from our borders. The threat would not even be relevant unless the local event were not only in the Soviet interest but under Soviet control. Liberals wanted a development of our conventional military capacity so that in our reply to a limited crisis we could choose among kinds and degrees of force. However tenuous may have been John Kennedy's connections with liberal Democratic programs, he spoke like a liberal in 1960, when in a campaign book, *The Strategy of Peace,* he wrote that the nation "must regain the ability to intervene effectively and swiftly in any limited war anywhere in the world." This, more than the issue of the missile gap that had the greater prominence in the 1960 campaign, was suited to the tastes and image of the war hero candidate who soon was to reveal his fascination for elite troops and light mobile equipment.

Educators, particularly in groups like the National Education Association and the American Association of Graduate Schools, joined the campaign for defense spending. Such organizations had constituencies that could profit from a flow of federal money into liberal arts, social science, and scientific technological research in response to the Soviet competition and could profit less tangibly from the honor of furthering a national purpose in a time of emergency. But there is no cause to doubt that the country's organized educators sincerely favored defense programs that could nourish science and technology and recognized the contribution that technical and scientific inquiry made to the nation's defense. Their endorsement of an advanced defense program symbolizes an alliance that had lasted several decades between political liberalism and the academy, in both its scientific and its humane fields. There was a sense of having made a common commitment to dispassionate investigation and to shaping the world around them into more rational patterns.

The mentality, in fact, bore on the way that liberals had looked on the cold war from its inception and on their conviction that the country should be bracing itself to confront the Communist bloc actively, deftly, variously across the globe. The stridency of the warnings of a missile gap, and the sonorousness of the calls to resolution in the face of peril, do not catch the tone of cold war liberalism. Liberal strategists during the Truman administration and liberal commentators since had argued, in answer to the political right, for policies of resistance to international communism that were measured, exact, cool, patient. It was as though the technological intelligence that maintained the economies and the weaponries of the great powers were to lend its sober competence and self-control to world politics as well. Modern technology itself, of course, occasioned and shaped the cold war, drawing the United States and the Soviet Union into every corner of the globe. The Truman presidency's efforts to shore up Western Europe against the Soviet Union appeared to some conservatives one more burdensome liberal exercise in taking on other people's troubles; then the diplomacy of Secretary of State Dean Acheson appeared a policy of weakness, with no satisfying results in sight, no Communists on the run. It was a Democratic, largely liberal administration that committed American troops to Korea; it was the administration's enemies who wished to bomb China and get the war over with. The conservatism of President Eisenhower, a distaste for activity that could not prove its necessity, was of another kind, and he despised McCarthyism, that emotional saturnalia of the right. But then the right wing of the Republican party had decided, before Eisenhower's nomination in 1952, that he was a liberal anyway. In their impatience at the government, liberals sounded as irritable as conservatives could sound. What they were calling for, though, was an extension of those American commitments abroad that conservative isolationists had detested and a further enlistment of the technology and resources that the Truman administration had been the first to deploy for the containment of Soviet and Asian communism.

So liberals remained true to the earlier premise that the cold war required not a spasmodic belligerence but steady, diverse, and extensive American engagements abroad. Yet between the Truman era and the late 1950s cold war liberalism had undergone significant change. The original policy of containment, as it was called, had aimed at holding back the Communist bloc at specific points where it threatened to expand: by a guerrilla movement in Greece; by the direct Soviet power that surrounded Berlin in 1948; through Communist parties elsewhere in Europe; by military proxy in Korea in 1950. The Republican party, winning the presidency in 1952, announced its intention of replacing containment with a policy of liberation; this was conservativism in its militant as opposed to its isolationist mode. The Republican administration, however, had no particular plan for liberating peoples behind the iron curtain and refrained from aiding the Hungarian revolutionists of 1956. The failure to intervene in the Soviet suppression of that uprising, along with the administration's refusal two years earlier to tolerate a leftist government in Guatemala, against which it then engineered a successful rebellion, meant that we had acknowledged the permanency of two regional spheres, each policed by a superpower that would decide which regimes were acceptable to it. The cold war was in a sullen deadlock. Liberals toward the end of Eisenhower's presidency did not specifically challenge the policy of containment that the last Democratic administration had crafted and the cautious Eisenhower administration had continued. Yet their determination to quicken the nation's economy, strengthen its military, and toughen its resolve implied that they were prepared not merely to put up with the divided world but as far as possible to change it, if only by the irresistible example of a free and prosperous West.

Before 1961, one critic of Kennedy writes, our policy was "essentially reactive"; under his presidency we sought to put our mark on events simply because we had the power to do so. If that is a valid contrast between Eisenhower's approach to foreign affairs and Kennedy's, one possible reason for the difference is that Eisenhower was a conservative in the direct sense of the word, desiring to conserve and tend, while Kennedy, though ambivalently, had enough liberalism in him, and his circle certainly had enough, to wish to set things in motion.[5]

Liberalism was actually becoming thoroughly enmeshed in its own contradictory best ideas and intentions. Liberals wanted the wealthiest nation on earth to be actively present throughout the world, and however injurious some of our objectives abroad may now seem, that was a commendable wish. They wanted the strongest nation on earth more actively to confront the expansion of communism, and however disastrous our effort in Vietnam was to turn out to be, the wish itself reflected a clear perception of the repressiveness and the arrogant appetites of Communist regimes, though it ignored the repressiveness of some of our allies. Yet the anticommunism of the liberals did not usually share the vision the right held of an absolute, changeless Communist evil, uncompromised by economic interests, internal conflicts, or varieties of nation and culture, devoid of any defensive, as distinct from offensive, objectives. By insisting, moreover, on the spread and variety of American commitments abroad that would be necessary for opposing Communist imperialism, liberals in effect were presenting a communism as diverse as the strategies in resistance to it. The anti-Communist militancy of the Kennedy years and the acts of conciliation at their end, the calls to action and Kennedy's remark, recorded by Richard Rovere, that the cold war would not be won or lost, were not conflicting but complementary. They proceeded from the assumption, which cold war strategists had made years before, that dealing with the Communists required not one belligerent response but a range of responses. Yet if there were many communisms and many ways of engaging them, then the very purpose of the cold war might be in doubt. The sophistication on which liberalism could insist more and more was to compound its difficulties in the Vietnam War. For liberals in the Vietnam years could not confidently claim to the public or to their own minds—as they would probably have done a decade earlier and the right certainly would have done—that the Vietnamese Communists were a mere function of an international Communist movement.[6]

Kennedy even before his presidency shared in the increasing awareness of the complexity of communism. In 1949 the young congressman, at least half a right-winger, had blamed the Truman administration for the loss of China; in 1957 a more mature Kennedy announced that it was not diplomacy but "underlying revolutionary conditions" that had "lost" China. There was not enough money to end the earth's poverty, and we could not buy poor nations away from communism, he had said in 1951; seven years later he was arguing for programs of economic aid to India and many other nations. Even in 1953, in the speech intended for delivery at the testimonial dinner for Hubert Humphrey and Eugene McCarthy, the words are those of a liberal Democrat. It complains of such failings in foreign policy as cutting funds for the United Nations technical assistance and children's relief programs and not working for reciprocal trade agreements and then warns, "This is a dangerous course indeed; for through it we have damaged the respect of our allies, unity among free nations, and our reputation [for being] a friend of underprivileged nations and . . . an enemy of colonialism." As early as 1957 Kennedy, calling for trade with Poland, was suggesting that we look on the Communist world not as a bloc but as containing different national identities. In the presidential campaign of 1960 he was to argue that our understanding of communism should qualify the developing antagonism between China and the Soviet Union—an antagonism that conservatives have viewed with much discomfort, as almost an impropriety within a Communist world that is obligated to be monolithic in its evil.[7]

At a time when liberalism was stirring with ideas and hopes, John Kennedy was stirring with ambition. Consoled that he would be the favorite candidate for the second spot in 1960, he replied coldly, "I'm not running for Vice-President anymore." The elder Kennedy worked all the more inconspicuously now. (Republicans gibed, "Jack and Bob will run the show, while Ted's in charge of hiding Joe.") Joe interested himself not in issues but in images conveyed by the press and television. He had a hand in persuading his friend Henry Luce to anoint Jack in cover stories for *Life* as the Democratic party voice of the future, and he encouraged Jack to take elocution lessons so that the young candidate would learn a dry understatement for the growing medium of television. In 1958, with Ted as nominal campaign manager, Jack won reelection in Massachusetts against Vincent Celeste by 875,000 votes, the largest margin of any senatorial race that year and the largest in his state's history. The same year he contributed to the campaigns of other senatorial candidates, looking to gain their favor for 1960.

Much of Kennedy's career in the national legislature had been politically nondescript, disclosing to the public little of what to expect of the senator who was now offering himself as a presidential candidate. His underlinings in Paul H. Douglas' *Economy in the National Government*, probably not long after the book's publication in 1952, reveal that he was thinking about the domestic issues that liberals and conservatives have quarreled over. But it would be difficult to place on a political spectrum a reader who marks both "If men are to be free, political and economic power must be diffused" and a declaration that the increase in spending over the past forty years was incompatible with liberty. The earlier years in the Senate suggest certain patterns. The belligerent anti-Communism could have been predicted of any American politician, certainly of a spokesman for Massachusetts Catholicism. An urban northern politician would subscribe to much of a northern progressive view of the race issue, and a politician responsive to the legal and social traditionalism of the Catholic community of the 1950s would manifest a measure of conservativism on the same race question, even as the church was beginning to press for integration in the South.

Kennedy's casting himself as leader of the New England Senators Conference was simply and sensibly designed to promote him as a spokesman of his region. But while as a whole Kennedy's record resembles the counters of a department store, over time his voting had shifted toward liberalism. And behind the compromisings lay a trace of the introspective maverick, or at the very least a political strategist thinking beyond immediate expediency.

When the American Legion opposed his public housing bill for veterans Kennedy denounced the Legion's officials for not having had "a constructive thought for the benefit of the country since 1918." He thereby set himself against the leadership of a powerful and respected organization. The bill, though, was for the benefit of veterans, and the mail in response to his fight ran ten to one in his favor, so the remark may not have offered a profile in courage. But Kennedy also voted against a popular pension increase for veterans. He refused to sign a petition asking President Truman to commute the prison sentence of former Mayor James Michael Curley. (Curley claimed illness requiring the rites of the church, but Kennedy determined that the prison doctor had found him in good health.) The young congressman was the only Massachusetts delegate not to sign, and his home district had been Curley's. Possibly he was acting in part on his family's traditional rivalry with Curley, or perhaps he simply disapproved of the plea on its own terms.

Kennedy supported President Eisenhower's program for the St. Lawrence Seaway, in what may have been a bid to show a larger public that he had more than a provincial vision. He risked his popularity in Massachusetts as the only national legislator from the state to vote for the Seaway, an action that the longshoremen, along with other labor unionists in Boston who had been his supporters, resented. A member of the Foreign Relations Committee, he was almost alone on the Senate floor in arguing that the French should leave Algeria. His statement commanded worldwide attention, making a large impact in France, and he visited war-torn Algeria. When, at the end of the decade, Eleanor Roosevelt asked Kennedy to go on record against the late Senator McCarthy, he pointed out with a candor not to be expected of politicians that for him to do so then would be hypocritical. There had been not only his own silence, he pointed out, but his brother's work for McCarthy's subcommittee. For the National Defense Education Act of 1960 he sponsored repeal of the requirement that graduate students take a loyalty oath before receiving federal loans. This might do for an apology. It also foreshadows the alliance that was to form between Kennedy and liberal academicians. Nor was he among those senators who worked tightly with party leader Lyndon Johnson, a club that socialized as closely as it worked.[8]

Kennedy was only a fair orator but a strong debater, once besting the veteran Socialist debater Norman Thomas. And now, as before in his life, an observer could glimpse an intelligence, and even an intellectual curiosity, at variance with his failure to commit himself to a clear philosophy. The liberal Senator Paul Douglas of Illinois would recall Kennedy as having one of the "best minds of the Senate." In 1959 Kennedy "made this speech on the labor management act and discussed secondary boycotts in a way which was a combination of politician and Ph.D."[9]

So whatever may have been Kennedy's motives, he could be fresh and interesting, unconventional in voting and in vocabulary. If he was not of a temperament to break publicly with popular attitudes, to be an Adlai Stevenson in public manner, a Hubert Humphrey pressing to the left within major party politics, a Wayne Morse challenging his own party, he did reserve for himself a private ironic distance from the demands of politics. After the 1956 convention he remarked snobbishly and unfairly of vice presidential candidate Kefauver, who had attacked him, that Kefauver "was prepared to speak at an intellectual level that will be comprehended by all of your audience regardless of education, I.Q., or literacy. . . . He and the American people got along well together because they demanded so little of each other."[10]

On a range of questions in foreign and domestic policy Kennedy ended by looking like a Democratic liberal. There was, of course, the general issue of growth. There was Kennedy's call in the Senate for Algerian independence. He advocated opening educational exchange programs with Poland. He voted against depreciation allowances for oil and natural gas and against giving to the states the rights to drill for oil more than three miles offshore. When Nikita Khrushchev visited the United States in 1959, Kennedy favored having him address Congress; Senator Eugene McCarthy was opposed. Kennedy's most complicated work was in behalf of labor legislation, an issue promising mixed reactions among liberals.

As chairman of a subcommittee of the Senate Labor and Public Welfare Committee—the most conservative Democratic member of the committee, his fellow member John Sherman Cooper of Kentucky has recalled—John was well placed to draft labor legislation. Robert, working for Senator John McClellan's crime committee, had directed a staff of forty-two investigating union corruption. It was good theater to pursue David Beck and his successor, James Hoffa, of the teamster's union, but the presidential candidate's aim was to write legislation to reform such practices. Kennedy may have been thinking about the liberals whose support he needed, with their quick hostility to financial corruption, and conservatives would like anything that put unions on the defensive. The resulting Kennedy-Ives bill died in the House in 1958, even though it had passed the Senate by a vote of 88 to 1. The following year Kennedy took his name off the bill, which under administration pressure had gone beyond its provisions against racketeering to become a general labor law that union leaders perceived to be unfriendly to organized workers. Kennedy lost on the issue, but so did Nixon, who had been forced to cast a tie-breaking antilabor vote as president of the Senate.[11]

Kennedy perceived liberal intellectuals, like labor, as a force in the Democratic party, which had twice nominated Adlai Stevenson for President. Their importance lay not in their numbers but in their influence, and during his presidency some of them could see in Kennedy, naïvely, a Harvard-trained author who could represent them and bring them to power. Kennedy would come to know Arthur Schlesinger, Jr., as an eager supporter without sycophancy. Schlesinger's various memoranda to the presidential candidate and President are tactful but always strong and often persuasive. Kennedy appreciated Schlesinger's crisp competence and came early to rely on him as a conduit to the liberal intellectual community.

A liberal with whom John Kennedy could not get along was Eleanor Roosevelt, who disliked his father and distrusted the family's Catholicism and its affinity for Joe McCarthy. In their first head-on encounter at the end of 1958 Kennedy got the better of the argument. The prospective candidate complained by letter about Mrs. Roosevelt's writing in her column that his father was lavishly financing his presidential campaign. She replied: "I was told that your father said openly he would spend any money to make his son the first Catholic President of this country, and many people as I travel about tell me of money spent by him in your behalf. This seems commonly accepted as a fact." Kennedy responded: "I am disappointed that you now seem to accept the view that simply because a rumor or allegation is repeated it becomes 'commonly accepted as fact.'" Kennedy's reply was a legitimate rebuke to a use of rumor suggestive of the tactics of Red-hunters; that the rumors happened to do some justice to the Kennedy family's employment of money is another matter. Mrs. Roosevelt's column lamely protested that "my information came largely from remarks made by people in many places," and privately she told Kennedy, "people will, of course, never give names as that would open them to liability." And in another letter: "My informants were just casual people in casual conversation. It would be impossible to get their names because for the most part I don't even know them." On the Associated Press wire in May 1959 she was quoted as saying that while it would be all right for a Catholic to become President, she was not sure that John Kennedy would be able to keep church and state separate.

Now that Kennedy's election and presidency have stilled the religious issue as it applies to the Chief Executive, it is easy to consider Mrs. Roosevelt's attitude as retrograde, a reflection not of popular hostility toward Catholicism but of the peculiar suspicions that liberals once harbored of the Roman Church. That may be beside the point. Some liberals, to be sure, shudder in uncomprehending amazement at Catholicism or any other religion that takes itself seriously. Mrs. Roosevelt was not among these. Other liberals, including Catholic liberals, have distrusted the church on reasoned grounds for its ambitions and for the obedience its priests and bishops could once expect of the laity. Mrs. Roosevelt was frank in her reservations. But there must have been liberals who remained silent on the issue, their doubts balanced against their abhorrence of conventional bigotry.

The national legislature can be a hard beginning for a presidential candidate since it sometimes forces its members to take stands, but by 1960 John Kennedy, even though he had occasionally made a reflective and intellectually independent comment and had taken on as formidable a figure as Mrs. Roosevelt, had no established political identification like Hubert Humphrey's or James Eastland's. He had been moving toward the politics of the liberals, but unobtrusively. An article by him in *Life* for March 11, 1957, looking to 1960, defines the problem of establishing a workable relationship between ideology and his party's politics. Kennedy observes that the Eisenhower administration, having moved to the left of conventional Republicanism, puts the Democrats in a peculiar position. If they move to the right of the Eisenhower forces, they will be abandoning their traditional progressivism. If they move to the left, they will lose the moderates they want to entice back into the party. If they stay in the center, they will have no separate identity. Scolding the nineteenth-century Whig party for its failure to take some definite political posture, the article does call on congressional Democrats to press such issues as aid to education and the relief of unemployment. But its logic is that such programs have become the property of the political center. Only in its advocacy of Medicare does the essay curve leftward or in any definable direction at all.

One issue Kennedy did not share with any other possible candidate, and that was his religion. From 1947 to 1950 he had sponsored federal aid to parochial schools, and until 1955 he had favored the appointment of an ambassador to the Vatican. Sorensen thought that Kennedy might have to break in as Vice President to condition the country to his religion. Some party professionals hoped that he might pull back into the Democratic party the many Roman Catholic voters who had deserted it in 1952 and 1956. Kennedy knew how to use the issue. In 1959 he told a group of Pennsylvania politicians that if he were to go into the convention with many delegates and then fail to get the nomination, the party might alienate enough Catholic voters to lose the election. Predicting a close race with Senator Stuart Symington of Missouri, he observed, "But if I won some primaries, it's going to take a lot of guts to give the nomination to him or anyone else. They are going to have to say, 'We won't give it to Kennedy because he is Catholic.'" Kennedy also had the good fortune to be a candidate at a time when religious sectarianism was in decline—and yet sufficiently in the public consciousness that a non-Catholic might consider it an act of decency to vote for Kennedy precisely because of the religious issue. During the 1928 campaign of Al Smith the story had circulated that if the Democrat were elected, the pope would have a tunnel dug under the Atlantic Ocean for a new Vatican City in the Mississippi Valley because Rome was too crowded. Wily Jesuits had installed cardinal red drapes in the White House, alleged another story of the period, or they had bought strategic land overlooking West Point, or they had inscribed rosaries on the dollar bill. A typical comment in the gentler campaign of 1960 was that the Statue of Liberty would be renamed "Our Lady of the Harbor." Then there was "Join the church of your choice while there's still time," a joke about jokes about religion. Kennedy used the issue of religion in the presidential primaries, as he had before the 1956 convention, as a weapon against his opponents. He brought it up repeatedly, and voters knew that if they voted against him for whatever reason, the national media might cast them as bigots.[12]

The first major test of political strength in 1960 came in early April, against Minnesota's Senator Hubert Humphrey in Wisconsin. Here, too, reprints of John Hersey's *PT 109* story flooded the state. The Kennedy forces also mailed anti-Catholic literature to Wisconsin Catholics, as supporters of Curley's gubernatorial campaign in Massachusetts had played to the Catholic vote by burning crosses on hills overlooking Boston. Kennedy money had bought a plane, the *Caroline*, that gave Jack a great advantage over Humphrey. But although Kennedy won a majority of the votes in the primary, the results were inconclusive, for the proportion of Catholics within the population was larger in Wisconsin than in the nation as a whole. He would have to prove himself again on May 10 in West Virginia.

Humphrey campaigned strenuously in that state on economic and social issues. A liberal of pure New Deal vintage, Humphrey let this state know that he had experienced poverty during the Depression and had memories of a mythic Roosevelt. Humphrey campaigned in front of a giant blowup of FDR. Kennedy, who promised West Virginia an interstate highway, called for a more active economy. He had the enormously impressive help of Franklin D. Roosevelt, Jr., as a speaker; West Virginians felt almost in the presence of the great President. And could it be that the handsome, upper-class Kennedy came nearer to the patrician FDR in awakening confidence among the state's poor people than plain, earnest Humphrey could hope to do? Kennedy's Harvard accent and manner may have also reminded older people of the great President, whom they had loved. The campaign repeatedly went beyond taste. It was natural that Kennedy's war record aided him in this mountain state, but the Kennedy camp pushed things along by Roosevelt's dark questions about why Humphrey had not served in World War II. (The answer is that Humphrey had been turned down for medical reasons.) The Kennedy machine was once more free with its money. For almost four years Kennedy money had been helping the campaigns of willing West Virginia Democrats. Sheriffs were courted with cash payments said to average $1,000, and Kennedy money arranged the positioning of candidates' names on the state's complicated ballots. Harry Truman was to remark later, "Joe thought of everything. Joe paid for everything."[13]

Kennedy worked the religion issue for all and more than it was worth. No one had questioned his religion, he said, when he spent two [sic] years in a veterans hospital; no one had questioned his brother's before Joe died in a mission over Germany [sic]. Theodore Sorensen, who had just finished calling out the Catholic vote in Wisconsin, now knew how to exploit West Virginia Protestants. "Make it clear," he advised the candidate, "that you are a victim of . . . bigotry by always so stating in passive tense, 'I have been called' . . . 'it has been suggested that' . . . 'people are being asked to vote against me because.' " Yet it was not as though Kennedy and Sorensen had to invent the religious issue out of nothing. The Humphrey forces played such hymns as "Give Me That Old-Time Religion" at some of their candidate's appearances. Kennedy's opponents might have made some progress if they had known that Cardinal Cushing had called priests throughout the state on Kennedy's behalf.[14]

Kennedy won 61 percent of the primary vote. The religion issue, it seemed, had been buried in the hills of West Virginia. That is not quite true, but West Virginia made it plain that Kennedy would be the nominee. Chicago Mayor Richard Daley's announcement of support made it all the plainer.

The candidate was proving himself not only effective as a campaigner but capable of a ruthlessness surpassing that of a conventional political boss and somewhat unexpected of the polished and withdrawn young man. There was the war record trick against Humphrey in West Virginia. Kennedy impressed seasoned politicos when he threatened to throw his support to a political enemy of Governor Michael DiSalle of Ohio unless DiSalle endorsed his candidacy. The endorsement added to his supporters the governor of an important state.[15]

The tumultuous greeting John Kennedy received outside the Biltmore Hotel in Los Angeles betokened the enthusiasm of his convention following. Senator Eugene McCarthy of Minnesota eloquently nominated Adlai Stevenson: "Do not reject this man who made us all proud to be called Democrats." Stevenson replied with some characteristically self-deprecating humor—he seemed, so said his detractors, to want to be appointed President. Perhaps Kennedy, as Schlesinger has argued, owed a debt to this pridefully humble man. Stevenson's oratory had aimed higher than the Democratic party appeal of 1948 with that year's slogan, "You never had it so good," and Kennedy's rhetoric, too, aimed high. The younger man defeated all comers on the first ballot of the convention.

Kennedy's acceptance speech contains the phrase "the new frontier." He got it, perhaps, from the title of a book in the Kennedy family library written by Guy Emerson and published in 1920, speaking of the resources and the bright future of American democracy. (Emerson had written: "Americanism means that *men and women are born to put more into their country than they take out of it.*" Kennedy said in his inaugural address: "Ask not what your country can do for you but what you can do for your country.") The speech does not make clear what Kennedy meant in the way of actual programs. But the platform drafted at the convention does anticipate a social frontier of the decades to come. It contained the strongest civil rights plank in the history of political parties up to that time; its most distinctive feature was a call for a federal employment practices commission having power to compel nondiscriminatory hiring in interstate business.[16]

The selection of Lyndon Johnson as vice presidential candidate has actually puzzled some political observers. Johnson, who had held second place in the presidential balloting, looked to some liberals from his Senate record like a provincial southerner, and liberals in 1960 had already begun to count Kennedy within their ranks. It is sometimes assumed that both the offer and the acceptance were sudden, and indeed, that is perhaps how they were made to appear at the convention with diversionary talk about other candidates. Bobby Kennedy, it is widely remembered, reassured delegates that Johnson would not be the choice and, after his brother and father had actually made the selection, urged the Texan to withdraw. Robert's version is that Johnson was offered the spot as a courtesy—in accord, perhaps, with the sensible Kennedy policy of embracing enemies after victory— and unexpectedly took it. The sense is conveyed that Johnson was ungentlemanly, if not greedy, in his behavior. Robert allegedly had the unpleasant job of trying to persuade Johnson to withdraw and head the Democratic National Committee instead; Johnson is supposed to have burst into tears at the suggestion. All this is in reference to a candidate whose presence on the ticket gained Kennedy the presidency. Perhaps what really occurred is that Robert had taken on the duplicitous job of reassuring liberals (and other vice presidential hopefuls), as he did, that Johnson would not be on the ticket or that the Kennedy forces were unhappy at the inclusion of Johnson; that strategy would require a cover story. Burke Marshall, later Robert's associate in the Justice Department, has remarked that Bobby was not opposed to having Johnson as the vice presidential candidate; that is an indication that his efforts against the Texan are perhaps not to be taken seriously.[17]

The arrangement joined two senators with like records, and both men must have contemplated it for some time. Richard Nixon had foreseen the choice. Johnson's name appears at the top of a list that Sorensen put forward not long before the convention. The ticket was patterned on that of 1928, when the northeastern Catholic Al Smith selected Senator Joseph Robinson of Arkansas, a choice Kennedy cited at the convention. To Johnson it offered the chance to break away from a primarily regional identity and politics. Kennedy had much to gain and little reason for hesitating. Whatever may have been the extent or character of his liberalism at the time, it had virtually no foundation in his political past that would have demanded consistency or symbolic purity. Johnson had not always spoken kindly of Kennedy (a "little scrawny fellow with rickets"; so wracked with Addison's disease he "looked like a spavined hunchback"); but by 1960 Kennedy was perceiving Johnson not unadmiringly as a "riverboat gambler," a tall Texan in ruffles and a black coat, a pistol and aces up his sleeve, moving gracefully in the saloon of a Mississippi steamboat. Johnson's leathery maturity went well with Kennedy's youthfulness, while the Texan's background of poverty complemented Kennedy's upper-class past and bearing, his down-home ways playing against the New Englander's Ivy League manner. Johnson was well thought of among farmers, businessmen, and conservatives. Liberals would not vote for Nixon in any event. Above all, Johnson could appeal to the South; as a Texas Protestant he might serve to neutralize somewhat the unpredictable issue of religion. Peter Lisagor on a plane leaving the convention remarked to Kennedy that the choice of Johnson must have been either inspired or cynical. The candidate bridled at the word "cynical," observing that Democrats always balanced their ticket with a Southerner. A liberal of more crystalline politics than Kennedy might have tried to avoid anything cynical; Kennedy's reaction was to deny the adjective.[18]

We speak often here of Kennedy's attractive public presence, but there was about him, as Norman Mailer has noted, the air of a young professor somewhat detached from his role of candidate, his mind occupied by some point of theory. Johnson was, in Mailer's description, "a political animal, he breathed like an animal, sweated like one . . . his mind was entirely absorbed with the compendium of political fact and maneuver." Johnson in his campaigning throughout the South was a fish in water. Starting at Culpeper, Virginia, he made 119 speeches from a train that reporters dubbed the Cornpone Special. He controlled every detail of popular speech making. He wanted the rostrum to be fifty-two inches high, the band to strike up "The Yellow Rose of Texas" the moment he ended his speech, the train to pull away from the station at the syllable of farewell. The speeches were as homey as the plans were crisp; to one reporter it sounded like "God bless yuh, Rocky Bottom. Ah wish ah could stay an' do a little sippin' an' whittlin' with yuh. . . . God bless yuh, Gaffney." On one occasion Johnson announced that he was the "grandson of a 'federate soldier." A reporter wired the *Chicago Tribune:* "The son of a bitch will carry the South." Johnson's was the style of a populist or midwestern progressive or a southern New Dealer, fit for a time when liberals or their predecessors had expected their politics to speak to hinterland crowds. It was not a style to appeal either to technocratic liberals or to those of a generation that associated populist democracy with McCarthyism or white supremacy. It is an irony in keeping with the perennial waywardness of political fortunes that this Texan whose style could so grate against the eastern liberal sensibilities was later, as President, to put his political energies to winning some of the nation's most advanced social programs. Father Theodore Hesburgh, chairman of the Civil Rights Commission, has observed that as a southerner Johnson was able to do for civil rights what Kennedy, widely disliked in the South, could not.

The absence in Kennedy of an assertive ideology could explain why he could be in tandem with Johnson, who, despite his southern identity, had been a moderate during the 1950s. On the other side was Richard Nixon, another politician not given to ideological pronouncements. The news commentator Eric Sevareid wrote of two "packaged products," devoid of conviction or passion. A bitter Gerald W. Johnson thought of the election as "the political equivalent of Burroughs against IBM. . . . Its outcome will depend not on the clash of ideas, but on the neat and accurate adjustment of ratchets, cams, and cog-wheels." And perhaps it is because Kennedy was a moderate, unmarked by any sharply defined public character beyond looks and vigor, that he came across as less a politician than a celebrity.[19]

As hard as it is for commentators to tell in retrospect exactly what Kennedy's campaign was about, every sharp and con-

fident New England syllable made it sound as though he knew.
And his opponent was a victim of enough bad luck and judgment to accentuate Kennedy's look of competence. In August
Nixon suffered an infected knee that postponed the beginning
of his campaign for two weeks and left him fatigued and a prey
to colds. Yet he held to his earlier promise to visit every state,
wasting valuable time in Alaska when he should have been in
the critical areas of the Midwest. Nixon's running mate, Henry
Cabot Lodge, Jr., was a slow-paced campaigner, at poles from
Mailer's Johnson, the breathing and sweating political animal.
That President Eisenhower's planned May summit meeting with
Khrushchev had collapsed after the Soviet Union had shot down
a U-2 reconnaissance plane deep in Soviet territory may have
added to the impression of the Republicans as losers. Later in
the spring anti-American sentiment in Japan led Ike to cancel a
visit to that country. To a reporter's question about what major
policy decisions Nixon had participated in as Vice President,
Eisenhower responded: "If you give me a week I might think
of one." In the closing days of the contest the President's health
kept him from active campaigning. When Norman Vincent
Peale, Nixon's own pastor, condemned Kennedy on religious
grounds, he made Kennedy seem a victim of prejudice.

A speech on September 12 arranged by Methodist leaders
before the Greater Houston Ministerial Association gave Kennedy an opportunity to prove by way of television to the nation
at large that non-Catholics had no reason to fear him on religious grounds. Kennedy now declared himself against federal aid
to parochial schools. The Houston address was an impressive
performance, but much of the Catholic press criticized his statement that "for the officeholder, nothing takes precedence over
his oath to uphold the Constitution." Kennedy's distinction between church policies and his presidential duties makes, on the
surface, a sharp contrast with the convictions of Martin Luther
King, Jr., and the ministers and rabbis who marched with him,
believing that their faith dictated what they must demand of the
state. What their faith dictated, however, was so simple an en-

actment of justice that the religious and the secular social conscience could agree on it. Kennedy's performance before the Houston ministers, in any event, can be commended for its statesmanship and political acumen, whatever may be said of its theology. "He's eating 'em blood raw!" exclaimed Sam Rayburn of the encounter. "This young feller will be a great President!"[20]

An enigmatic note in Drew Pearson's diary for March 14, 1949, indicates that Kennedy earlier in his life may have been more submissive, and to a more restrictive church. Kennedy, reveals the entry, had accepted Pearson's invitation to speak at a dinner honoring the four chaplains, representing the Protestant, Catholic, and Jewish faiths, whose common death at the sinking of the *Dorchester* in World War II is remembered as a moment of religious fraternity. Then Kennedy had withdrawn from the commemoration, "stating that the Church had forbidden him to speak. He said he must follow the dictates of the Church." The diary does not tell more about the occasion or explain the prohibition. Someone in ecclesiastical authority had perhaps found the event too ecumenical for a good Catholic to participate in. Kennedy's withdrawal from a gathering that might have gained him some capital among Americans outside his religion suggests a faithfulness as simple as the prohibition was archaic.[21]

That incident had been many years in the past. In 1960 Kennedy was speaking with ease to Americans who did not share his faith. The contrast between John Kennedy and Al Smith, who had been clearly ill at ease, is compelling. Smith discussed the issue only once during his campaign. In a speech at Oklahoma City he accused a hostile audience of hiding under the cloak of anti-Prohibition. Using explosive gestures to match his words, he behaved as though the issue were an attack on him. Kennedy, on the other hand, spoke often and directly to critics of his religion. "My experience . . . shows it is a matter of great concern," he said. "I am delighted to answer any questions about it. . . . There is nothing improper in discussing it. . . . All questions that interest or disturb people should be answered."

Kennedy's speech to the Houston ministers respected the doubts of his audience. He was specific, moreover, in his remarks about what worried his listeners. "No church or church school," he now said, should be granted "public funds or political preference." Nor did Kennedy compound the religious problem, as Smith had done, by politically amateurish appointments. As national chairman, for example, he named Senator Henry M. Jackson of Washington, after passing over a prominent Catholic congressman. Undoubtedly Kennedy profited from Smith's mistakes, as he also profited from the liberalization of his church since Smith's time and the decline of provincial anti-Catholicism.[22]

Nixon made the error of agreeing to a series of four television debates with Kennedy, who as the lesser-known candidate was likely to profit from the exposure. Nixon had been successful in comparable situations: the appearance on television in 1952 when, evoking the name of his dog, Checkers, he had replied to charges of financial misconduct; and then, in 1959, the "kitchen debate" with Nikita Khrushchev in Moscow. But Kennedy, too, had debated successfully, notably against Lodge in 1952. For the first campaign debate Nixon was in poor physical condition, and Kennedy appeared fresher and more vibrant, natural, and relaxed—"grace under pressure" was the Hemingway phrase columnist James Reston used soon after. Kennedy spoke to his audience, while Nixon, who had been on a debate team, addressed his opponent in the style of a high school contest. It was a clash of images rather than of significant ideas. Kenneth O'Donnell claims that a main effect of the debates was to present Kennedy as disdainful of his opponent. If so, the encounter suggests the element of aloofness that from time to time distinguished Kennedy from his colleagues. Each candidate dealt in traditional pieties and inarguable aims. The one assertion in the debates that related to a salient issue was Kennedy's often repeated claim of a missile gap, and this turned out to be inaccurate. Yet the debates, especially the important first one, viewed by seventy million people, were a polemical, though not an intellectual, defeat for the Vice President. He had provided his opponent with a respectable forum in which to overcome charges of inexperience and to look brisk, assertive, purposeful, independent.

Whether or not Nixon lost the formal debate, the process was not necessarily a disaster for his candidacy. There is no clear measure of the effects of the debates on the November vote. One woman, while admiring Kennedy's stance on bread-and-butter issues, shrewdly remarked, "I don't know whether to vote for the man who may do too little or the man who may try to do too much."

It was perhaps more the electoral process itself than either candidate that benefited from the debates. For if they did not achieve a sophisticated confrontation of issues, they did provide a national public, for the first time in our history, with candidates visibly together, each trying to say something in response to concrete questions and each looking like a creditable contender. Nixon, despite his physical condition, demonstrated rationality and intelligence. The debates, then, gave to the presidential campaign process a new character and authenticity. The series also heightened the respectability of television, winning recognition for the medium as a principal means of political discourse. And the prominence of television within the campaign presaged its prominence during the sixties, when crisis after crisis entered the homes of the American people so as to appear to create a national community of viewers and participants, at the same moment that demonstrators on the streets were drawing a portion of the populace into a community of political action.

While the campaign was not productive of well-defined issues cleanly separating the candidates, Kennedy did speak for concerns and preferences that he had shared with liberals for some time, concerns that prefigured the mentality of the Kennedy and Johnson administrations. When Kennedy endlessly repeated that it was time "to get this country moving again," he referred principally to the national economy. But he connected the issue of economic growth to that of national prestige, contending that a booming economy was necessary to the maintenance of an American presence and credibility in the face of the Communist powers. In voting in a good liberal cause, the removal of the loyalty oath provision in the National Defense Education Act, he had argued that the people whom the loyalty oath would exclude from federal funding would have the kind of intelligence the country needed in its scientific competition with the Soviet Union. It was also appropriate to the liberalism of the time, and to Kennedy as a war hero, that he was interested in military matters, specifically in military technique and technology. The talk about a missile gap was to be subsequently proven inaccurate. But Kennedy was taking an intellectually respectable side in a serious controversy when he argued for ending our reliance on massive retaliation and for complementing our nuclear arsenal with a mobile conventional force.

Kennedy's demand for a more prepared and more flexible military made him look like the candidate of energy and action, and even the civil rights controversy, which apparently did not greatly interest him, evoked a fresh gesture. When the Reverend Martin Luther King, Jr., was sentenced after a traffic offense to six months of hard labor in a Georgia penitentiary, there was wide comment internationally and at home. At the suggestion of Harris Wofford, campaign adviser on civil rights and later White House special assistant on the issue, Sargent Shriver suggested that Kennedy phone Mrs. King to express his concern. So the candidate made the famous call to the pregnant wife of the rights leader. Wofford writes that Robert Kennedy was angry at first, fearing alienation of the white South, while Lyndon Johnson told John, "Well, we'll sweat it out—but you'll have the privilege of knowing that you did the right thing." Finally, Robert, acting on the advice of Governor S. Ernest Vandiver of Georgia, called the judge. Shortly thereafter King was released on bond, probably for procedural reasons unconnected to Robert's intervention. But the actions of the Kennedy brothers, extraordinary for the time in their symbolism, had a political effect. King's father announced his intention to switch from Nixon to Kennedy.

Joe Kennedy paid for the printing of nearly two million leaflets recounting the event, to be distributed at black churches the Sunday before the election. Wofford sent out thousands of copies of a restrictive lease Richard Nixon had signed on a home; the words "Jews" and "Negroes" were circled, and "Shame" was printed in red. In violation of election law the mailing contained no return address. Black leaders had cared little for Kennedy's record on civil rights, and Robert Kennedy, according to one source, regarded the party's strong civil rights plank as a mistake. In response to southern support in the 1956 convention John Kennedy had said, "I'll be singing 'Dixie' the rest of my life." But most black votes went to Kennedy, and since the election was close, expectations among black leaders of what he would do as President were high.[23]

Kennedy defeated Nixon by 303 to 219 electoral votes but received only a hair's breadth more of the popular vote, which at 62.8 percent of those eligible was the heaviest turnout since 1908. The victor, at forty-three, was the youngest and the richest candidate ever to win the office. Allegations of fraud in the counting of close returns in Illinois and Texas made Kennedy's victory uncomfortable; Mayor Daley had told Kennedy on election night, "With a little bit of luck and the help of a few close friends you're going to carry Illinois," but Nixon made a responsible choice not to pursue the matter. The results of the Senate races increased the Democratic majority, which now was to stand at 64 to 36. Democrats won in the House 261 to 174, numbers that look impressive but represent a loss of about 20 seats.[24]

What remains a great puzzle about the November election is the closeness of Kennedy's margin of victory; at a time when the economy, despite its affluence, was sluggish, a Republican candidate could have lost heavily to the party that in any event had the loyalty of the greater portion of the electorate. The popular vote for Democratic House candidates averaged 54.7 percent, about five points ahead of Kennedy's. The University of Michigan's Survey Research Center decided that the religious is-

sue had cost Kennedy 2.2 percent of the popular vote while helping him in critical large states with substantial Catholic blocs
and many electoral votes. Instinct suggests that the cost was
greater, but instinct has no statistics at its command. It was apparently not the religious issue, however, but the domestic and
foreign peace that had prevailed in the Eisenhower years, and a
prosperity that late in the decade had been subject to only a minor threat, that accounted for the thinness of Kennedy's margin.[25]

The Kennedy administration commenced on a chilly January day in Washington. "It began in the cold," writes Arthur
Schlesinger. First came the poetry of Robert Frost, his white
hair gleaming in the sunlight. The bright light occluded his vision. The poem he had intended proclaimed:

> *It makes the prophet in us all presage*
> *The glory of a next Augustan age*
> *Of a power leading from its strength and pride,*
> *Of young ambition eager to be tried,*
>
> *Firm in our free beliefs without dismay,*
> *In any game the nations want to play.*
> *A golden age of poetry and power*
> *Of which this noonday's the beginning hour.*

In prose presentation, Frost declared, "Our new world diplomacy has been afraid of its responsibility. The prediction is an
era . . . of more confidence in our power and the right to as-
sert it." The inaugural address, written largely by Theodore Sorensen and partly in response to Khrushchev's bellicose speech
two weeks earlier, set the tone for a presidential administration
as few such addresses have ever done. It committed a free people to "pay any price, bear any burden, meet any hardship"; it
recalled the "graves of young Americans who answered the call
to service" around the globe. There was a chill in the words of
the address. Beneath the conventional and inevitable commit-

ments to strength and freedom and peace was a solemnity curious at a moment that was no grimmer than any other in the era
of the cold war. Much has been made of the speech: first the
praise from liberal intellectuals—158 artists and "thinkers" had
been invited to the occasion—delighted at the intelligence of the
rhetoric; then, in reaction to the praise and the administration
itself, a debunking of the address, with its gratuitous vision of action and sacrifice and the contrived balance of its phrases. It
stands, nonetheless, as a remarkable effort, not so much for any
specific definition of programs as for a mood that seems in retrospect to accord with that biting cold winter day.[26]

It also reveals that John Kennedy and his advisers had crys-
tallized into a vision the concern of *Why England Slept* and
Profiles in Courage, the combativeness instilled by parents and
brothers, a preoccupation with discipline and self-testing tracing
back to Kennedy's upbringing and his subjection to illness and
pain. These and an accompanying dry reserve had been, for
many years preceding 1960, the only qualities about Kennedy
that suggest any definite character and preference. The presidency, an office that requires its occupant to embody strength in
crisis and to recall the nation to its primal republican virtues,
presented Kennedy with an opportunity to translate into action
a set of tastes that he had not been able to express in the national
legislature. A study of recurring words in Kennedy's speeches has
indicated a frequent coupling of "peace" with a vocabulary of
strife—as though he were not at home with peace even as a state
of mind except as something to be won and sustained against
the violence of Addison's disease or an elder brother's taunts.
The talk of warring for peace may have been an effort toward
that political image making that the Kennedy forces had carefully engaged in during the campaign of 1960, to the extent of
running a computer survey of voter attitudes for the constructing of a composite image. But the image that Kennedy seized on
was consonant with his most private wishes. And the call to
growth—economic, military, intellectual, cultural—was another
call to combat, an international competition with the Soviet

Union, a combat at home against that sloth and that mediocrity Americans perpetually fear they have succumbed to and John Kennedy had been bullied into despising in himself.[27]

The administration was to be brief; it was 1,036 days from the "trumpet summons" of the inauguration to the muffled drums and caissons marching slowly up Pennsylvania Avenue in November 1963.

4

An Imperial Presidency in Foreign Policy?

JOHN KENNEDY WAS A FOREIGN POLICY PRESIDENT. IT HAS BEEN common for the presidency in this century to receive much of its definition from the global events that impinge so dramatically upon it. Kennedy, even among recent Presidents, has been distinctive in the degree of his identification with those events.

That Kennedy, an occasional reader of Ian Fleming's James Bond novels, has been associated with them in the Kennedy image is appropriate to the cold war mentality of his times. Fleming's fiction is about more than an arrogant practitioner of secret war. The violence of his stories notwithstanding, they were early efforts in a spy genre that looked beyond the simplicities of a time when militant Westerners had resolved all the details of international politics into confrontations between a free world and a solid Communist bloc. The antagonists in a Fleming story play a game in which they act for larger forces, but these are shadowy and vary from one tale to the next. James Bond, moreover, is armed with light and dazzling mechanical devices that evoke the increasingly sophisticated technological world of the cold war itself. And this understanding of power and politics found a presidential spokesman in a war hero, the skipper of a small craft, who wanted a quicker, more mobile, more expert military capable of fighting in limited wars. Major General Chester Clifton has remembered: he "made me gather up all [the weapons] we had that might be used for guerrilla warfare. . . . There were about twenty weapons . . . the most recent of them was something that had been invented in 1944. This was 1961."

The "torch has been passed to a new generation of Americans, born in this century, tempered by war, disciplined by a hard and bitter peace"—so go the famous words of the inaugural at the transfer of power from the oldest elected President in the nation's history to the youngest. The new generation, or much of it, had served under Eisenhower or MacArthur in a war. The claim is now familiar that the war had schooled the Kennedy people, made them quick to react to crisis, impatient with bureaucracy, swift to improvise. After victory in 1945 it must have seemed to the war generation that the world's ills would yield to the competent marshaling of power, and that the United States, the most powerful victor of the war, had the ability and the obligation to shape events. There was another side to the thought of this generation. Elvis Stahr, secretary of the army under Kennedy, reports that the President wished that every military officer would read *The Guns of August*, Barbara Tuchman's account of the world that stumbled into war in 1914. "It is a dangerous illusion," he said at Berkeley on March 23, 1962, "to believe that the policies of the United States, stretching as they do worldwide, under varying and different conditions, can be encompassed in one slogan or one adjective, hard or soft or otherwise." It was a "simple central theme of American foreign policy," Kennedy once said, "to support the independence of nations so that one bloc cannot gain sufficient power to finally overcome us." John Gaddis in *Strategies of Containment* calls this "the most precise public explanation by an American president of what all postwar chief executives had believed, but rarely stated: that the American interest was not to remake the world but to balance power within it." This belief has activist implications if the balancing is carried out in the Kennedy manner, by an incessant watchfulness, an infusing of military or economic aid to one region, an encouragement of progressive reform in another, a neutralization of a dangerous conflict, as in Laos, a development of a swift and versatile military, and the sending forth of a skilled force of Peace Corps volunteers. A world to be balanced and rebalanced, indeed, invites an activity more extensive and exact than a world to be remade once and for all.[1]

"In general," writes the journalist Carey McWilliams, "the liberals Kennedy attracted to Washington were more aggressively anti-Communist than the bureaucrats they replaced." But their anticommunism sought more sophisticated expression than Washington had previously employed. In wanting to renovate the military so that it would be a defter instrument for use in a complex power politics, Kennedy was taking the same position that Generals Maxwell Taylor and Matthew Ridgway had earlier expounded in the Pentagon against the view that we should rely primarily on the nuclear deterrent. The United States, said Taylor, should be able to fight two wars and a half at once. Having retired in 1959, subsequently becoming president of the new Lincoln Center for the Performing Arts, Taylor returned in 1961 as an important presidential adviser. Taylor was a liberal's general. A scholar who could speak several languages, he argues in *The Uncertain Trumpet* against founding national policy simplistically on the threat to use nuclear weapons. During the Berlin crisis of 1961 he was free enough of chauvinism to be able to say, in a note of July 7 to Secretary of State Dean Rusk, that it was not our rights in Berlin but our responsibilities to the West Berliners that mattered. A combination of the warrior, the seasoned critic of force, and the technician in Taylor favored tactical over strategic nuclear weapons, for the incorrect reason that they would produce virtually no fallout or danger to civilians. The Robert McNamaras of the administration, no spokesmen for the rhetoric that equated internal subversion with Soviet troops and negotiation with surrender, were given to the new militancy of surgical antiguerrilla tactics.

The counterforce strategy soon announced by the administration, the plan to prepare our missiles for strikes not at enemy cities but at missile bases, was equally expressive of the technocrat liberal mind. It trusted in the precision of which missile technology is capable, it was supposed to allow for greater flexibility of action, and McNamara apparently sincerely preferred it as more humane than a policy aiming weapons at civilians. In July 1962 Kennedy and McNamara finally equipped overseas nuclear missiles with electronic locks so that their crews could not fire them without information from the government. Advances in missile construction decreed the eventual use of the device, but it was fitting to an administration that looked to technology for power and for the restraint of power.[2]

As if in preparation for a presidency that aimed at displaying splendid virtues in foreign policy, the young John Kennedy had read and been much taken with *Pilgrim's Way*, published in 1940 by John Buchan, an official within the British Empire, an admirer of the imperialist Cecil Rhodes, and a novelist (among his works was *The Thirty-nine Steps*, one of whose characters prefigures James Bond). *Pilgrim's Way* is full of the zest of life, somewhat innocently perceived, even after a career that included the battlefields of Europe. It is copious in descriptions of countryside, particularly the rough Scots country of Buchan's youth, and the robust virtues that the author applauds seem associated with the health of nature itself. John Buchan, Lord Tweedsmuir, was not a champion of the upper classes; he admired virtue and steadfastness wherever he found them. But the book could find an avid reader in any young aspirant to aristocratic deeds and style. The British, of course, are accustomed to distinguishing between aristocracy and money, and it is even easier to differentiate both from an elite of skill, training, and talent. The Kennedys themselves knew that their money could not propel them from the ranks of the merely rich into the world of the Anglo-

American Brahmins. But money, aristocracy, and skill have ways of converging, as they did in the commander of a PT boat.

As President Kennedy seemed to relish elitist competence and aristocratic gesture singly and in compound: his was the administration of experts, of the Special Forces or, as the service was popularly known, the Green Berets. An early plan for training the Green Berets, it seems, projected that troops parachuted into Hungary should be able to talk about the principal Hungarian poets and know the correct words for romance. (James Bond becomes an expert lepidopterist.) The President, who had our remaining PT boats routed to Vietnam, made suggestions for the equipping of the Green Berets, the substitution, for example, of sneakers for heavy combat boots. When the sneakers were found vulnerable to bamboo spikes, he recommended their reinforcement with flexible steel inner soles. He shared fully in the family regard for strength and courage, a regard that made Robert Kennedy respond longingly, on hearing his brother read from a citation for bravery Douglas MacArthur had received in World War I, "I would love to have that said about me." Like James Reston, John was aware of Hemingway's succinct definition of courage, "grace under pressure" (he remarked that it reminded him of a girl he had known). But to locate courage in an expert's or an aristocrat's conduct that is at once resolute and perfectly restrained makes for a precarious balance. The restraint could be the hard part. It has been observed that President Kennedy's fear of appearing weak could tempt him to overreact, as after his first confrontation with Khrushchev about Berlin.[3]

The first days of Kennedy's presidency were a time not of militancy abroad but of domestic reconciliation. In a manner reminiscent of bringing Lyndon Johnson on the presidential ticket for balance, he met with Richard Nixon in Florida after the election. He later appointed Nixon's running mate and Kennedy's 1952 Senate race opponent, Henry Cabot Lodge, Jr., ambassador to South Vietnam. The inaugural address omitted a specific discussion of domestic issues for fear of divisiveness. Kennedy retained staple figures of government, such as Allen Dulles of the Central Intelligence Agency and J. Edgar Hoover of the Federal Bureau of Investigation, and appointed the conservative William McChesney Martin chairman of the Federal Reserve Board.

Robert McNamara, the cost-accounting president of the Ford Motor Company, became secretary of defense. "He really runs, rather than walks," even "running up and down the escalator steps"; so Kennedy's secretary of agriculture Orville Freeman has described McNamara. For secretary of state the President wanted William Fulbright of Arkansas, chairman of the Senate Foreign Relations Committee. He had worked with Fulbright in the Senate and found him capable. Robert Kennedy and others argued against the appointment on the ground that the southerner's civil rights record would make him undesirable to new African countries, while one source recalls that it was the opposition of supporters of Israel, thinking Fulbright too sympathetic to the Arab interest, that kept him from becoming secretary. President Kennedy also passed over Adlai Stevenson, who as early as the middle fifties had called for an end to nuclear testing; Stevenson instead became ambassador to the United Nations. Following the advice of the tough-minded foreign policy experts Robert Lovett and Dean Acheson, Kennedy chose imperturbable Dean Rusk for secretary.

For undersecretary of state Kennedy picked a liberal of strong convictions, Chester Bowles. After less than a year, during which he was instrumental in selecting able ambassadors, Bowles was to be eased from his post into an ambassadorship himself. In the discussions preceding the administration's launching of the exiles' invasion of Cuba, Bowles was almost alone in opposition. Beyond that, he was the kind of liberal, in the Stevenson vein, with whom John Kennedy was uncomfortable. But that does not seem to have been the main trouble. A comment in the *Kiplinger Washington Letter* for December 2, 1961, in a discussion of inefficiency in the State Department, suggests a general incompatibility between the government and Bowles's administrative style: "*Bowles made the situation worse* with fireworks of bright *ideas*. . . . That's the real reason he was fired, then kicked upstairs." Kennedy himself confirmed that view in an interview with Robert Estabrook of the *Washington Post*. "I told Alsop," the President observed, "that he had made sure that Bowles would stay." Bowles was capable of serving as the conscience of the administration. In a letter to Kennedy dated September 30, 1961, he voiced his concern that the government's training of foreign military personnel was neglecting to inculcate "an understanding of the values and practices of a democratic society" and that "our aid programs have woefully underemphasized an integrated attack on poverty and despair." He later wrote Kennedy brilliant memoranda on the dangers of American involvement in Vietnam. Bowles's difficulties were one of few exceptions in remarkably warm relationships between a President and his advisers.[4]

McNamara, a graduate and at one time a teacher at the Harvard Business School; Rusk, a Rhodes scholar and an academician who had published in *Foreign Affairs*; Elvis Stahr, another Rhodes scholar and after his services in Washington president of the University of Indiana; Walt Rostow of Yale University and MIT; McGeorge Bundy, dean of the faculty of arts and science at Harvard; the historian Arthur M. Schlesinger, Jr., a White House adviser; Bowles, an editor of the *Encyclopaedia Britannica*: these were among the people who constituted for the administration virtually a university faculty presided over by Norman Mailer's young professor. It was the right assemblage for a government that gave promise of quickening the scientific, technological, and intellectual instruments of national growth.

Dean Rusk's later connection with the Vietnam War has turned liberals against him, and during Kennedy's presidency his careful steadiness made him unpopular with the Kennedy White House advisers who prized their own bright, quick decisiveness. Rusk had a strong liberal background. Peace advocate before World War II (though also a member of his college ROTC), open opponent of McCarthyism, supporter of Stevenson even in 1960, he belonged to a now almost forgotten company of old-line southern liberals and, when such gestures meant something, once broke a color barrier by going with Ralph Bunche of the United Nations into the officers' mess at the Pentagon. As secretary of state he tried to reestablish the China experts purged in the Redbaiting days, but Robert Kennedy stopped him.[5]

Rostow, Rusk's subordinate, was of a different character. At his worst he was capable of proposing in a note to the President during the Berlin crisis that we increase the risk of armed conflict by probing within Khrushchev's territory. That way both leaders would "share the burden of making sacrifice to avoid nuclear war." (Yet in a memorandum of August 14, 1961, to McGeorge Bundy, Rostow in proposing broad negotiations between the West and the Soviet Union on Germany and Berlin remarked, "This approach requires that the President reverse the bad Western postwar habit of regarding negotiation as a sign of weakness.") Later Kennedy apparently titled Rostow the Air Marshal for his inclination to advocate bombs as answers to our various troubles abroad. But he was a spokesman for peaceful competition with communism through aid for economic development. That idea, along with his notion that the military of the underdeveloped nations could be their hope—providing a leavening of educated and idealistic officers—represents the compound of toughness, progressivism, and trust in trained intelligence that the Kennedy circle expected to dictate foreign policy.[6]

McNamara had a mind as severe and clean as a statistical table, so clean that because of Franklin D. Roosevelt, Jr.'s, conduct in the West Virginia primary McNamara would not countenance the President's making Roosevelt Secretary of the Navy. Once during his days at Ford McNamara had upset a few of his corporate superiors with a passage in a commencement address at the University of Alabama that seemed to question whether money was a sufficient motive for going into business. "Today progressive taxation places limits on the earning power of the businessman, and hence upon his purely monetary motivation," said McNamara with an engaging innocence. "More and more he draws his incentive from a sense of public responsibility." Mc-Namara would typify the liberal technocrat side of the administration in his pursuit of efficiency and his apparent belief, so his conduct during the Vietnam War demonstrates, in information gathered by experts. His combination of militancy and respect for complexity represents what cold war liberalism was coming to.

Among the technocrats and new frontiersmen of the administration appeared a figure out of another time and style, New Dealer Adolf A. Berle. He now had a reputation for being a conservative, but it was not illogical for a New Dealer to be well content with American business civilization as the Roosevelt era had modified and confirmed it. But Berle could think like a postwar liberal, faithful to the spirit of New Deal progressivism. He was both a cold warrior and, toward the American continent, at any rate, a supporter of the Democratic left—a formula the New Frontier groped toward. Head of a task force for advising the President-elect on Latin America, Berle presented to Kennedy and Sorensen on January 6, so his diary entry for that day relates, a summary of the report that contains the injunctions: "Stabilization of social revolution at left-of-center. . . . U.S. cannot support dying dictatorships . . . or plutocracies—or any group including Communist parties." A portion of the summary attributed to Berle alone suggests this position on Cuba: "The '26th of July' revolution has the sympathy of U.S. It is incomplete, and should succeed. Castro aborted it; he is now dictatorial obstacle to be removed like Batista." Berle's entries for the years of the Kennedy administration reveal a grumbling hard-liner, complaining late in the fall of 1961 about the failure of the West to require the dismantling of the Berlin Wall—"The evidence coming in now suggests that a little nerve would have stopped the maneuver"—and noting just after the Cuba missile crisis that we had not completely expelled the effective Soviet presence from the island: "A half-done job."[7]

Some of the new administration's mentality quickly revealed itself at the Bay of Pigs. In the Eisenhower years, the Central Intelligence Agency had prepared an invasion force that it believed would bring a Cuban uprising against Fidel Castro. Cuban refugee guerrillas awaited orders on a coffee plantation in a mountainous region of Guatemala. In the campaign debates, Kennedy had come out as the hard-liner on Cuba, implicitly holding the Eisenhower administration responsible for letting Cuba go Communist, while Nixon, the liberal Republican, observed that we were obliged to work within the Organization of American States. Conservative columnists praised Kennedy; liberal commentators lauded Nixon, somewhat inaccurately, for the Vice President knew of the plans for invasion. So Kennedy as President had to make a decision about a scheme that his opponent had needed to shroud with soft language. Several liberals dissented from the plan. Arthur Schlesinger and William Fulbright voiced their objections to the President. Others did not get to make their case: Chester Bowles, intelligence expert Roger Hilsman of the Department of State, and George Kennan, the intellectual architect of the policy of containment. Another set of advisers got through to Kennedy.

Notable among these were the Joint Chiefs of Staff, including Arleigh Burke, the legendary navy chief, whom Kennedy admired. As Kennedy would soon discover, all the chiefs had a habit of favoring belligerent operations. Allen Dulles told him that the probability of success for the act was higher than could have been predicted of the Eisenhower administration's successful intervention of 1954 in Guatemala. In April 1961 Kennedy gave the order for the assault on Cuba.[8]

The landing spot, surrounded by swamps and allowing the rebels no opportunity to retreat to the mountains, was familiar in detail to Castro, for it was his favorite fishing spot. Maps studied for the invasion had little grasslike figures that one CIA participant could recognize as symbols for swamps. The other planners apparently did not possess the useful art of map reading and so could not see that the exiles would be pinched in. "I don't think we fully realized," writes Schlesinger, "that the Escambray Mountains lay *eighty miles* from the Bay of Pigs, across a hopeless tangle of swamps and jungles." He has also noted that one road believed to be important ended in a swamp. The force of 1,400 was challenging an army of 250,000 to 400,000, powerfully equipped by the Soviet Union. The invaders, using old freighters supplied by the United Fruit Company, carried radio equipment and much of their inadequate supply of munitions in a single boat, which was blown up; air cover by the exiles was inadequate. Coral reefs ripped the hulls of some craft. In its spirit the enterprise recalls some of Kennedy's moments in World War II. Yet the President had the restraint not to provide major United States air support. Or perhaps it was not self-restraint but, as Senator George Smathers of Florida has reported Kennedy's telling him, Adlai Stevenson's threat to resign from the ambassadorship to the United Nations. Another possible reason for Kennedy's forbearance was a message from Khrushchev that in the event of a more direct intervention the Soviet Union would take action—perhaps it would be in Berlin or Southeast Asia: "Cuba is not alone," Khrushchev announced. Kennedy's indefatigable champion Schlesinger was later to tell Robert Estabrook that while Eisenhower had contemplated American air and sea support and even American ground forces in a strike against the island, Kennedy had rejected that idea in March, before the invasion. Castro, in any event, destroyed the assault.[9]

Just after the Bay of Pigs an analogy appeared several times in the press between the Russian invasion of Hungary in 1956, intended to protect the Soviet Union's sphere of influence, and the attempt on the part of the United States government to preserve its own international domain. As an exercise in *realpolitik*, the invasion was comparable. It would have been morally comparable only if the Soviets, instead of sending their own troops to kill thousands of Hungarians in order to crush a movement unpleasing to them, had sent in an army of Hungarian exiles, expecting them to rally the people in a coup against a repressive government. In 1961 the Cuban regime had more people in prison than the rightist former government had confined for an equal period, and the treatment of political prisoners was often brutal. Not only former supporters of Batista but anyone at whom the new order took political offense became a victim of the mass trials and mass executions of the early days of the Castro regime. Kennedy was acting on one of the most generous, and most naïve, of American cold war beliefs. He assumed, in effect, that every people in the world wishes to be free in the way that the Western democracies understand freedom: with elected parliaments, a diverse and argumentative press, competing political parties, and a citizenry that conducts itself not by neighborhood committees ruthlessly enforcing ideological orthodoxy but by private choices. It may be that Cuba under Castro is free in ways that it was not before: free from extremes of hunger, disease, illiteracy; free to participate in local forms of self-management. The freedom that Cubans do enjoy, if freedom is the right word, must be preferable to a life of malnutrition and sickness under governments that provide a measure of democratic debate for classes prosperous enough to relish or profit from it. Yet the beliefs that led legions of Americans to expect that nations would be content with nothing less than constitutional, parliamentary, civil libertarian freedom expressed the pride of the West in some of its finest political achievements of recent centuries. Kennedy would have had no patience with the species of radicalism that dismisses the liberties of the Western republics as merely bourgeois.

It "is not the first time," Kennedy said just after the crushing of the invasion, "that Communist tanks have rolled over gallant men and women fighting to redeem the independence of their homeland." An in-house memorandum presented to Kennedy early in his administration illustrates this perception of the mood of populations under Communist regimes. It includes the suggestion that leaflets be dropped in North Vietnam. To urge defections from a popular regime? No, to keep up the morale of the North Vietnamese populace. Perhaps in memory of the Hungarians gunned down in 1956 in their misguided belief that we would rescue their insurrection, the same document warns against doing anything that would spark an outbreak we would not support. At a meeting of presidential advisers at the beginning of the missile crisis of 1962 recorded on the White House tapes, McNamara warned that an air strike against the Soviet missiles in Cuba might bring an uprising that would oblige us to invade the island and "prevent the slaughter of . . . the free Cubans. And we would be prepared to do that." McGeorge Bundy in an oral history in the 1970s has recalled the thinking of the Kennedy administration about Cuba: "Anytime you had a Communist takeover . . . most people in that country wouldn't like it and would be in favor of liberation." Astonishing of a Harvard dean? Possibly. But within a very few years prestigious university professors would be looking to Hanoi as the leader of a liberation movement—an opinion that had some reasoned if insubstantial foundations, but then so had Bundy's.[10]

If the expectations that led to the Bay of Pigs reveal the political thinking of cold war liberalism, they also demonstrate a liberal's, and a Kennedy's, faith in expertise. The Central Intelligence Agency, founded under President Truman in 1947, had been an outgrowth of the Office of Strategic Services, the American spy organization of World War II staffed with many scholars and often thought to lean leftward. In its own way the CIA was a liberal's institution, with its cluster of scholars and analysts of the sort who have historically staffed twentieth-century liberalism. During the Eisenhower and the Kennedy years, it is estimated, at least 10 percent of the agency's members held Ph.Ds. The chairman of a CIA supervisory board reorganized under Kennedy was James R. Killian, president of the Massachusetts Institute of Technology, and among the board's members was the liberal historian William Langer, formerly of the OSS and then of the CIA.

The CIA was "the only place in the Eisenhower Administration that had room for the young activists who wanted to work with youth and labor movements abroad," says Roger Hilsman. It had attracted champions of a strategy of supporting popular progressive movements abroad as alternatives to communism (though it was also instrumental in effecting the 1954 coup against a progressive Guatemalan regime. It is to be expected that in the process of implementing agrarian reform, explains an indignant CIA paper of 1953, "the large Guatemalan landholders and the United Fruit Company will be victimized." It then observes, with reason, that neither the landholders nor the company can hope for the sympathies of the public.) Joseph McCarthy included the CIA among the innumerable American institutions corrupted by the left. Richard Nixon's memoirs describe it as a stronghold of liberalism. William Sloane Coffin, chaplain at Yale in the 1960s and among the leading activists against the war in Vietnam, has reflected without lengthy apology about his connection with the early CIA. Arthur Schlesinger, Jr., has observed, "In my experience its leadership was politically enlightened and sophisticated. Not seldom CIA representatives took a more liberal line in White House meetings than their counterparts from State. A great deal of CIA energy went to the support of the anti-Communist left around the world—political parties, trade unions and other undertakings." And in Robert Kennedy's own words: "During the 1950s . . . many of the liberals who were forced out of other departments found a sanctuary, an enclave, in the CIA. So some of the best people in Washington, and around the country, began to collect there. One result of that was the CIA developed a very healthy view of Communism, especially compared to State and some other departments. They were very sympathetic, for example, to nationalist, and even Socialist governments and movements."[11]

CIA people, having turned their intellects outward from scholarship to the virile business of counterinsurgency, had nothing about them of the pallid, introspective hesitancy that a Kennedy despised in liberalism. The most enthusiastic of the experts who designed the Bay of Pigs was Richard Bissell, impatiently brilliant, eccentric, a former economics professor, a sailor and a mountain climber who appealed to the elitist in Kennedy. Bissell in an interview about a year after the attempt said that he had favored air support for the invaders, which he acknowledged could have brought a wider involvement. This Stevenson Democrat and friend of Chester Bowles believed with much of the administration that Castro was a traitor to a revolution that had drawn support from liberal and democratic elements. He once said of opponents of Castro like himself: "We're the real revolutionaries." Kennedy in *The Strategy of Peace*, published early in 1960, had called Castro "part of the legacy of Bolivar," the liberator of much of Latin America from imperial rule. But during the campaign he had accused Castro of betraying the revolution. Bissell and others told Kennedy that if the Cuban invaders did not succeed militarily they could become guerrillas. Perhaps the Kennedy circle had succumbed to the twentieth-century romance of the guerrilla, the Che Guevara or the black-clad NLF insurgent, who will win because he is of the people.

The *Kiplinger Washington Letter* for February 18, predicting an invasion and composed with material in quotation marks suggestive of an inside source, indicates that the planners had projected a progressive government: *"Castro's successor* will be 'radical, but not anti-the-U.S.' "; *"Some stolen U.S. property will be returned* . . . factories, banks. But expropriated land and utilities will be kept . . . and 'socialized.' " Possibly some CIA planners did project such a future, but the agency would deserve little credit. A memorandum of May 6 by Adolf Berle claims, "All known Batistianos had been filtered out" of the revolutionary front, and the exile movement included former participants in Castro's revolution, former supporters of Batista, and students opposed to both. But opinion, Louise FitzSimons writes, ranged from "extreme left to extreme right"; and the CIA inclined to favor Batista officers with military training. Whether it was ideology or practical considerations that dictated this preference, Kennedy had to insure the inclusion within the *frente*, the exile front, of a progressive element that not everyone in the CIA wanted. Arthur Schlesinger's Kennedy was in all this, as in most other things, a nearly impeccable liberal. While under Eisenhower the government's contacts had been with right-wing Cubans, Robert Estabrook reports Schlesinger as telling him, Kennedy's government dealt predominantly with liberal and left exiles, counterparts of the Americans for Democratic Action. Yet a letter of March 29, 1961, from Schlesinger to Tracy Barnes of the CIA complains that a manifesto prepared for the invasion has too much on "free enterprise" and the rights of property, to the neglect of discussing what the new regime will do for the poor.[12]

The Bay of Pigs turned Kennedy angry at the CIA and skeptical of officialdom. Some agency officers, in Robert's later description of them, had been disobedient, saying before the invasion that if the President were to call it off, they would arrange for the rebels to get American weapons—"virtually treason," in Robert's words. President Kennedy had insisted that no United States troops be used; the first two people on the beach were his countrymen, sent by the CIA. In the opinion of Robert, who after the disaster headed the program for building counterinsurgency forces, the Bay of Pigs may have been the best thing to happen to the administration, teaching his brother to trust only his own judgment and keeping the United States from a heavy commitment of troops to Laos. Here, in rough, is Robert's rendering, something of a parody, of an exchange between the President and the military eager to send troops to Laos. How would the troops get there? asked the President. Two airports could land them, he was told. How many could be landed? Under perfect conditions, came the response, a thousand a day. How many Communist troops would be in the area? At a guess, three thousand. How long, wondered the President, would it take the Communists to bring up four thousand? The answer: in four more days, five to eight thousand. What if we have landed three thousand on the third day and the Communists bomb the airport and concentrate five or six thousand more? Bomb Hanoi, was the military advice; use nuclear weapons. Chester Bowles has said that while Marine Corps Chief of Staff David Shoup could be reasonable on Laos, other chiefs wanted something major, such as air attacks on South China. Following the crisis of the Cuba missiles, Robert recounts, Navy Chief of Staff George Anderson, Jr., lamented, "We've been sold out," and Air Force Chief Curtis LeMay wanted to bomb Cuba anyway.[13]

John Kennedy had remarked to Richard Neustadt at the beginning of his administration that he could not be a good President if he limited himself to one set of advisers. He did come to seek varieties of opinion, balancing Robert Kennedy and Sorensen, for example, against the military. The President, writes Adam Ulam, "became increasingly impressed by brilliantly reasoned, but not always realistic, academic theories and memoranda bearing on insurgency and nation-building." Upon the retirement of Allen Dulles from the directorship of the CIA, Kennedy appointed John McCone. The performance of the new director pleasantly startled liberals who had known him to be only a right-winger. Yet the incurable agency was still intruding on the administration as late as April 2, 1963, when Sargent Shriver called the President to ask that he restrain the CIA from planting people in the Peace Corps. Kennedy, the White House tapes record, agreed to do so.[14]

Among the advisory agencies to which Kennedy looked after the Bay of Pigs was the INR, the bureau of intelligence and research that was the intelligence arm of the State Department. At its head was Roger Hilsman, later to become Kennedy's assistant secretary of state for Far Eastern affairs. Hilsman was an adviser consummately in the spirit of the liberal cold warrior elite. He belonged to the generation of World War II, a West Pointer, the leader of an OSS mission behind enemy lines in Burma. The war, he was to remark after the end of Kennedy's presidency, like the plantation system, had trained people at an early age for administrative responsibility; Hilsman, for example, had been a battalion commander at twenty-five. His kind, he has said, "were activists. . . . We thought one man could make a difference. . . . [This] is the Kennedy thesis. . . . Pragmatic, idealist, activist."[15]

Hilsman embodied the unstable compound of militancy and restraint that prevailed in administration thought. He was a main contributor to an issue of the *Marine Corps Gazette* filled with discussion of guerrilla warfare. An INR study group working after Hilsman's departure suggested that assassinating Castro might merely turn him into a martyr and that the object should be an "independent, democratic, and socially progressive Cuba." So far, sensible enough. But at this point unchecked imagination took over. We should discredit Castro, demolish his self-esteem, and drive him to irrationality, proposed the group. Mock him for needing a beard when his "proprietor Khrushchev" needs none; "dare [the] vassal to be man enough to shave." Deny publicly that Castro, as some medical authorities say, is insane. Where these ideas came from in an agency on which Hilsman had impressed his stamp is unclear. But Hilsman in recollection has criticized the Central Intelligence Agency for its adventurism. On one occasion it had contaminated Cuban sugar destined for the Soviet Union. The INR bought up and destroyed the sacks. As it took over functions of the CIA, the INR tried to cut back the agency practice of subsidizing political parties abroad, as well as the practice of giving money to students, professors, and magazines, which, according to Hilsman, might have been reasonable to do at the height of the cold war. The very purpose that Kennedy, in Hilsman's understanding, assigned to the INR accords with the liberal concept of the agencies of the cold war. It was to put the President in touch with the academic community, and this Hilsman interpreted as a mandate to provide ideas and interpretation as opposed to sheerly technical work. Here in retrospect is Hilsman on Vietnam: "Our three pronged policy is to protect the people; don't chase the Viet Cong, just use your troops to protect the people. Then, behind that screen, you have social and political reform, land reform—and very deep reform—education, everything. And then the sea of the people in which Mao says the guerrillas swim like fish will have dried up. And if necessary, you can arm the people, but it probably won't be necessary. Now, the point is that we were all grossly misinformed about the convolutions, the thickness, the obstacles, that Vietnamese culture represents."[16]

Kennedy, turning after the Bay of Pigs to such advisers as Hilsman, continued his early policy of hostility toward Cuba and of defense against the possibility of any further movements in the hemisphere allied to the Soviet Union. A memorandum from Dean Rusk urges the government to "tighten the noose around the Cuban economy and to increase the isolation of the Castro regime from the political life of the hemisphere until the regime becomes a complete pariah." Washington requested Western nations not to trade with the island state. On military spending, too, Kennedy was acting like the hard-liner of the 1950s. Discounting the argument that building up our weaponry would provoke the Soviet Union into a like program, the President pushed for greater funding for defense, and Congress passed a fifteen percent increase. The Russians did ultimately respond to our growth in weaponry as well as to the crises of these years with their scheme for placing missiles in Cuba and with a long-term increase in their military expenditures. The obsession with Cuba has been one of the worst legacies of the Kennedy administration. Yet even in his belligerence the President, who during his campaign had said that we should "create a Latin America where freedom can flourish," adopted also the strategy of economic assistance that had reconciled the anticommunism of the liberals with their social progressivism.[17]

Using the Bay of Pigs as a reason for acting, Kennedy pressed for an Alliance for Progress, a $10 billion decade-long program of economic aid to Latin America. At Punta del Este in Uruguay during 1962 the alliance committed itself to land and tax reform. Though the administration was never to carry its support for progressivism to the point of abandoning right-wing regimes that promised stability, the plan at its origins was assertively social reformist. Richard Goodwin, one of Kennedy's advisers, was instrumental in fashioning the alliance and worked to make it address political and social problems as well as economics. State Department officials had cooperated with rightist Latin American governments and were repelled when the President, in a speech of March 13, 1961, talked of "revolutionary ideas and efforts." The *alianza,* in Hilsman's words, "is saying a revolution is inevitable in Latin America. If you don't do it peacefully, you'll end up with blood." Juan Bosch, a progressive leader in the Dominican Republic whose politics Lyndon Johnson was to push aside with marines in 1965, has said of the Alliance, "That was the only time the U.S. ever followed a correct policy in Latin America."[18]

Elsewhere as well the administration acted to the left of its defense spending. The Development Loan Fund in 1961 provided more than $1 billion in aid to underdeveloped nations. The administration united diverse foreign aid programs under the Agency for International Development. An objective of AID was counterinsurgency, but its plans for training local police in advanced technology were combined with progressive measures for emergency economic assistance to threatened areas and for technical aid for sanitation and transportation. Yet Congress in 1963, against Kennedy's wishes, sharply cut foreign aid in response to the recommendations of a conservative study group headed by General Lucius Clay that the President himself had appointed. Kennedy's hope had been that the committee would win conservatives to foreign aid, but the plan went askew. In the opinion of John Sherman Cooper, foreign aid benefited little under Kennedy, aside from some additional funds for Latin America. In Africa Kennedy did not seek out the kinds of rightist regimes that over the years have so beguiled us in Latin America. Washington showed no sympathy for the white supremacist government of South Africa and strongly supported the efforts of the United Nations to put down a secessionist movement in Katanga considered to be more friendly to Western neoimperialism than was the new government of the Congo.[19]

It was not, however, these initiatives that preoccupied Kennedy's presidency. More sudden necessities of confrontation and conciliation determined the character of its foreign policy.

A major crisis began in June 1961, when the President went to Vienna—in "excruciating pain," O'Donnell reports, from dislocated muscles at the base of the spine—for a summit conference with Premier Khrushchev. The main object of the Soviet leader was to get a permanent separate status for Communist East Germany. That meant an abrogation of the original agreement among the Allies for a reunification of Germany under free elections. Khrushchev was particularly disturbed at the flow of East Germans through the passage from East to West Berlin, a migration that included much of the professional classes within the Russian satellite and threatened to collapse its economy.

Khrushchev's concern was understandable. Recent history had instructed the Russians to fear a strong Germany, which in this case would mean a strong West Germany with no Eastern European buffer. They feared also a Western thrust into the vulnerable Eastern European corridor that flanks the Soviet Union, a thrust that could come from Germany in alliance with the NATO powers or could follow economic and consequent political chaos in East Germany. The politics of the West German government and the speeches of its politicians had been so provocative that they would disturb any Kremlin government—czarist, Communist, or democratic. Soviet spies had even seen German pilots warming up planes that carried American nuclear weapons. Eisenhower as President, agreeing that Berlin was "abnormal," had proposed negotiating the size of the Western military presence in West Berlin and the uses of the city for West German propaganda and intelligence. Now the premier threatened to sign a separate peace treaty with the East German Communist state unless the Western powers gave him a satisfactory alternative. The American reaction was as understandable as the Soviet position. Years of cold war and Communist ruthlessness toward Eastern Europe had conditioned Americans to an inability to conceive of the Soviet Union as having any foreign policy interests that were defensive rather than aggressive. The Russians, moreover, were tearing up the original Allied plans. That may have been justifiable; conditions and needs change. Yet a generation of commentators excoriates the United States for going against the Geneva accords of 1954 on Vietnam, which Washington had not signed but was obliged not to disrupt, and it is not surprising that in 1961 Americans held Khrushchev to a similar accountability. Khrushchev's designs for a German settlement contemplated making West Berlin a free city under the supervision of the United Nations on condition that East Germans not be allowed egress through it. But the United States feared that a German Communist state would swallow up West Berlin, a possibility that the rights of Berliners and the honor of the Allies made unacceptable.

At Vienna Kennedy argued for the stabilization of the two blocs, while Khrushchev, who was working to insure that Eastern Europe would remain safely closed, insisted that the rest of the world be open to the spread of Communist revolution. The two leaders also discussed a developing confrontation in Laos, where the United States had been supporting a rightist, and the Soviet Union a Communist, faction. On that issue, at any rate, they managed to agree to some disengagement, actually effected later under a troika government composed of the right-wing, the Communist, and a neutral party. But on the overriding issue of Germany Khrushchev and Kennedy went home empty-handed. The meeting is remembered for an ideological argument between the two leaders, one of them by general account having little taste for abstraction, the other a spokesman for a society steeped in the language of ideology.[20]

It was a prelude to some of the sharpest verbal and diplomatic clashes of the cold war. The Soviet Union had its reasons for arrogance. The Bay of Pigs had discredited the United States, and the Soviet space program, after years of spectacular success, had just launched the first of all manned satellites. But who, precisely, was confronting Kennedy? There was Khrushchev himself, possessing something of the belligerence, as well as the hearty good fellowship, of a peasant out of folklore. Yet it is a question how much of the truculence that he was to show throughout the crisis expressed his own personality and how much was for the sake of politics at home. Khrushchev, having presided over the ending of political terror in the Soviet Union and its replacement by a milder and more stable repression, was working to put the economy at the service of the population, while his more chauvinistic opponents, led by V. I. Kozlov, wanted the resources of the economy to flow into the military. Khrushchev's political situation bears a resemblance to that of Dean Acheson, Truman's secretary of state, who had been relentlessly firm toward the Soviet Union even while right-wingers accused him of appeasement. Khrushchev apparently needed to win enough from the West, and to be aggressive enough about winning it, in order to appease or outflank his domestic enemies, just as American politicians have to prove that they are not soft on communism. So Kennedy had to face a country confident in its recent achievements, resolved to settle the German danger, and speaking through a leader whose verbal manner and political troubles made him the image of bellicosity.[21]

The first reactions to Khrushchev's demands were angry. Samuel Beer, head of the Americans for Democratic Action, said in the liberal manner of the time, "The crisis in our affairs is no less serious than that confronting the nation in 1933. Nothing less is at stake than the survival of freedom." Even before Vienna Dean Acheson, calling the Berlin question a "simple contest of wills," had recommended sending a division of American troops on the Autobahn through East Germany to Berlin and had urged Kennedy to declare a national emergency and make it clear that we would fight a nuclear war, if necessary. Since there was nothing to negotiate, a willingness to go to the conference table would be taken as a sign of weakness. After the meeting with Khrushchev, Kennedy seemed to be of like mind with such pugnacious advisers as Acheson. The President believed that Khrushchev was using the German question to probe Western resolve. He demanded a crash civil defense program that led to a popular stir about bomb shelters: the government, reported the *Kiplinger Washington Letter* for July 29, was testing NEAR (National Emergency Alarm Repeater) boxes, to be plugged into household wall outlets, that would receive from a central office warnings of impending attack. The President re-

quested estimates on casualties in the event of nuclear war.
Aided by the nation's reaction to the recent launching of a
manned Soviet space satellite and possessed of a keen sense of
historical event, he began a multibillion dollar effort that aimed
at reaching the moon and, as a side effect, quickening the economy. It was in the atmosphere of Vienna and Berlin that he
turned to heavy increases in defense spending. On July 25 he
proposed a growth in military expenditures and an increase in
the armed forces by 217,000 and announced doubled draft calls
and a mobilization of 51,000 reserves. "We do not want to
fight," he said, "but we have fought before." Berlin was "the
great testing place of Western courage and will."[22]

One incident that summer, though, was or seemed to be
curiously at odds with the administration's announcements of
its resoluteness. The large immediate issue was that of emigra-
tion from East Germany. Washington knew that the threat of
the economic ruin of the Communist satellite could push the
Soviet Union very far. On July 30 William Fulbright, chairman
of the Senate Foreign Relations Committee, remarked on television that a Communist closing off of East Berlin might be
acceptable. After widespread indignation in Germany, Fulbright
retracted his statement. In answer to a question that referred to
Fulbright's comments, the President in his press conference of
August 10 was noticeably silent on the question of whether the
East Germans had a right to free exit. Khrushchev was losing
East Germany and could not allow that to happen, Walt Rostow recalls the President's remarking to him early in August.
The premier would have to halt the stream of refugees, perhaps
by a wall, Kennedy observed, and he could not stop Khrushchev
from doing it, though he could muster the Western alliance for
defense of West Berlin. On August 28 an annoyed Kennedy,
speaking to Robert Estabrook, was to deny the truth of a story
in that day's paper that the closing of the border in Berlin had
caught the United States by surprise.[23]

Is it possible that the administration, having recognized
how dangerous the situation had become, was giving signals that

it would tolerate a sealing off of the passage into West Berlin, signals that could amount to encouragement to the Communists to do so? Then its policy would be a study in the dilemma of how to balance one evil against another. Should history, for example, be more understanding of those realistic antebellum statesmen who to preserve domestic peace would return fugitive slaves to the South? When in August East Germany, acting with the blessing of Khrushchev, began the construction of the Berlin Wall, thereby presenting itself as the sovereign force in an East Berlin in which the four-power arrangement no longer existed, Kennedy responded as though the act was uninvited and an outrage. McGeorge Bundy remembers the President as being surprised by the wall. Probably Fulbright's speculations and Kennedy's lack of response to them had not been meant after all as a message to the Soviet Union. Or perhaps the administration had contemplated something less harsh on the part of the Russians, possibly a negotiated slowing of the migration from the Eastern sector. Or was Kennedy attempting, through belligerent gestures, to reassure West Berliners that their allies would not also abandon them or to warn Khrushchev against trying his luck further?[24]

Kenneth O'Donnell, summing up the remarks his cautious John Kennedy made in the course of the crisis, reports that the President, having read Barbara Tuchman's account of the beginning of World War I, commented, "All wars start from stupidity," and reasoned that it would be especially stupid to risk American lives over the question of access to an Autobahn or over the desire of Germans for unification. "Before I back Khrushchev against the wall, . . . the freedom of all of Western Europe will have to be at stake." Kennedy, according to O'Donnell, remarked "Why should Khrushchev put up a wall if he really intended to seize West Berlin? . . . This is his way out of his predicament. It's not a very nice solution, but a wall is a hell of a lot better than a war." In a memorandum to Bundy that summer the President observed, "I'm somewhat uneasy to have refusal to negotiate become a test of firmness." Kennedy chose a show of force. Aware of the possibility of a confrontation with the Communists, he sent 1,500 troops along the Autobahn from West Germany to West Berlin. Vice President Johnson went to the city to pledge American lives to its defense. To strengthen the confidence of the Berliners the President appointed as his representative to them General Lucius Clay, the determined organizer of the defiant and victorious airlift of 1948. The airlift, the rescuer of West Berlin, had been Clay's idea, pressed upon Truman in the face of more conciliatory advice. With reason, the Berliners considered the general their special friend and champion. Yet the wall solved a big problem for the Soviet Union and perhaps a big problem for the United States. It also circumvented the wishes of Khrushchev's domestic enemies for some policy that would force all Berlin into Russian hands, and allowed him to compensate in part for having backed off from his six-month deadline for a separate treaty with East Germany.[25]

But his decision not to press for a fully satisfactory solution must have remained a domestic political problem for him. Kennedy's stridency in his July 25 speech, Khrushchev later remarked to the banker John McCloy, put the premier under great duress from Kremlin militants to resume nuclear testing. His nation lagged behind the United States in nuclear weaponry. On August 30 the Soviet Union announced that it would begin tests. Thereupon a new issue compounded the crisis that Berlin had wrought. Kennedy and Britain's Tory prime minister, Harold Macmillan, appealed to Khrushchev not to set off further nuclear bombs in the air, adding that they would not insist on standard schemes for monitoring tests. The September 15 issue of Life carried an article by the President on fallout shelters, a subject that simply in being raised was an expression of militancy. The administration, meanwhile, had to decide on its own policy of nuclear tests. If the Russians really wanted a treaty on the issue, Rusk reasoned at a meeting of the National Security Council, we should not test. But Rusk guessed that they did not, and he argued that the hazards from fallout were minimal beside the hazards that misunderstandings about our nuclear strength might bring. Kennedy expressed concern that fallout might kill even a single person, but Rusk doggedly insisted, "Our security must be the primary consideration." In September Kennedy, angered at the intransigence of the Soviet Union on the issue, began a round of tests. Robert Kennedy's explanation is that his brother, though unenthusiastic about testing, feared that the Soviet Union would perfect an antimissile before we did. Our first explosions were underground. The next spring, after a presidential decision in February, atmospheric testing followed, most spectacularly with the Starfish, which turned the Hawaiian night into day, flashed the skies of Australia, and temporarily altered the Van Allen radiation belt.[26]

Still, even as the tests were threatening to move the two superpowers toward confrontation, their leaders were seeking a formula to avert it. On September 5 the Soviet premier, telling C. L. Sulzberger of the *New York Times* that he would be happy to meet with Kennedy, suggested a resolution of the power struggle between Russia and the West in Laos in return for a settlement of the Berlin crisis. On September 25 before the United Nations, Kennedy made a conciliatory speech. And a letter on September 29 from Khrushchev to the President was part of a long correspondence between them that bypassed the usual institutions of negotiation and may in the end have considerably softened for a time the relations between the two powers. Then, in mid-October there was a tense moment in Berlin. On the border between the Western and the Eastern zones, American and Soviet tanks faced each other after a dispute over what rights the East German authorities had to restrict the movement of Western military between the sectors. The tanks pulled back and the Berlin crisis eased. Robert Estabrook, reflecting on an interview of November 11 with General Clay, recorded the conviction of the President, at odds with Clay, that insistence on the details of Western rights could be unnecessarily provocative.

Clay early in 1962 pleaded for greater authority to make

decisions in any future clash; Clay told Dean Rusk that had he been there to take immediate, unilateral action on the ground, he could have stopped the wall. The general wired: "If we fail to exercise [our power] properly, we here are at fault. If we exercise it improperly, almost any error of judgment here can be corrected immediately by the prompt removal of the responsible official." Kennedy, after sending his brother to Berlin, pointedly praised Clay's "coolness" and assured him that his "convictions" were not being "lightly overridden." On another occasion the President told the General, "The clear impression of determination, calmness and unity which we have all sought to convey in recent actions is, I think, a major element in the success which we have had in sustaining our access and making Soviet tactics ineffective." Clay was home by May 1962.[27]

Kennedy's words here come as close as anything to indicating how his handling of the Berlin crisis accorded with the style of a liberal cold warrior—a style presuming that both resolve and restraint, and more particularly a close balancing of the two, are the way of disciplined maturity. And either Kennedy's forbearance or his determination or both could claim at least one result: Khrushchev had withdrawn the deadline for Western assent to a separate East Germany as a condition for our continued access to West Berlin. Was there a victor? The Soviet Union, certainly, had not gotten all it wanted. But during the crisis furious voices had risen in the West, as they have from the beginning of the cold war no matter how strong our actions, complaining of the weakness of the Western posture. Bonn university students had sent Kennedy an umbrella symbolic of British Prime Minister Neville Chamberlain and his appeasement of Hitler at Munich. To such people, doubtless, the West was losing; to Khrushchev's Kremlin opponents, the Soviet Union was being sold out. At the end the superpowers had played out their tests of will, at no cost in blood to either, and with no harmful consequences at the time to anyone except, of course, the East Germans, who no longer could go West.

To a generation accustomed to the Vietnam War or to

Reagan's war on Central American leftists, the Berlin crisis is a reminder that in the early years of the cold war the major objective had been to save a burned and broken Europe from Soviet domination. By the time of Kennedy's presidency Western Europe, having long since ceased to be a convalescent, was a powerful economic and military force. Kennedy encouraged Britain to enter into the European Common Market, and since a strengthened Common Market could become tariff-encased against the United States, he asked Congress for legislation, which late in 1962 he obtained, permitting him to bargain for tariff reductions. In 1962, going along with a plan conceived before his presidency, he worked without result for the formation of MLF, a multilateral European and American nuclear force that was supposed to operate within NATO.

The gravest incident of the cold war, however, was to come not in Europe but close to the United States. Earlier in 1962, several months after the United States had stopped altogether the importing of Cuban sugar, Castro had decided to allow the Russians to set up a great military installation on the island. The Soviet leaders secretly began preparing for forty-two medium-range (1,100-mile) ballistic missiles, twenty-four intermediate-range (2,200-mile) missiles—these, as it happened, would never arrive—forty-eight out-of-date bombers, and some 22,000 advisers. Access to the missiles was controlled by electronic locks much like those that Kennedy had installed on our missiles abroad. By October, none or few of the sites yet had the nuclear warheads intended for them. For the first time the Soviet Union was doing what the United States had done many years before. It was installing missiles outside its immediate sphere. Air surveillance revealed the sites as their construction neared completion. Thereupon the Kennedy administration, early in the autumn of 1962, was in the midst of a crisis of immeasurable magnitude.[28]

The incident of the Bay of Pigs, it may be supposed, had given Khrushchev two somewhat contradictory impressions of the United States, both of them invitations to bellicose action: that this country was an adventurist nation against which the

Soviet Union would have to fortify itself, and that we knew how
to back off and therefore would not overreact to the emplacement of the missiles. It would once again have been to Khrushchev's advantage, moreover, to win a power play so great as to
silence the Kremlin right. But why Cuba and the missiles?

One gain from the venture would be the strengthening of
Soviet credibility with Cuba. In Moscow Raúl Castro, brother of
the Cuban leader, had pleaded for more aid. The island had reason to want aid. By this time the Kennedy administration, obsessed with Cuba, was waging something close to undeclared
war. Operation Mongoose it was called. Robert Kennedy championed it. In the course of the early sixties the CIA by one
estimate launched hundreds of commando sabotage raids in
Cuba involving 2,000 exiles working with 600 of the agency's
people. Bombing of Cuban embassies in Latin America and Europe was plotted. Circumstantial evidence, moreover, indicates
that both before and after the Bay of Pigs Kennedy, at the insistent nudging of elements in the CIA, had contemplated the
assassination of Castro. If so, it is one of the seamiest stories of
American foreign policy in recent years, and not because the
plotting of an assassination is especially brutal—nations continu-
ally effect policies that bring widespread death and suffering—but
because it would violate one of the implicit rules of good behavior that keep international relations from being even worse than
they are.

Former Florida Senator George Smathers has recounted a
conversation with Kennedy that took place after mid-March
1961, when the agency gave toxic pills to a Mafia chief in Miami,
a second supply to be delivered in April. The President asked the
senator how Latin America would respond to the killing of the
Cuban premier. Smathers, answering that the United States
would be held accountable, opposed the idea, and Kennedy replied that he was also opposed. The chief of the Cuba desk office
of the CIA in 1961 has summed up the impression Richard
Bissell passed on to him of a September meeting that year between Bissell and the Kennedy brothers: "They wanted the CIA

to get rid of Castro, and they meant *get rid of Castro.*" In a talk with a *New York Times* reporter in November, at a period when the CIA was again in touch with the Mafia on the matter, the President had a near repeat of his conversation with Smathers, asking for an opinion of Castro's assassination and then again, perhaps for the record, rejecting the idea. Whether or not the President was at odds with himself on the idea of assassination, in January 1962 he said of the removal of Castro, reports Thomas Powers, CIA officer at the time, "it's got to be done and will be done." McNamara once openly suggested Castro's assassination. Castro was a continuing preoccupation of the government. By the time of the missiles the CIA had been deeply involved in Operation Mongoose. Robert Kennedy, it seems, was angry at the CIA scheme for eliminating Castro, but what angered the purist and crime-fighting Bobby was the use of the Mafia. And whoever may have been behind them, in the middle seventies a select editorial committee chaired by Frank Church of Idaho was to document eight attempts on Castro.[29]

In face even of the administration's overt sentiments about the island regime, the missiles could have appeared to Soviet and Cuban minds as defensive, rescuing Cuba from the threat of an invasion from the north. What Khrushchev actually did, it would turn out, was to rescue the United States, as Norman Mailer observes, from the moral disadvantage the Bay of Pigs had put us in.

The larger reason for installing missiles was that however much they might actually increase relative Soviet power at a time when additions to the destructive capability of nuclear weapons were becoming meaningless, they would at least add to the look of Soviet military might. Khrushchev's memoirs describe the venture as an attempt to establish a balance of power.

Kennedy, even after discovering that the missile gap so important to him during the campaign did not exist, had increased the nation's nuclear strength. The President and McNamara might have realized that the Cuba missiles were a response to that increase. Their failure to recognize that our build-up would bring a Soviet reaction belongs to the dreary history of a cold war in which each bloc has believed again and again that one more increase or show of force will right matters. It is known, too, that the Soviet military leaders had been alarmed to learn that the United States could measure Russia's nuclear strength. Kennedy's announcement of the counterforce strategy had been his way of informing Moscow that we knew where its missiles were and could take them out of action—possibly in a first strike—instead of making war on the whole population. Our intention was to tell the Soviet Union we were aware that there was no missile gap and thereby to restrain the Russians from any adventurism, especially toward Berlin, that they might be tempted to effect if they believed that the West thought itself too weak to resist. The placing of missiles so close to the United States could appear to compensate for the inferiority of Soviet long-range striking capacity to ours. Particularly provocative to the Soviets, too, were the American Jupiter missiles in Turkey, installed during the previous administration. Taking hours to fire, and so vulnerable that a sniper's bullet could disable them, they were virtually useless as a deterrent weapon, to be used in retaliation for a Soviet nuclear attack on the alliance. They were the ugliest of nuclear weapons, a missile having no effective purpose aside from beginning a nuclear war. President Kennedy, for once more cautious than his predecessor, had ordered a study of whether they should be removed.

That the Soviet Union was behind in the arms race undoubtedly constituted Khrushchev's biggest problem, bigger than the specifics of Berlin and Cuba, and could explain much of the urgency with which he pressed for advantages in both instances.

The format for the White House discussion preceding the Bay of Pigs had provided not a free and continuing conflict of ideas but orchestration by the CIA. Kennedy recognized that he now needed a broad exchange of ideas. For the mid-October strategy sessions to plan an American response to the missiles, Kennedy pulled together a group of advisers under a new heading, the Executive Committee of the National Security Council, or Ex-Comm as it was quickly and coldly termed. Sessions were informal and at times would break into groups, each having its own conversation, after which the participants would come back together for cross-examinations.

Ex-Comm spent much of its time on the issue of how much military force was necessary. On the one side was the alternative of air strikes against the missile bases or a larger military action. On the other was the policy the administration finally chose: a naval quarantine of Cuba for the interdiction of further weaponry, to be accompanied with the threat of bombardment or invasion if the bases were not dismantled. As the discussion proceeded, some participants switched from one plan to the other or back and forth.

All this sounds like a debate between belligerent advisers and those favoring relative restraint; between hawks and doves, to use terms that became popular in the sixties. Air raids were, of course, the more technically belligerent course, although the dovish Senator Fulbright argued in favor of air strikes that as a defensive measure they would be less provocative than attacking a Soviet ship in the open seas while it ran the quarantine. And in tone the debate sometimes divided as could be expected. Dean Acheson favored an attack on the missile sites to show that we were not to be cowed. The Joint Chiefs were set on air strikes, and the air force was urging the bombing not only of the missile sites but of other military installations. McNamara, proposing the quarantine as an alternative, suggested on October 16 a diplomatic way of presenting it to the world: we would declare a policy of open surveillance. Robert Kennedy argued that an air attack against a small nation unable to retaliate would be treason to the American ethos and comparable to the Japanese attack on Pearl Harbor. He was McNamara's and the President's indispensable partner in facing down the military.

The debate, however, did not separate hawks from doves so neatly. There was, with the possible exception of Averell Harriman and Adlai Stevenson, no one who would have forsworn force or put off its use for long and risked giving the Soviet Union time to complete construction and to add the nuclear warheads.

The goal was limited and technical: defining the proper economy of force that would insure the quick dismantling of the sites with the least likelihood of retaliation. That outcome, not the satisfaction of parading a triumphant American will, was what most of the President's advisers set themselves to achieving, not because they were above humiliating the Soviet Union but because the moment was too serious for self-indulgence. The President at first thought that we would have to take out the missiles, and he left open the question of whether to have a more general air attack. Walt Rostow, relishing the advanced and the unusual in military tactics and technology, contributed the suggestion, disordered but humane, that we drop nonexplosive pellets "of the kind we used to shoot out of BB guns." Thickly deposited, they would "quickly convert both the missiles and the installations into worthless junk." Toward the very end of the crisis, when it was uncertain whether Khrushchev would dismantle the missiles, the participants floated an idea that defied the categories of dove and hawk: we would unilaterally start dismantling the missiles in Turkey and let the Soviet Union know that we were doing it; then we would bomb the Cuba sites.

The Jupiter missiles in Turkey gave Ex-Comm virtually the only opportunity it could discern for diplomacy. If it could find some way of offering their removal that would not tempt Moscow to decide that its Cuba venture had been profitable and would be a model for future behavior, the crisis would have a peaceful resolution with no material loss to the United States, which was dissatisfied with the Jupiters anyway. They may have been a better touchstone than the air strikes for distinguishing hawkish from dovish sentiment, for while most advisers probably were prepared to accept whatever force was necessary for elimination of the Cuba bases, they could disagree over whether to present a plan of genuine or at least contrived reciprocity. Averell Harriman, once ambassador to the USSR and shrewd in his knowledge of that nation's leadership, had remarked to Schlesinger that we should not stop Soviet ships—that would injure Soviet pride—but instead ought to help strengthen the position of the more conciliatory Kremlin people. Now he suggested, on October 26, as a means of releasing Khrushchev from the confrontation without our backing down, that we proffer the dismantling of the Jupiters in Turkey not as a trade but as the beginning of a more general process of disarmament. But Thomas Finletter, American ambassador to NATO and a member of New York State's Liberal party, opposed the exchange, which is an object lesson in not confusing liberal with dove.[30]

The discussions, as White House tapes and other records reveal them, catch the minds and temperaments of Kennedy's advisers in crisis. Dean Rusk, who today is measured by his stony defense of the war in Vietnam, showed on October 16 a careful sensitivity to diplomatic questions. He observed that an air strike would entangle our allies in the consequences, and he suggested approaching Castro and talking to the Organization of American States, from which the administration did obtain support for a blockade. McNamara on that day was insistent on close examination of what each action might bring and recommended writing down the possible result of every alternative the country might choose. Throughout the crisis the most pacific counselor was Adlai Stevenson, who wanted the United States to turn back to Cuba our naval base at Guantánamo and to negotiate the elimination of Soviet and American missile bases. His scheme would have the United Nations send inspection teams to all missile bases outside the homelands of the three major nuclear powers as insurance against secret attacks before the achievement of a broader agreement. Schlesinger remembers that as he was about to go to New York for the UN discussions of the crisis, Robert Kennedy told him, "We're counting on you to watch things in New York. That fellow [Stevenson] is ready to give everything away. We will have to make a deal at the end; but we must stand firm now." Yet Stevenson in United Nations debate that week pursued the Soviet delegation relentlessly. McGeorge Bundy has argued that reliance on the United Nations could have undermined our whole position at that desperate moment: "in public comment, especially in the United Kingdom, there was evidence of the difficulties we should have faced if we had been less clearly strong, restrained, and right."[31]

Events, meanwhile, were unfolding before the public. Appearing on television on Monday, October 22, the President announced the presence of the missiles and informed the public of his response, the institution of a naval quarantine against Russian ships bringing additional missile equipment to Cuba. Kennedy set the barrier as close to the Caribbean as he dared, hoping that Khrushchev would decide not to risk an incident. He also placed McNamara in charge of supervising the details of the quarantine very closely, much to the distress of the chief of naval operations. The White House further provided that every ship enforcing the quarantine carry Russian-speaking personnel. Thereupon the events of the week made for a country at war but not at combat, a people at once participants and spectators. The United States permitted a harmless tanker to enter the quarantine area. After that the first ship carrying equipment applicable to the missile bases drew back. That was in radio and television reports by Wednesday evening, October 24. Still Americans waited, those in the big cities going about their work with resignation or affected nonchalance.

The navy, meanwhile, had been playing games. It had ignored instructions from the White House to pull the line still closer to Cuba. In contravention of the President's orders, its ships were on top of Soviet nuclear-bearing submarines in the Atlantic, keeping them from surfacing, which that generation of Russian submarines would have to do before it could launch missiles. An American U-2 plane accidentally strayed on Friday over Siberia, and our fighter-bombers sent to escort the plane met up with it over Soviet territory. Khrushchev's mild response was confined to complaining to Kennedy about American recklessness. On Saturday night, after an American spy plane had been shot down over Cuba, members of Ex-Comm argued again for an immediate assault on the missile bases. Kennedy rejected the idea.

Then, on Sunday, Americans awakened to hear of Khrushchev's announcement that he was removing the missiles, and they realized that for a time at least they could go back to a workaday universe in which nuclear weapons could seem remote and abstract. Khrushchev may have responded not so much to the quarantine itself as to an implicit warning by the President on Saturday night that the United States would not continue to refrain from military action against the Russian presence in Cuba. We were successful, according to Kennedy's later observation, because by then we had a conventional military capable of invading Cuba. In 1961 our forces would not have been equal to the task without reinforcement with troops sent home from Europe. The appraisal is consonant with the arguments put forth by liberals during Eisenhower's administration for a development of our conventional forces and with Kennedy's conviction in response to the Berlin trouble that we needed a larger military. But if the threat of a bombing or an invasion was the immediate reason for Khrushchev's backing off, it was the quarantine that made that threat credible.

What the American public had not known about during the crisis week was an intricate diplomacy between the United States and the Soviet Union. In one telegram received by President Kennedy the premier offered to take the missiles home in return for a promise that we would not invade Cuba. Events, Khrushchev warned, would join the "knot of war" tighter and tighter. Another telegram asked for the removal of the American missiles from Turkey. Robert Kennedy championed this response: publicly this nation ignored the question of the Turkish bases but promised to stay out of Cuba; privately Bobby went to the Russians with the word that dismantling of the sites on the island would bring the withdrawal of the American missiles from Turkey. President Kennedy then told the world what he had indicated to Khrushchev: that the United States would not invade Cuba—though that December he was to tell the released prisoners from the Bay of Pigs that the battle flag of a free Cuba would be returned "in a free Havana."

To his countrymen Kennedy's performance appeared flawless. It made Americans feel good that their nation had stared down a major danger. It must have made Kennedy feel good that the humiliation of the Bay of Pigs was now behind him. That the outcome of the event did not make the Russians feel good, and that this might in time have dangerous consequences, were not at the moment considerations. Since the crisis occurred just before the midterm elections, it probably helped the Democrats gain seats in the Senate and hold their losses in the House to two, no small achievement for a first-term party in power. Khrushchev's position was left more precarious. This leader who had made life measurably better for the Soviet people by ending the worst terror of the Stalin era and by nourishing the consumer economy, and who toward the end of his career would make the world a little safer by following a policy of détente, had committed one inexcusably dangerous act from which his country was forced to retreat with embarrassment. Within a few years of the crisis he was out of power, replaced by a more militaristic leadership determined to increase Soviet arms so that the USSR would never have to back down again. Khrushchev's decline also slowed the course of de-Stalinization.

Some critics have called President Kennedy irresponsible for taking a military course, and if the horror that the quarantine could have brought is weighed against the probable benefits that it did bring, there can be no satisfactory answer to those critics. It is a partial vindication of Kennedy that among all the military actions available, his was the most restrained—so much so that military people were muttering even after the resolution of the crisis that he had settled the affair too mildly. At the President's suggestion Navy Chief of Staff Anderson, who had disregarded instructions to pull in the quarantine boundary and at the end of the crisis was complaining bitterly, resigned and was named ambassador to Portugal. The President had determined during the crisis to avoid anything that might invite from the Russians a "spasm reaction." Still, the proper measure of Kennedy's actions is not what other people would have done, but what the dangers were in his own course of action. The recollections of John Sherman Cooper catch the President at one moment saying that if the missiles were not removed, "they will be destroyed and Cuba will be destroyed."

Walter Lippmann on October 25 had made a more limited criticism of the President for bringing the issue to public light, which made it more difficult for Khrushchev to get out of the crisis gracefully. But then the public revelation and challenge may have been a way of subjecting the Soviet Union to world opinion, an alternative to military action. Lippmann also objected to the "suspension of diplomacy." Much secret diplomacy would be going on, but Lippmann cannot be faulted for ignorance of it. In failing to pursue a more formal diplomatic course, Kennedy was acting consistently with his larger decision, which was to treat the missiles as an intolerably dangerous adventure that must not be allowed to become a precedent. That decision may have been wrong; it was not separately wrong to avoid a public process of bargaining that would have legitimized the missiles as objects to be bargained over. During the time public negotiations would take, moreover, the Soviet Union might have completed the emplacement of the missiles. The administration had needed to act quickly. The White House tapes for October 16 have McNamara concluding that since photography revealed land still unfenced, the warheads were probably still not in place, then remarking that he would strongly oppose an air strike against completed weaponry. Another accusation would fault Kennedy for refusing during that dangerous week to make public his agreement to dismantle the Turkish sites. That refusal, it can be claimed, increased the threat that the Russians, seeking some other means of not looking as though they were backing away, might draw out the crisis or do something brash. To this the same response applies as to the claim that Kennedy should have publicly negotiated: the proposition that the missiles were unacceptable meant that nothing—in public, at any rate— could be traded for them.[32]

Khrushchev had been the aggressor in his attempt to overturn in a stroke the status quo. That in itself, however, is not a sufficient answer to the critics of Kennedy. Scorched and flattened cities at the end of a technically defensive American act would still be in cinders. The same would hold for any attempt to defend Khrushchev for wishing to place missiles not many miles nearer to United States soil than separated American warheads from the Soviet Union. A nuclear world has too much to worry about to indulge the kind of reasoning that demands technical parity of that sort. Khrushchev had violated the precarious nuclear peace that obtained, and that, in a nuclear age, was an aggression that risked inviting a nation-killing response. Kennedy gave Khrushchev an ultimatum, and an ultimatum is so very humiliating for a nation to submit to that Kennedy was risking a nation-killing response. Khrushchev gambled, and Kennedy gambled, and not much more is to be said than that.

In a reply appearing in the *Christian Science Monitor* for November 25 to the question of what made our missiles in Turkey different from the Soviet missiles in Cuba, the administration explained that we had not deployed our missiles secretly and had put them there only after a Soviet threat of a nuclear attack on Europe. The response indicates much about our perceptions; it is less useful as an answer to the question. The West values openness, and the secrecy of the Russian maneuver, which reflects the character of Soviet officialdom, gave the undertaking all the more malevolent a look. But an overt emplacement of the missiles would not have made them acceptable to Washington either. The argument that our missiles in Turkey had been in reaction to a Soviet threat says only that the United States saw itself and its allies as peaceful and their weapons as defensive; that is, of course, the way nations see themselves. The administration could have pointed out that the Cuba missiles were much closer to Washington than our missiles were to Moscow. A sufficient accuracy in delivery would make this technically unimportant, but it does emphasize how politically provocative the Cuban weapons were.

One thing that the missile crisis and the events leading up

to it did demonstrate is that short of the actual firing of nuclear weapons, both the Soviet Union and the United States will as like as not respond to signs of strength or aggressiveness not by turning away from conflicts but by inviting them. The superiority of our nuclear force, along with the revelation of our ability to spot bases in the Soviet Union, should have frightened Moscow, and it did—into installing the missiles in Cuba. Khrushchev, in setting up the missiles, should have frightened the United States, and he did—into setting up the quarantine and finally into delivering an ultimatum. It is a continuing source of curiosity that some of our more hawkish political commentators expect American shows of force to produce Russian retreat, while they demand that Russian shows of force be met with American bellicosity. Out of the era of Khrushchev they have one incident to enforce their claim: when Khrushchev did not choose to push the confrontation farther to preserve his pride. And an eventual result of the crisis was a further increase in Soviet armaments, and a remote result of that has been an American arms policy designed to face down the Russians.

Yet if the missile crisis put the world at the edge of catastrophe, it is not because either side remotely considered or suspected the other of considering a nuclear strike under the circumstances. The danger rode on the momentum of the crisis itself. The event shaped the period of partial détente that followed because it revealed to the antagonists what they had probably been coming to know half-consciously: that they were in the end allies of a sort in the presence of a weapon that threatened to wrench itself loose from all control. The crisis gave Kennedy another occasion for that perception, which seems so inappropriate to what his presidency was supposed to mean: that the world will not go the way we wish it to go. Asked by a reporter in 1963 whether after the crisis he was more or less pessimistic about the future, he answered, more so: "I believe that sooner or later someone is going to make a mistake."[33]

The two powers nevertheless started behaving as though they were not going to let that mistake happen. A hot line between the Kremlin and the White House insured instantaneous communication in emergencies; it was a fitting complement to a diplomacy of personal correspondence that Khrushchev and Kennedy had been carrying on. However angrily and however fearfully the Russians were to arm themselves in the years after the missile crisis, they also opposed the Maoist stridency. The administration had wanted to step up subversion within Cuba; then, in the midst of the crisis, it ordered a cessation. On June 10, 1963, Kennedy at American University in one of his most important speeches urged an era of cooperation between our country and the Soviet Union: "We all inhabit this small planet. We all breathe the same air. We all cherish our children's future. And we are all mortal." The address had the courtesy to refer to the sufferings of the Soviet Union in World War II, and the reference may have contributed to the good feeling that attended the test ban treaty that year. Then came a speech in the confrontational vein, in Berlin on June 26. Kennedy's famous announcement *"Ich bin ein Berliner"*—"I am a Berliner"—was warranted; the encircled people in the free part of the city were entitled to an assurance that the West would stand by them. Less called for was the declaration "There are some who say that communism is the wave of the future. Let them come to Berlin. And there are some"—Kennedy actually was now among them— "who say in Europe and elsewhere, 'We can work with the Communists.' Let them come to Berlin."

But two months before his death the President made a major speech against the proliferation of nuclear arms. Elsewhere he proposed that the Soviet Union and the United States make a joint flight to the moon. In October 1963 he initiated the first sale of surplus wheat to the Soviet Union. After the shaping of the wheat deal Khrushchev announced a reduction in Soviet defense funding. In his final days Kennedy, with the aid of Republican conservative Senator Everett Dirksen of Illinois, got ratification of the test ban treaty outlawing atmospheric testing of atomic weapons, and bringing to an end, so it seemed, the hopes of the right wing for a future of uncompromised hostility to all things Communist. The treaty was also a victory for Khrushchev over Soviet hard-liners, whose political position had been weakened by the illness of Kozlov.

The Kennedy policy or style, the working toward a perfection of force and restraint, had achieved about as full a vindication as any politician could dare wish for. The Kennedy image, whether programmed or spontaneous, had its final polish, and technocratic liberals could argue confidently against both rightists, offended at the very thought of negotiating coexistence, and whoever to the left might reject the entire strategy of negotiation from a posture of military strength. Meanwhile, in a corner of Asia were unfolding events that would turn much of a whole generation of liberals against the memory of the Kennedy style.[34]

In 1953 Kennedy had argued against aiding the French in Vietnam, insisting that we had no business supporting a colonial regime, and in 1957 he had denounced as imperialist the French war in Algeria. He once commented that the feelings of the Indochinese for "the white man who bled them, beat them, exploited them, and ruled them" would make it difficult for the United States to aid them. But now South Vietnam had its own government. Kennedy had been a founding member of American Friends of Vietnam, an organization that supported Ngo Dinh Diem. Kennedy believed that this government was under attack by the Communists. He was right. While differing political persuasions contributed to the insurgency, by the time of Kennedy's presidency it was drawing on guerrilla units of southerners trained in Communist North Vietnam. The revolutionary forces in South Vietnam, and their northern comrades, could claim that the Saigon regime had blocked the elections promised at Geneva in 1954 for the unification of the country. But the Kennedy people, even as they were moving toward a perception of a planet more variegated than their cold warrior predecessors had imagined, were not ready to see the Vietnamese situation in that way. If they had in mind a primary division within a Communist world once presumed to be monolithic, it was between Soviet and Chinese communism. And in the 1960s Americans, doubtless remembering the Chinese masses that had swept south into Korea in 1950, thought the Vietnamese insurgency to be in the Chinese interest; they would not have imagined the Communist Vietnam of the next decade, an ally of the Soviet Union and an active military enemy of a China that had become a near ally of the United States. Asked in a television interview on September 9, 1963, whether he still believed in the domino theory, Kennedy replied: "I believe it. . . . China is so large, looms so high just beyond the frontiers, that [the fall of South Vietnam] would not only give [the Chinese] an improved geographic position for guerrilla assault on Malaya, but . . . also give the impression that the wave of the future in Southeast Asia was China and the Communists. . . . What I am concerned about is that Americans will get impatient and say because they don't like events in Southeast Asia or they don't like the government in Saigon . . . we should withdraw. That only makes it easy for the Communists. I think we should stay."[35]

For a brief time in the mid-sixties, after Kennedy's presidency and before Richard Nixon's rapprochement with China, the Cultural Revolution in that country was to awaken among Americans who were aware of events abroad a sentiment unique in the history of the cold war. As Maoist crowds harassed Soviet diplomatic representatives and Russian troops faced the Chinese, fiction and journalism here presented the Soviet Union as a sensible country with a mob at its borders. The Cultural Revolution itself made the major contribution to that perception. But the détente begun in the Kennedy administration had prepared Americans for it, prepared them more particularly to see the Russian leaders as disciplined technicians of power who thought in cool tones against the shriek of the Maoists. By now, however, the United States was also fully at war in Vietnam with forces that both the Soviet Union and its Maoist rival were supporting.

At the beginning of President Kennedy's involvement in Vietnam the preoccupation was with the USSR. In May 1961 Kennedy received an oral report from Maxwell Taylor on the

Bay of Pigs disaster. Robert Kennedy, CIA Director Allen Dulles, and Admiral Arleigh Burke had aided in its preparation. The gist was that the United States, locked in a "life and death struggle" with the Soviet Union "which we may be losing," must carry any cold war policy "through to conclusion with the same determination as a military operation." General Taylor and Walt Rostow went to Vietnam at Kennedy's request late in the same year and recommended an increase in troop support. At a meeting of the National Security Council on November 15, Rusk and McNamara argued for a firmer American commitment in Vietnam. But here Kennedy questioned "the wisdom of involvement in Viet Nam since the basis thereof is not completely clear." He noted, "Korea was a case of clear aggression which was opposed by the United States and other members of the U.N. The conflict in Vietnam is more obscure and less flagrant." The President compared the obscurity of the issues in Vietnam to the clarity of the positions in Berlin. McNamara on November 8 nonetheless pressed Kennedy to make an unqualified commitment.

Nearly a year later Maxwell Taylor, who lacked such doubts as Kennedy had revealed on November 15, became chairman of the Joint Chiefs of Staff. At the end of the Eisenhower presidency the general had spoken for what would be a major strain of thought within the Kennedy administration when he talked of demonstrating to the Russians that wars of national liberation were not "cheap, safe and disavowable" but "costly, dangerous, and doomed to failure." Before becoming chairman of the Joint Chiefs he had recommended sending 8,000 regular combat troops to Vietnam and making the United States "a limited partner in the war." Like the French generals, Taylor insisted that the Communists would not retaliate in any major way against substantial troop involvement. Robert McNamara, who wanted to send 200,000 men, at least had a better sense of scope. But Taylor and Rostow talked of a counterinsurgency program, sending Saigon guerrillas against the insurgents, that would have been much in the spirit of the Kennedy rhetoric, combining imagination, an elite military trained by the American elite, and a popular progressivism—the cold war fought to its furthest liberal possibility. Nation-building was one of Rostow's catchwords for the policy.

The administration from its earliest days had treasured the concept of counterinsurgency. On January 30, 1961, in fact, Kennedy had proposed that guerrillas operate in the North. But the administration was unable to shape and confine the war to a struggle of guerrillas against guerrillas. In January 1962, 2,646 American military personnel were stationed in Vietnam; President Eisenhower had roughly adhered to a figure of 700, permitted under the Geneva accords. For a time an increase in American equipment stopped the degeneration of Saigon's strength. William Manchester describes a split over Vietnam, McNamara and George Ball against Taylor and the advocates of extensive intervention. The split could be clean. In September 1963 the National Security Council sent one more fact finding mission. The marine general on it praised Ngo Dinh Diem and said that the war was being won; a foreign service officer reported the regime near to collapse. An idea of the direction the war was taking was Kennedy's introduction of artillery and fighter-bombers. By October 1963 the total American military presence had risen to 16,732, though these were not regular combat troops. At the time of Kennedy's death more were on the way. By then 69 Americans had died. These figures do not reveal much about what Kennedy thought we were doing or could do in Vietnam. Nor do Kennedy's own observations indicate any clear idea.

Dean Rusk reports that in the "hundreds of times" he talked with Kennedy about Vietnam, "on no single occasion did he ever whisper any such thing" as withdrawal "to his own secretary of state." The President, Rostow comments, thought that the loss of Southeast Asia would make for an even more acrid debate in this country than had the loss of China. When in September 1963 Kennedy remarked, "in the final analysis it is their war," the *New York Times* chided him: it was *our* war— "a war from which we cannot retreat and which we dare not lose." But Kennedy also said, "For the United States to withdraw . . . would mean a collapse not only of South Vietnam but [of] Southeast Asia. So we are going to stay there." Yet General Taylor has said that the President was the only member of the administration opposed to sending combat troops to Vietnam. That does not contradict the opinion of those who believe that Kennedy was committed to the defense of South Vietnam; it would mean only that he was not prepared to undertake a conventional American military solution.

Kennedy could sound very eager to leave Vietnam. "If the Vietnamese win it, okay, great," Hilsman reports Kennedy's saying to him in midspring of 1963. "But if they don't, we're going to Geneva and do what we did with Laos." In conversation with Senator Mike Mansfield of Montana that year, Kennedy expressed agreement with the senator's insistence that a complete military withdrawal from Vietnam was necessary, adding that such action before the coming election would bring a "wild conservative outcry," and Mansfield agreed. Kennedy partisan Kenneth O'Donnell recalls of the same occasion that the President said that in 1965 he would "become one of the most unpopular Presidents in history. . . . If I try to pull out completely now from Vietnam, we could have another Joe McCarthy red scare on our hands, but I can do it after I'm reelected." On October 2, 1963, Kennedy asked McNamara to announce to the press an immediate withdrawal of 1,000 troops and to say that by the end of 1965 we would probably take out all American forces. As the secretary was setting off to talk to the White House press, Kennedy called out, "And tell them that means all of the helicopter pilots, too." McNamara gave the reporters a less definite statement. But critics of the lengthening war still remember with some puzzlement that we were both adding troops and planning to withdraw. Kennedy once told his secretary of defense that he would "close out" Vietnam in 1965 "whether it was in good shape or bad." The President toward the end of his life was groping, unwilling to accept a clear and final loss of South Vietnam, unwilling to make a heavy and an irreversible involvement for the rescue of that country that would raise the cost in American lives. In the course of his presidency, however, the administration did succeed in a more limited and temporary way in making real policy toward Indochina.[36]

In Laos Kennedy did so by the direct communication with Khrushchev that offered more real promise during these years than did the staffs of experts who were pulling us, with the President's permission, further into Vietnam. The collaboration of the two leaders firmed up the device of a troika and for a moment Laos appeared to be settled. In South Vietnam Kennedy intervened to change a government as he had attempted to do in Cuba; this time his target was not a popular, successful, and effectively authoritarian regime like Castro's but a corrupt and failing one. On August 21, 1963, on the eve of the arrival in Vietnam of newly appointed Ambassador Henry Cabot Lodge, the government of Diem made a sweeping arrest of Buddhist monks. The Kennedy administration had no further hope that the regime could either rally its people or be a creditably progressive recipient of American aid. An administration to the right of Kennedy's might have tried to go on shoring it up. Instead, Washington instructed Lodge to tell the South Vietnamese generals, in effect, that in case of a coup the United States would assist an interim government. A later cable qualified the previous instruction, but on November 1 the generals acted, and two days later Diem was killed; his death had not been Kennedy's desire.[37]

The President's troubles with Diem exemplify the difficulties of conducting a foreign policy as carefully responsive to complexity as liberals wished it to be. John Gaddis' *Strategies of Containment* describes the tight balances that the administration had tried to achieve: it aimed to moderate the Saigon government without weakening it, to give enough American aid for Diem's survival without making him out to be our puppet, and to insure that our interests in Vietnam would not turn our country into his puppet. "In the end, the line proved too fine to walk," writes Gaddis. *I. F. Stone's Weekly* for December 9, 1963, soon after President Kennedy's death, was harsher: "Have we not become conditioned to the notion that we should have a secret agency of government—the CIA—with secret funds, to wield the dagger . . . ? How many of us—on the left now—did not welcome the assassination of Diem and his brother Nhu in South Vietnam? We all reach for the dagger, or the gun, in our thinking when it suits our political view to do so."[38]

In the wake of the coup *Time* suggested the possibility of neutralizing all Southeast Asia along the lines of the settlement in Laos, and in a meeting of the National Security Council Robert Kennedy asked whether this might be a good moment to leave South Vietnam. When the President at this time gave his order for the withdrawal of 1,000 American advisers, he promised continued aid only "at this time"; in 1963 he showed a larger concern than liberal journalists like David Halberstam who wished solely to get rid of Diem. Kennedy, faced with the further weakening of Saigon, would probably have acted as Johnson did. He, too, was captive to the conviction—which still plagues the nation's foreign policy—that any victory anywhere of any movement that the Soviet Union supports or speaks well of is our dishonorable loss. His actual responsibility for that future lies in his incremental involvements. Once the American presence had been established, it was unlikely that its size or character could be limited. Kennedy seems to have realized this. He once observed that sending troops is a little like taking a drink: the effect wears off, and you have to have another. The toppling of the Diem government morally entangled this nation further in the fortunes of South Vietnam.

Kennedy had known that leftist movements are not invariably enemies of the United States and their own people. And he had not been part of the earlier events that led to the denouement of the 1960s: the absurd decision at the end of the Second World War to bring the French back into Indochina in the face of a vigorous nationalism; the defense of the French imperialist war there, which, in fact, Kennedy had urged us not to support. In his copy of Ellen J. Hammer's *The Struggle for Vietnam*, published in 1954, he underlined the observation that in Indochina "nationalism has come to be largely identified with Communism." His encouragement of the removal of the Diem regime suggests that his administration was less prepared than others, liberal and conservative, to ignore the character of governments that passed the one test of being spotlessly anti-Communist. The involvement in Vietnam under Kennedy was probably among the least insensitive of American meddlings abroad. By that time there existed in South Vietnam an indigenous government allied to at least part of the population and tolerating, possibly because it had not the power to crush, much more dissent than Hanoi permitted. In his hesitancy about troop increases in Vietnam, as in his rejection of hard-line advice during the missile crisis, Kennedy seems more reflective and dependable than much of his advisory circle. But he never came fully to realize that being born throughout the world was something that would not take orders from Moscow, Peking, or Washington. It was a revolutionary condition sprung from the soil of each land it inhabited. The administration did not ever come to satisfactory terms with neutralism, which American foreign policy during the fifties had treated as selfishly opportunistic and weighted in favor of the Soviet Union. Kennedy did arrive at a temporary neutralization of Laos. Yet through ignorance or consent he allowed the CIA to attempt to subvert the Cambodian leader Prince Norodom Sihanouk, who drew on popular loyalties and represented the best hope for a peaceful Cambodia. The world was divided into Communist and anti-Communist blocs, but it was also a patchwork of Cambodias. This was a truth that liberalism, in its increasing insistence on a diplomacy more sophisticated and sensitive than right-wingers could endure, ended by turning against the cold war policies and mentality of liberalism itself.

What Kennedy left in foreign policy, besides the Peace Corps and the arrangement of the wheat deal, besides the escalation in Vietnam and his part in a missile crisis that offers no lessons anyone would care to try out again, was the treaty ending atmospheric testing of nuclear weapons. Negotiations for an agreement limiting tests go back to Eisenhower, but the treaty owes much to the sobriety that the missile crisis had brought. The reputation of the treaty, like the repute of Kennedy's policies on civil rights, has suffered from its being perceived by standards that came into their own as the decade progressed. Rather than getting praised for moving away from the policy of massive nuclear retaliation that the previous administration had followed, Kennedy stands accused now of committing an act of power politics, an attempt to freeze the nuclear arms race at a moment favorable to this nation. Any negotiations about nuclear weapons are necessarily a function of power politics, and a nation is not to be expected to forgo terms favorable to it; still, the object of the administration was not to freeze the balance of power but, through the test ban treaty, to loosen relationships between the two countries and make for a continuing process of negotiation. The treaty represented the furthest implication of the technocratic liberalism that would substitute sober considerations of power for the military and ideological confrontations that the American right appeared to yearn for and Kennedy himself at times had seemed to seek. The President had wanted a treaty banning underground as well as atmospheric test detonations, but our conservatives and military insisted on inspection adequate to insure that no such tests were going on, and Soviet conservatives and military feared that inspection would be a device for spying. Kennedy, however, had rejected Rostow's proposal that the resolution of diplomatic issues other than nuclear testing be a condition for the agreement.[39]

At home the treaty was recognized as at the very least a major symbolic affirmation that something beyond a taut military stand-off was possible. Kennedy looked for opposition from the political right, and the administration's successful effort to get Senator Dirksen, known as a conservative, to support ratification was both a means of undercutting the right and a measure of the character of Dirksen's conservatism. That both Dirksen and House Republican leader Charles Halleck of Indiana had favored the quarantine of Cuba in place of the more aggressive alternative of an air strike, and in a few months would be instrumental in the passage of the civil rights bill, suggests the breadth of the political changes that seemed to be happening. Indeed, Kennedy discovered during a western tour in 1963 how enthusiastic a response the impending treaty evoked with crowds —even, it seems, in Salt Lake City near the Mormon Tabernacle. Yet many on the right and even such liberal cold warriors as Nelson Rockefeller opposed the treaty.

In the years that followed the treaty the debate over foreign policy would divide in a new way. An old conservatism wanted the cold war back, a new left despised the whole business, and liberalism in the wake of a succession of diplomatic and political triumphs foundered and broke apart over Vietnam, torn between its anticommunism and its growing awareness that no ideological formulation can describe the wayward contradictory world.

5

Kennedy Liberalism

IT WAS SO SUDDEN. THE FRONT OF A BUS WHERE NO BLACK PERSON had dared to sit, a lunch counter operated by and for the South's master race, a white southern high school class—each had a black occupant free in that instant of centuries of subordination. The country had seldom known such freedom: the stepping across of an invisible line that had been a chasm, a moment astonishing in its revelation that a new thing could happen so quickly.

That sudden freedom, of course, had the enormous press of history behind it. A century before, a great war had been fought. Then had come decades of massive oppression and the apparent irrevocability of custom, accompanied by a burden of guilt and a knowledge that things could not stay that way. So when black people, at times with some white companions, stepped across that invisible line while other Americans watched from as far as 3,000 miles away, all of them could know that a long history was reaching fulfillment even in the act of reversing itself.

The civil rights revolution prefigured and prepared for other events of the 1960s, some of them trivial beside it while others had their own significance. To hear a song of political protest over a radio that a decade earlier would have carried only that week's hit songs; to hear the Roman Catholic service in English with the strum of a guitar: such moments and a hundred others captured, for those who were not offended, the sense that life could be immediately more spacious. And if that was so, politics and social criticism could address themselves to issues that shortly before would have been beyond imagining.

Kennedy was President at the very beginning of all this—a few years after the Montgomery bus boycott and just at the time that other rights protests were happening. We have no way of learning whether he ever knew the meaning of the sudden freedom that was to be a distinctive political and cultural experience of the 1960s. Surely his trust went to the more sober twentieth-century forces of technology and expertise, forces that as the decade progressed would seem antithetical in spirit to the rebellion that was taking place in one component of American culture after another. But these technological forces, too, have a power quickly to make things new, to transform a landscape, to remake a city, to change the chemistry of a rock, to plant a ship on the moon. And the President who breathed such energy and could suggest, without details or a coherent program, so much national renewal contributed something large to what was occurring in the American imagination.

Kennedy was still fresh from his triumph of 1960 when the columnist James Reston asked him "what he wanted to have achieved by the time he rode down Pennsylvania Avenue with his successor. He looked at me as if I were a dreaming child. I tried again: did he not feel the need of some goal to help guide his day-to-day decisions and priorities? Again a ghastly pause. It was only when I turned the question to immediate, tangible problems that he seized the point." "Your predecessor," a reporter observed at a press conference on February 1, 1961, "had called himself a moderate; how do you define yourself?" "Well [no], I don't call myself anything except a Democrat who's been elected President of the United States," came the unhelpful response, "and I hope I am a responsible President." Among the few hints that the new President offered of what austerities he had in mind, in this administration that was supposed to be making a call to sacrifice, was a comment at the same press conference that could be taken to suggest that the unpoor should share some of their resources with the poor. That could have meant something, if Kennedy had been specific and insistent enough about it. On May 5 the President who was later to effect a tax cut observed that Americans contribute to the general good when they "pay heavy burdens as they do in taxation to maintain programs which they may not always agree with but which at least many of us feel to be in the national interest." How would domestic liberalism come into its alliance with John Kennedy, who was so unclear right after his election about what he wanted for a country that was already in the first days of a social revolution on the race issue? What did liberalism have in common with the politician who in the 1950s had not been able to break with Senator Joseph McCarthy and had voted to weaken a civil rights bill and with the President who was to go for more than two years before endorsing new civil rights legislation?[1]

Kennedy's temperament and manner define as much as anything else his elusive relationship to the liberalism that gained a temporary confidence from his presidency. The side of him that came closest to being romantic, expressing itself in a taste for the military expertise that antagonizes many liberals as well as in a propensity to picture the world as edging toward some moment of danger and promise, lent itself to the energetic progressivism that for a time increased after his death. But the respect for the expert—the Robert McNamara at a computerized command center or the counterinsurgent soldier alone in the jungle—is by conviction antisentimental, certain that the world is to be managed not by emotion but by skill. And Kennedy shuddered at a liberalism that drenches its rhetoric with compassion and outrage or parades its purity. He was impatient with the kind of genteel liberal who speaks too tremulously of suffering or calls for selfless dedication to the world's needs. He resented liberals who had attacked his father, as had Eleanor Roosevelt, for being a crude businessman. He was aware of Mrs. Roosevelt's thinly disguised assumption that Roman Catholicism means political reaction. His respect for Adlai Stevenson, Chester Bowles, and Hubert Humphrey was mixed with irritation: at Stevenson's indecisiveness, Bowles's long and reasoned pronouncements on world problems, Humphrey's tears. In 1952 Kennedy had encountered what must have seemed an act of extraordinary moral presumption on the part of academic and journalist liberals when, two years after speaking by invitation to a Harvard seminar and saying a couple of good words for Joe McCarthy and Richard Nixon, he found himself cited and attacked in the *New Republic* for his remarks. "I'd be very happy to tell them I'm not a liberal at all—I never joined the Americans for Democratic Action. . . . I'm not comfortable with those people." Kennedy was, in fact, from the start something of a liberal because he was an urban Democrat, just as he was also from the start something of an anti-Communist superpatriot because he was an urban Catholic Democrat. He became more of a liberal as events compelled him to take stands on concrete issues. In these respects, at least, and not in temper he remains the ally to liberals more preoccupied with poverty and injustice.[2]

John Kennedy came upon his public at the right moment. In 1960 the nation was restless and irritable. The economy was sluggish. Civil rights forces were stirring, and their presence was hinting at a national moral reformation. The Warren Court, after its great 1954 decision *Brown* v. *Board of Education*, declaring segregation in the schools to be unconstitutional, had shown that it was ready to implement its judgment and so to press the federal government more directly into confrontation with southern custom than national authorities had dared since Reconstruction. American education was thought to be lagging. American technology was at once humiliated by *Sputnik* and bursting with color TVs, flashy cars, and the beginnings of computers, as though a whole nation's energies were ready to take some quantum leap. A brilliant technology had the space program as its most visibly daring expression, and as its most pressing demand a renovation of the public schools.

Cool and crisp, a war hero, combatively eager if not very

clear about what he was eager for the nation to do, John Kennedy spoke exactly to the national mood. The salient events of the early sixties—the civil rights marches, the manned space explorations, the missile crisis—that appeared to test or affirm the national will found in television a means of making themselves immediate public phenomena. So for a moment in the 1960s much of the country came close to achieving a shared public experience such as it had not enjoyed for years. And it is fitting that Kennedy came to prominence at a time of political movement toward more elusive cultural and ideological questions. For he presented himself with the aid of television less as a traditional politician, speaking for a party and articulating a specific politics, than as a voice or an embodied energy ready to be expended as a national need arose. This, after all, is what Ronald Reagan has represented for the right, and it may now be a continuing component of American politics.

Americans remember the early 1960s with some embarrassment. The optimism and self-confidence reveal an element of contrivance, of politics by mass media and the pieties of advertising. We can particularly recall the enthusiasm for culture and the arts that seized on these things as though a poem by Robert Frost could be a national embellishment like a space satellite. But judgment of those years should consider the atrophy of purpose that has been more recently the dominant condition of American politics and recognize that the partially contrived political mood of the early sixties ultimately produced some of the finest social legislation and social change of the century.

So it was in good part the times, probably in conjunction with his own northeastern, urban, Democratic formation, that carried Kennedy to a liberal politics. The events, for example, that led to his request for civil rights legislation, and thereby joined him to the great liberal cause of the decade, began far away from Washington, in the deepest South, with mobs and politicians whose response to the sit-ins and freedom rides forced the government into confrontation. There, its evils manifest and challengeable in moments of sudden freedom, segregation could be treated antiseptically, and the rest of the nation could enjoy a somewhat unearned moral pride.

In 1960, before Kennedy's election, black and white students defied segregation ordinances by drinking coffee together at southern lunch counters. A year later freedom riders were assaulted on their peaceable, though morally revolutionary, bus journey through the South. In the fall of 1962 the governor of Mississippi raged, for Mississippi public consumption at any rate, and mobs took over the campus of Ole Miss in answer to the enrollment of the first black student, and Kennedy, who delivered a speech that denounced not prejudice but the violation of the Constitution, sent marshals and troops to the campus. In Birmingham the following spring fire hoses and police dogs were turned upon children, and in September a fire bombing killed four black children in a Sunday school class in the basement of a Baptist church. Even before that bombing civil rights activists had compelled segregation to disgrace itself so publicly that a President with any claim to Democratic liberalism had to call for a legislated end to the discredited system. Southern white liberals, meanwhile, having finally encountered a movement that forced them to choose between their regional loyalty and their consciences, between their doubts about the efficacy of efforts for social change and their hopes for it, were turning with relief to desegregation. They, like the black community, were among the liberated. John Kennedy responded as circumstances, politics, and morality required.

Television brought the civil rights movement before the public, and without it the 1960s would be unimaginable. That medium is faulted today for replacing the most subtle, analytical, and elegant means of conversation, the written word. But for a time two decades ago television became an instrument of analysis, making possible one of the most remarkable experiences of self-awareness and self-criticism in the nation's history. The nineteenth-century abolitionists, in contrast, had been forced to rely on a religious and Victorian moral rhetoric that defined the evil of slavery but seldom could describe its psychological and moral corruptions as precisely as do the best parts of *Uncle Tom's Cabin*. And for generations after abolition, white American politics rarely discussed racism at all except, of course, to approve of it. When the advent of television as a mass medium almost exactly coincided with the earlier days of the civil rights movement, it gave to a whole nation, perhaps even to blacks and to southern whites as never before, clear images of the racial issue as immediate, national, morally inescapable. That is not to say that television itself is the best vehicle of criticism and analysis; brief, violent images on a screen—black protesters falling under the force of fire hoses, white mobs screaming at black children entering public schools—are not in themselves more conducive to intelligent political thought than the images of Iranian crowds that in 1980 endangered rational discussion of foreign policy in this country. But in the early 1960s the images on the screen worked with the civil rights movement itself, with a responsiveness on the part of politicians, and with such reflective writers as James Baldwin to elevate rather than to degrade the public consciousness.

Television, meanwhile, made for the ersatz familiarity with which the Kennedy family entered millions of American homes, and it was just the right family: beautiful, well mannered, well favored. TV allowed Kennedy to be so visible to the public as a whole that he seemed to be outside the party structures and the backroom maneuverings that his people managed so well.

It is easy to forget that during the early days of television another older visual medium was in its prime. Photojournalism, along with photography in general, can be at once brief and analytical; it can study the exact placement of individuals in a crowd, the look on a black child's face, the twist of hatred on the face of a white woman. During the Birmingham civil rights crisis President Kennedy commented that a photograph of a German shepherd leaping at a black woman made him "sick." Photojournalism, like television, cannot look into the ambiguities that the word can explore; it needs dramatic events, striking figures, exact moments of pain and triumph, or larger cultural events that express themselves flamboyantly. And in the 1960s Selma, Vietnam, Haight-Ashbury, and the photogenic Kennedys supplied precisely the materials with which it could do its most effective work.[3]

The Kennedy forces knew the power of a good visual image. John Kennedy had seen Democratic governor Paul Dever of Massachusetts go down to defeat in 1952 because on television he came across as a cartoonist's rendering of an old pol, and the President knew what his own election had owed to the television debates. The administration was friendly to the press cameras. Kennedy opened his press conferences to live television coverage. The Executive Mansion initiated ideas for picture stories. It was at the suggestion of the White House that during the missile crisis a photographer snapped the reassuring picture through a rainy window of the President in thought.

In this early time of the image, President Kennedy and the civil rights movement were the most important subjects of television and photojournalism, and while the media were studying both, each was doing something for the other. At the push and tug of events, President Kennedy lent to the movement enough of the protection of the federal government to make it slightly freer to operate in the South, and his presidency made the preliminary decisions that would grow into the important legislation of the Johnson years. And civil rights would eventually bestow on the Kennedy administration a moral meaning beyond anything the government had at first planned for.

Kennedy liberalism was born in the presumption, which turned itself into a fact, that there was in John Kennedy's person and programs a force for social reformation. Black leaders increasingly looked to him for whatever he had to offer, whether it was the tangible support of marshals and federal troops in the South when their presence was essential, the partial symbolic desegregation in 1962 of federally funded public housing, or in 1963 Kennedy's espousal of civil rights legislation. Opponents of the civil rights movement, in their very fear that the President favored the rights cause, contributed to defining him as the embodiment of a liberalism that would go beyond the established New Deal programs. Liberal intellectuals could think that a youthful Harvard graduate with a beautiful and socially accomplished wife must be one of them. Pushed by the experience of the presidency to adopt a Keynesian economics, Kennedy was thereafter identifiable with the fiscal policies of twentieth-century liberalism. The teen-agers who screamed at Kennedy's approach the way they screamed at the Beatles aided in the perception of him as a fresh and energetic presence in American politics. More politically involved young people responded to him. "The biggest single influence that helped the formation of SDS," recalls Robert Greenblatt, a member of the Students for a Democratic Society, "was John F. Kennedy." This and similar testimonies appear in Peter Joseph's *Good Times* and in other oral histories of the 1960s. Only the young could reinvigorate the nation, asserted the Port Huron Statement, the 1962 founding document of SDS. The final and perhaps most important contributor to the making of Kennedy liberalism was Lyndon Johnson, who evoked the memory of the President to further his own remarkable program of social reform, even while some members of the Kennedy circle were abrupt in their dealings with the successor to their mourned President.

In his prepresidential years, Kennedy had given little promise of awakening a progressivism of this sort. Voting often as a bread-and-butter Democrat, he had acted politically as a moderate, being apparently detached, for example, from the civil rights questions of the 1950s. *Profiles in Courage* actually preaches not maverick independence but political temperance as necessary for the maintenance of democratic processes. Until after the missile crisis President Kennedy trained his abundant energies largely on foreign policy. Toward domestic issues he was not combative. Having spoken indignantly in a Buffalo campaign speech about the plight of laundry workers, he assented early in his presidency to exempting their employment from minimum wage legislation. His own claim was that a minimum wage would throw laundry workers out of jobs; but most of the laundry workers were black, and the exemption would please southern legislators. Yet some initiatives did come with the new administration and Congress. Kennedy got Congress to authorize money for food stamps. The administration supported liberals in their successful effort to enlarge the membership of the House Rules Committee, through which bills are filtered to the floor of the lower house. Congress in 1961 passed several measures that continued the Democratic traditions of the New Deal: a selectively higher minimum wage; an easing of eligibility for Social Security; a grant of almost $5 billion for urban renewal projects; funds for retraining in areas of high unemployment; and increases in money for treating water pollution. Some of Kennedy's cabinet appointees, such as Stewart Udall of the Interior Department, promoted conservation programs. John Kennedy ended the practice of preventing Communist propaganda mail from entering the country—not, if Robert Kennedy's later explanation is accurate, because he was "liberal" or "emotional" but because the restriction was "silly." Yet the new President did not press hard for welfare or social legislation.[4]

Kennedy's temperament militated at first against his instituting a progressive program. Udall, after speaking to the President about conservation, remarked in the summer of 1961, "He's imprisoned by Berlin." Kennedy could be impatient with the details of legislation. Orville Freeman, his secretary of agriculture, has observed that the President was "restless and uncomfortable" talking about farm issues. When Secretary of Health, Education and Welfare Anthony Celebrezze tried to speak to him about proposed laws, Kennedy was brief: "You were the mayor of a large city. You know how to handle these problems. Now handle them." (Celebrezze's look of a man halfway lost hindered his effectiveness. At his celebrated press conference on the relationship between cigarettes and cancer he chain-smoked.)

Political realities were also unfavorable to bold legislation. The last Congress of the Eisenhower years, though weighted toward the Democrats by 280 to 155 in the House—a larger majority than they would enjoy in 1961—and by 66 to 34 in the Senate, had defeated a Medicare bill sponsored by Kennedy, along with a public housing measure, minimum wage legislation, and aid to schools. Since 101 of the 261 Democratic congressmen in the new national legislature were southerners, many of them conservatives, perhaps Kennedy could do no more, as his defenders have claimed. He had won the election of 1960, moreover, by a very slender majority. "The reason" for not pressing bills, Sorensen has written, "was arithmetic." The *Kiplinger Washington Letter* for January 6, 1962, observing that labor and liberals would criticize Kennedy for not holding to his campaign promises for spending on welfare and public works, explained that he was cleverly presenting a "hazy target" to the Republicans. "They hoped he'd emulate Truman and come at 'em swinging and cussing. But no. Kennedy won't look for trouble. He will try to step around it." The same publication for April 28 predicted that Kennedy, after winning a stronger Democratic position in the midterm elections in the fall, would be able to work for a more liberal program.

Apart from Kennedy's major activities in foreign affairs, it is his performance in the civil rights controversies that has led to the most extensive judgments of him, favorable and condemnatory. That this should be so is a commentary on the early sixties. No President before John Kennedy, Abraham Lincoln included, could meet more than the smallest test for racial justice, or for forthright public discussion of the racial issue, on the terms that are now acceptable. But then no President had been put to the test by any movement as highly visible as the civil rights forces of the sixties. Kennedy's presidency coincided with the early years of a rights activism that demanded an absolute and uncompromised equality, a disappearance of private as well as official discrimination, an end to stereotypes and to the whole range of cruelties that had attended racism in this country. The Kennedy administration connected with that movement—furthering it, Kennedy's supporters say, dragged along, as more skeptical commentators insist, or growing with it. But it is at least beyond dispute that the administration's activity for civil rights differed fundamentally in character from that of the protesters in the southern streets and the rights workers in the southern back country. Not one but two forces were arrayed against segregation, one of them hesitant, legalistic, calculating, while the other acted out of a simple and relentless moral witness. The result of the administration's caution is that in the presence of the rights workers and demonstrators it looked timid and temporizing; the result of its activity is that the rights movement gained a solid body of federal practices to supplement the sit-ins, the freedom rides, and the marches.[5]

Kennedy brought to his presidency a record of compromise and expediency on civil rights. As a senator coming to national prominence he had seemed scarcely aware of the Supreme Court desegregation decision of 1954 and the Montgomery bus boycott. For a northern liberal, Kennedy's record in the Senate was, even on balance, unsatisfactory. He said of Little Rock that a greater planning and leadership on Eisenhower's part could have prevented the trouble. In his vice presidential and presidential campaign he sought support from the South's most truculent segregationist governors. Kennedy omitted civil rights from a list of the "real issues of 1960" that he presented near the beginning of his presidential contest. His sympathy call to Coretta Scott King while her husband sat in a Georgia jail was a gesture of great political value, but there is no evidence that it was anything more. During the weeks after the election he created a number of task forces to make recommendations on pressing national problems, but he appointed none on civil rights. The pessimism of a conservative oddly coexisted, even in Kennedy's words, with the vocabulary of will and action. "There is always some inequality in life," he observed at a press conference in Greenfield, Massachusetts, on March 21, 1962. "Some men are killed in war, and some are wounded, and some men never leave the country, and some men are stationed in the Antarctic and some men are stationed in San Francisco. It is very hard in military or personal life to assure complete equality." Such pessimism Kennedy could also bring to the rights question.[6]

Harris Wofford was, by Robert Kennedy's explanation, "so committed to civil rights emotionally" that the administration decided against appointing him assistant attorney general in charge of civil rights in the Justice Department. Wofford instead became a White House assistant on civil rights. He was to say of the position in retrospect that what President Kennedy had most liked about it, and he had least liked, was his task of serving as a buffer between the President and the civil rights forces. For the civil rights position in the Justice Department Byron White, the conservative Rhodes scholar from Yale, friend of Kennedys, and future Supreme Court justice, recommended Burke Marshall, another Yale Law School graduate and a member of a distinguished corporate law firm in Washington, D.C.

Marshall, like so many educated Americans, understood the moral problem and was a patient negotiator. He also brought to the job a liberal record; he had been a member of the American Civil Liberties Union and an originator of the idea of federal registrars who could insure enrollment of southern black voters. But he believed in the ways of compromise and agreement and despaired of addressing the question of civil rights with the means available to a federal system of government. Marshall later opposed the Civil Rights Commission's plan to hold hearings in Mississippi that would publicize conditions there, and he opposed the commission's wish for a halt in all federal money to that and other states. He was also to observe that a major nationwide effort for integrated housing would have been too frightening. In *Federalism and Civil Rights*, published in 1964, Marshall concludes that the central government's police power cannot deal effectively with the complex race problem. And for generations, legal and social conservatives, following similar reasoning, had refrained from using governmental power to challenge unjust social institutions, so the injustice, in all its complexity, remained. The moralistic and relentless Robert Kennedy was making use of legal power, first against radicals in the Redbaiting days of the early 1950s and then against labor racketeers, long before he discovered a real "enemy within" that had long made a mockery of American ideas of justice. Yet even Burke Marshall could draw limits to compromise. He was later to observe that while some liberals were too aggressive for civil rights, others, such as Hubert Humphrey, were too conciliatory.[7]

The earliest of the administration's measures were symbolic acts of integration. Having seen no blacks in the Coast Guard contingent of the inauguration march, Kennedy instructed the academy to recruit more. The government increased the number of blacks at social functions, desegregrated the White House press and photography pools, multiplied the appointment of Negroes to important government posts. In the spring of 1961 Secretary of Labor Arthur Goldberg attacked the practice of racial segregation in private clubs. Afterward the economist John Kenneth Galbraith, Kennedy's ambassador to India, resigned from Washington's Cosmos Club, an association of writers, scientists, and other professional people, when the club, which at the time had no black members, refused to admit the columnist Carl Rowan. At the resignation the name of John Kennedy, whom Galbraith had been sponsoring for membership, was automatically withdrawn. When for a time later in the sixties a scornful anger became the moral fashion among leftists, black and white, the well-meaning social gestures of white liberals fell victim to a studied contempt. But that has gone the way of other fashions, and it is perhaps now safe to suggest that the efforts of the Kennedy liberals to extend the common civilities had some role in the rights revolution.

Soon after two black students had integrated the University of Georgia, Attorney General Robert Kennedy in 1961 gave a speech there depicting the two as freedom fighters. (The phrase recalls the Hungarian insurgents of 1956; that is how strongly the struggle against communism gripped the imagination of the times and the Kennedys.) At the university Kennedy announced his intention to work for racial justice, and his speech decried inequities in the North as well as in the South. It was the first time a modern attorney general had spoken in the South for civil rights. Robert Kennedy's Justice Department made or was forced to make many of the day-to-day decisions bearing on civil rights. He brought in a handful of black attorneys, along with Archibald Cox as solicitor general, Ramsey Clark, John Doar, John Seigenthaler, and many others of note. But Robert shared Burke Marshall's caution about sudden federal assaults on local customs. It was the demonstrators and the rights workers, and more particularly the assaults on them, that pushed the Justice Department forward.

The freedom riders, organized by James Farmer's Congress of Racial Equality, pressed the cause of civil rights. CORE's northern black and white demonstrators, beginning in the spring of 1961, went through the South in busloads, defying segregation of terminals enforced by state and local officials. Farmer, before the trek through the South, sent an itinerary to the President, Robert Kennedy, and the FBI, in addition to Greyhound and Trailways, and got no response. The attorney general did not like the freedom rides and tried to discourage them. Possibly the lawyer and politician in him, which in other cases his anger could overwhelm, predominated at the moment, recoiling from tactics of confrontation and defiance of local officials. If so, freedom riders would have had a ready response. Their intention was to compel the enforcement of the law, for the Supreme Court decision in *Boynton* v. *Virginia* had declared illegal any segregation in interstate bus and train terminals. The freedom riders were aware of the violence their journey might provoke but calculated that the violence would make the federal government intervene. That is precisely what Robert Kennedy did not want forced upon him.[8]

The attorney general did not get the peace he had wished for. When a freedom bus was fire-bombed in Anniston, Alabama, he ordered the FBI to investigate the arson. Bull Connor, the hostile chief of the Alabama police, was directed to protect the riders in Birmingham. On May 21 patrolmen and police helicopters escorted them to Montgomery. Governor John Patterson had promised continuing protection. The governor was not an unenlightened southern politician. He had acquired his political prominence when, upon becoming Alabama attorney general in 1954, he finished cleaning up vice-ridden Phenix City, completing the work for which his father as a district attorney had been murdered. More recently he has revealed sufficient contrition, or at least embarrassment, about racism to observe that while he did use the race issue in campaigning for governor, he would have preferred not to do so. Yet he was sufficiently of his own culture that he could not bring himself to act promptly in defense of the riders. When the riders arrived in Montgomery, a mob set upon them. John Seigenthaler, the Justice Department official and friend of Robert Kennedy, was clubbed as he was trying to protect a female demonstrator, and he lay unconscious for about twenty-five minutes. The FBI, meticulously staying within the letter of its mandate, as it sometimes did·to its own advantage, stood by and took comprehensive notes. (Therein the bureau acted consistently with its inconsistent conduct during the civil rights years, when it was censorious of the movement, legalistically slow to discover violations of racial justice, and at times energetic in support of civil rights.) That evening some fifty marshals tried to protect Martin Luther King and civil rights supporters as King led a vigil in the city's First Baptist Church until Patterson at length discovered his responsibilities, declared martial law, and sent the National Guard. Nicholas Katzenbach, an assistant attorney general in Robert Kennedy's Justice Department, has remarked in another connection that neither he nor his chief liked to take away from local officers the job of protection, for they knew how much that is resented. But local authority, in Montgomery and elsewhere in these violent times, refused to act on its obligations, so there was to be street war, of sorts, between the Justice Department and the segregationists.[9]

But in 1961 Robert Kennedy remained aloof from the tactics of confrontation and peaceful rebellion that gave to the civil rights movement its distinctive character. Byron White, who thought that blacks needed a higher standard of living rather than civil rights, explained at a press conference in Birmingham that marshals would not intervene if the police arrested the freedom riders: "I'm sure they would be represented by competent counsel." Robert actually countenanced the arrest of riders in Jackson, Mississippi, on whatever charge the local officers used against violators of segregation. Apparently he thought that the arrests would rescue the riders from the dangers they were inviting upon themselves. "Do you know," he exclaimed to Wofford, "that one of them is against the atom bomb—yes, he even picketed against it in jail!" After the arrests the attorney general urged a cooling-off period; he cited the forthcoming summit conference between the United States and the Soviet Union. Martin Luther King, Jr., agreed to a momentary respite. But hundreds of arrests followed later in the summer.[10]

The administration was unwilling to make demands on Congress. The President appointed to southern federal districts, especially in the deep South, judges so traditionalist that they obstructed the work of his brother's civil rights lawyers. He was, of course, constrained in his selections by the custom, almost never violated, of obtaining approval from the states' Democratic senators. The political commentator Tom Wicker has argued that Kennedy could have risked presenting Congress with a civil rights bill early in his administration. Republicans, he contends, would have had no good reason to oppose it, and southerners were already as alienated as they could be, antagonized by the liberal rhetoric of the presidential campaign, by the administration's support of the fight to widen the membership of the House Rules Committee, and by liberal legislation having the endorsement of the White House. But when Senator Joseph Clark of Pennsylvania and Representative Emanuel Celler of New York introduced six bills to implement the Democratic platform of 1960 on civil rights, the White House disavowed the very bills Kennedy had asked for during the campaign.[11]

Almost as cautious about the use of executive power, the administration canceled no contracts for reasons of job discrimination. Speaking of such new regulations as withholding federal funding from highway construction that practiced discrimination in working conditions, the President once urged that the rules be enforced only when essential. In 1961 the NAACP had proposed that the government withhold funds from states using them in a discriminatory way. The report of the Civil Rights Commission recommended that Kennedy explore his authority to hold back funding from Mississippi. The President, calling the idea "unbelievable" and "almost irresponsible," urged the commission not to make its statement public. At a press conference he said that he neither had nor should have the authority to stop funds going to recalcitrant states. "They ran away from it," Roy Williams said of the scheme, "like it was a rattlesnake." Yet the Civil Rights Act of 1964 was to give the President the power Kennedy had rejected. In 1960 Kennedy had attacked the previous administration for tolerating segregation in federally funded housing. But it was almost two years before he acted on his promise to eliminate it with "a stroke of the presidential pen" (he had received thousands of pens and floods of ink through the mail), and even then he acted circumspectly, burying the order in the midst of public announcements covering other subjects and phrasing it to apply only to future FHA and VA mortgages. Probably he knew that the desegregation of suburban housing was a dangerous issue; it took Lyndon Johnson until 1968 to get any legislation on the subject, and suburban desegregation is still notoriously slow to proceed.[12]

Three times the Civil Rights Commission was ready to hold hearings in Mississippi, and three times Robert Kennedy stopped the hearings, claiming that impending legislation would be endangered. Even while pushing voter registration, the attorney general feared race riots in the South and thought that hearings might set them off. He complained, Wofford recalls, that the commission was not objective: "It was almost like the House Un-American Activities Committee investigating Communism." The commission, disregarding the wishes of the President and the attorney general, published a report on violations of civil rights in Mississippi.

Robert Kennedy and his Justice Department did take or respond to initiatives in the furtherance of civil rights. When King and other civil rights leaders involved in the freedom rides complained to him that the Interstate Commerce Commission was not enforcing the Supreme Court declaration in terminals, he had explained to them that the commission was both independent and slow to move, but in the wake of the rides, he disproved his claim, persuading the ICC to forbid discrimination. By the end of the year every airport and nearly every bus and railroad station had been desegregated. Hoping that the voter registration movement for black southerners would bring less violence than the freedom rides, the attorney general joined in the call for the project, which the NAACP announced to the press in a statement that included the phrase "ask what you can do for your country." The need was plain: in Mississippi the percentage of blacks registered to vote had been declining for seventy years even as literacy among Negroes had been steadily rising. When the question of voter registration became central, Burke Marshall's civil rights division sent lawyers into the South to investigate violations of voting rights, and in another innovation he permitted them to initiate actions, which numbered about seventy by late 1963. Government lawyers went into Fayette County in Tennessee to sue landlords who had forced black sharecroppers off their land for trying to register for the vote, and the Agriculture Department gave food to the dispossessed.

The voter registration campaign, which put the administration at odds with white supremacists it had appointed to federal courts, was in its defense of traditional constitutional rights an eminently conservative program; and even Americans relatively indifferent to race issues could acknowledge its justice. It therefore accorded with that streak of caution that had marked Robert Kennedy's initial management of the race problem. But in the self-consciousness and militancy it awakened in black southerners, in the political organization it spawned among them, and in the power base it ultimately provided, the voter registration project was revolutionary.

John Kennedy's administration as a whole was moving incrementally and yet at a rate unprecedented within this century on the issue of civil rights. In the early sixties motor travelers between Washington and the Northeast still had to use Route 40 in Maryland, and those travelers sometimes included diplomats from the new African nations. The government, its attention fixed on international politics, successfully urged the state of Maryland to pass a public accommodations law and persuaded the governor to apologize to a black diplomat who had been turned away from a restaurant. In the days when the District of Columbia still practiced much de facto segregation, the President appointed the first black District commissioner. He also made some notable selections of blacks elsewhere, choosing for the court of appeals Thurgood Marshall, who had argued the great school desegregation case of 1954. Kennedy strengthened the President's Commission on Equal Employment Opportunity, charged with working for more equitable hiring in the government and in the firms with which the government did business. It won some voluntary agreements from businesses contracting with the government to survey and improve their hiring practices. President Kennedy asked Congress to forbid literacy tests for voting, and at his behest the national legislature sent to the states the Twenty-fourth Amendment, outlawing the poll tax. The government warned universities receiving federal money for language institutes that the program funding would be contingent on an absence of discrimination; as a result, a half dozen schools withdrew. Washington also resolved to withhold federal aid from segregated school districts in areas "impacted" by federal installations. The President appointed Robert C. Weaver as housing administrator and worked hard but unsuccessfully to have his office raised to cabinet status. To the Civil Rights Commission, which President Eisenhower had made a more effective body than had been expected, Kennedy made some appointments that strengthened its activist character, and the commission, of all government agencies the most aggressive on the rights issue, was a goad to the administration.

The administration, in sum, was sending contradictory signals, and that may have given hope to elements in the South of winning a battle that they had already lost. The presidency had chosen to act with some responsiveness to that first moment in American history when it appeared possible that racial equality could actually prevail, and now rather than in an indefinite future to which Americans of good will could look wistfully. That may explain both the activity and the reticence of the administration. It was active because an increasingly insistent segment of the black population and numbers of white allies were urging it into action and because a growing number of white Americans were showing that they would not, at the slightest progress toward integration, turn into a mob. And the administration could afford to be reticent, prepared to compromise for the sake of keeping its friendship with white southerners, because it believed that the revolution in attitudes and practices had its own momentum. Every small gesture on the part of the government made the revolution appear, and therefore be, all the more an irresistible reality. The Kennedy presidency might have gone its entire tenure in the way it and events had set, forceful enough to win popularity among black Americans, politic enough to keep the popularity among southern whites that opinion polls registered for it until mid-1963. But in the end violence by southern bigots brought the President to speak and act against racial injustice with a militancy that he may once have intended only for confrontation with communism.

In the autumn of 1962 James Meredith pursued his plans to enter the University of Mississippi, its first black student. He has recalled that he might not have applied to the University of Mississippi had Kennedy lost the 1960 election. Meredith worked out his plan on his own, claiming later to have received inspiration from the cadences of John Kennedy's inaugural address—which said not a word about civil rights. At least not intentionally. The famous Lincolnesque phrase borrowed by Kennedy—"We shall have to test anew whether a nation organized and governed such as ours can endure"—looked to foreign affairs, but events played it out in the deep South.

After resistance from the state a federal court ordered Meredith's admission. On the night preceding his enrollment Assistant Attorney General Nicholas Katzenbach was on the campus at Oxford, Mississippi, along with Justice Department marshals armed with tear gas. For several hours marshals were under siege in a pitched battle, while Governor Ross Barnett, instead of sending sufficient police or militia forces, declined to deviate from his public posture of antagonism to integration—though his phone conversation with the President in the evening reveals a worried and hesitant man hoping for some solution: he told Kennedy that his defiant words were directed "just to Mississippi."[13]

The President, still unaware of the violence, went on television, urging compliance with the court order, appealing to sportsmanship on the gridiron and to southern honor won in battle. That evening—that terrible evening, in Robert Kennedy's memory—Washington learned that two people had been killed on a campus in anarchy. The White House waited and fretted while federal troops sent by the President took much longer to arrive at Ole Miss than he had expected. Katzenbach asked over the phone whether the marshals could fire on the rioters. No, answered Kennedy, except to protect Meredith. That evening Bobby thought of the killing that might take place, and he thought of the Bay of Pigs. So did the President. "I haven't had such an interesting time since the Bay of Pigs," he said. And Robert composed a bulletin: "The attorney general announced today he's joining Allen Dulles at Princeton University." John Kennedy spoke of *Seven Days in May*, the taut 1962 thriller about a general who tries to overthrow a President to prevent a conciliatory arrangement with the Soviet Union. "The only character that came out at all was the general," said Kennedy. "The president was awfully vague." The novel's general reminded Robert of General Edwin Walker, who had been retired from a European command after his broodings about communism seemed to be prodding him toward making his own separate war on it. Robert's association was apt on that night of Ole Miss: Walker, by now connecting communism with integration or both with the crumbling of Western civilization, was among the rioters. In the end the federal soldiers quelled the mob. Walker was arrested on a federal warrant charging him with seditious conspiracy and insurrection for spurring the rioters, but the government did not get an indictment. The army remained on the campus for months. It had taken some 23,000 troops to do the job.[14]

Robert Kennedy was to remember that after Ole Miss the President said that he would never again believe stories about terrible federal troops in the Reconstruction era. Yet the federal government was so new to the task of enforcing civil rights that Burke Marshall had worried about whether the President had the constitutional authority to send troops without first calling on the governor to act.

The following spring Vivian Malone and James Hood entered the University of Alabama under the protection of federal soldiers. In Alabama, where the attorney general went to prepare for the integration, a state trooper jabbed him with a nightstick, and he was asked at a press conference if he was a member of the Communist party. In a remarkable effort that recalls the administration's earlier mobilizing of its resources in a war with the steel industry, cabinet members and directors of agencies called 375 business executives in Alabama to request that there be no more trouble. Similar calls were to be made to Birmingham businessmen later in 1963 with reminders that the economies of Little Rock and Oxford had suffered after racial troubles there.

The impending riot at Ole Miss had put President Kennedy for the first time before the national television audience on the subject of civil rights. Yet conceivably for strategic reasons at a moment when the threat of violence was the immediate problem, he had stressed not racial justice but obedience to the Constitution. Events the next spring so intruded the race issue into the national consciousness that a moral vocabulary was at last inescapable.

Federal efforts in deeply segregated Birmingham had been virtually unavailing; aside from the post office and Veterans Administration hospital, blacks held fewer than one percent of federal jobs in the area. George Wallace, now Alabama governor, was moving into the leadership of southern segregationists. The strategy of the rights workers in 1963, the only workable one, was to confront the city with massive demonstrations. What transpired placed an overwhelming demand on the national conscience: police dogs, electric cattle prods, fire hoses, and rioting. Burke Marshall, at his best when the patient arts of negotiation were required, talked endlessly with white business leaders and won at least a segment of civic opinion to the cause of peace. The administration, meanwhile, had entreated King to call off the demonstrators on the ground that they were hindering the negotiations with the whites, as the two Kennedys, never pleased with the tactics of confrontation, had wanted him in 1962 to ease off in Albany, Georgia, so that a moderate Democratic candidate for governor might win. Kennedy, foreseeing the "fires of frustration and discord . . . burning in every city, North and South," responded as the occasion demanded. By now he, the churches, a majority in Congress, and much of the nation had awakened. Kennedy on June 11 gave an eloquent address on television: "I ask you to look into your hearts—not in search of charity, for the Negro neither wants nor needs condescension—but for the one plain, proud and priceless quality that unites all as Americans: a sense of justice."[15]

That same night in Mississippi a white racist murdered the civil rights leader Medgar Evers. His was only one of innumerable murders of black people since the coming of slavery to the continent, but now there were awakened media to give the killing nationwide prominence.

Shortly after his television talk the President, who had presented to Congress a mild civil rights bill after Ole Miss but before Birmingham, requested the national legislature to place a partial ban on discrimination in public places, empower the Justice Department to sue for school desegregation upon a request that it do so, and give the executive broader authority to withhold funds from federally assisted programs in which discrimination occurred. The President, who had been politic enough not to want Johnson to speak out inordinately on the race issue, was bold enough to deliver his historic speech against the judgment of most of his White House advisers. Johnson had argued for some preparatory work to soften up Congress. Afterward civil rights leaders persuaded Kennedy to strengthen the proposed legislation to give the attorney general power to intervene in all civil rights cases. The Civil Rights Acts that followed his death were to go well beyond the initial Kennedy program.

Though the President never perhaps came to see the issue as absolutely and morally central—he told a press conference that tax reform was more important than anything else—he did work hard to pass the legislation, meeting with some 1,700 people that summer. After House liberals tried to revise his legislation with provisions that the administration feared would bring its defeat, Kennedy persuaded conservative Republican leader Charles Halleck to agree to a moderate version and thereby, according to the recollections of Robert Kennedy and Burke Marshall, presented the liberals with a political situation so promising that holdouts came over. If they had compromised their virtue, Halleck in the view of many conservatives had compromised his. He found a furled umbrella on his desk in the House. Senator Everett Dirksen made passage nearly certain by agreeing on November 2 that the Republican leadership would not support a filibuster. By the time of the President's death the bill had already cleared its most difficult hurdle, the House Judiciary Committee.[16]

Martin Luther King, Jr., was to comment privately in an oral history that at the President's directions Robert Kennedy had done much more than his office of attorney general obliged him to do. But he remarked before Kennedy's June 1963 speech that while the President had perhaps done "a little more" for blacks than Eisenhower, "the plight of the vast majority of Negroes remains the same." When 250,000 people under King's leadership marched on Washington that August in support of the proposed legislation, John Kennedy first tried to dissuade them and then avoided addressing the assembly. Burke Marshall, however, has claimed that the attorney general did much of the real work of organizing the march: providing water and toilets (which a government is virtually obligated to do anyway) and insuring—whatever this means—"that the character of the people who were coming was in close touch with the police." Upon learning that John Lewis of the Student Nonviolent Coordinating Committee was going to give an inflammatory speech—"It attacked the President," Robert laments—the theologically conservative but socially progressive Roman Catholic archbishop of Washington, Patrick O'Boyle, was going to decline to participate. Marshall went to Walter Reuther, who enlisted the help of King, James Farmer of CORE, and others to persuade Lewis to temper his speech, which satisfied O'Boyle. The final version omitted the announcement that the civil rights forces would "march through the South, through the Heart of Dixie, the way Sherman did." The contrast is inviting: the heroic and visionary rights activists in a triumphant moment; the worried administrators who rushed about to keep everything safe and orderly. The generation of the sixties reveled in such contrasts. But if the movement that called the march could reach beyond the caution that guided the administration, the government, by keeping O'Boyle in the march, rendered the demonstration a service.[17]

On August 28 King addressed the marchers: "I have a dream that one day on the red hills of Georgia the sons of former slaves and the sons of former slaveholders will be able to sit down together at the table of brotherhood. I have a dream that one day even the state of Mississippi, a desert state sweltering with the heat of injustice and oppression, will be transformed into an oasis of freedom and justice. . . . I have a dream that one day the state of Alabama . . . will be transformed [and] little black boys and black girls will be able to join hands with little white boys and white girls and walk together as sisters and brothers." John Kennedy never gave voice to such a dream. But he allied himself with King's, and the alliance brought forth after his death the great civil rights legislation of the mid-sixties. Congress approved the first law in 1964, and others followed in 1965 and 1966.

Robert Kennedy's later commentary on the administration's race policies gives a plausible, though self-interested, justification of the caution. State by state, he was to claim, the government had to accommodate southern senators on federal judicial appointments. The reason the administration did not send more civil rights legislation to Congress, by his explanation, is that there was so little effective demand for it. In 1962 the attorney general went to the Hill to testify for a bill that would insure voting rights for people literate at the sixth-grade level, but interest in it was insufficient. Robert was wary of expanding the power of the federal government to defend civil rights, believing that a gradual resolution of issues was healthier than sudden confrontations of the South by rights workers under federal protection. His idea of a well-managed policy was the federal pressure and discussion that brought about the desegregation of rail and air terminals. The strategy-tempered idealism of the administration, as Robert's recollections present it, was typified in the determination to protect the right to vote: the federal government had the authority, accomplishment would bring much good, and there could be relatively small opposition to so clearly fundamental a right.

Robert Kennedy's observations in his oral history on the House liberals who tried to stiffen the administration's civil rights bill (which include his comment that the epithet sons of bitches that his father had applied to businessmen applied also to liberals) put neatly the difference between two perceptions of morality. The liberals preferred failure to a reasonable bill. "An awful lot of them, as I said then, were in love with death," the motive, perhaps, that some of them had for liking Adlai Stevenson; they thought only of their own goals, not of the needs of others. This moralistic denunciation of liberal moralism comes from a man in whom virtuous anger seemed forever close to eruption. It may not be a just interpretation of the House liberals of 1963, and it does not take into account the demonstration provided by the civil rights activists that a will to strain beyond the limits of the sensible and the possible may have the practical effect of widening the limits. But Robert Kennedy makes a good moral case against the virtuousness that thirsts after purity. The argument is also applicable to those right-wingers who were offended at President Kennedy's attempts to reach accommodations with the Soviet Union. And it is applicable later in the decade to the seekers after purity whose antiwar, antiliberal, antigovernment, and anti-American convictions could express themselves only in superlatives chasing after superlatives. In those days could be heard the most tremendous denunciations of the United States as a genocidal country and of its people as rotting in corruption, as if any accusation more measured would be a compromise.

George McGovern has commented that President Kennedy's respect and desire for power led him to conserve it for essential uses and to refrain from expending it on anything that could dissipate it. If the observation does not describe the President who agreed to the Bay of Pigs, it does suggest the administration that finally spoke for a sophisticated understanding of the architectures of world power. Kennedy had something of the sense of federal power as a force to be calculatingly and subtly deployed against racism. And the other, contradictory component of John Kennedy's feeling for power, his tendency to react to crisis rather than to the stubborn detail of a problem, may be further explanation for the peculiar pace of his dealings with the race question: conciliatory, slow, incremental reform punctuated in the end by dramatic televised responses to the great civil rights events of the day.

Critics have accused the Kennedy presidency of indulging, especially in foreign policy and in administration, a taste for activity in itself, a contempt for slow continuity, an impatience with existing channels. It is curious that the will to break through the boundaries of the given, to make a new thing happen in the simple doing of it, had its greatest expression in the sixties not in the Kennedy presidency but in the civil rights movement that the Kennedy liberals have been blamed for being slow to understand. And it is an irony that the chief aid the administration could give to the movement was not to join in as witness against the given but instead to enforce the given, the laws and procedures that lend a stable foundation to civil rights.

The United States has traditionally and somewhat romantically understood one of the meanings of its history to be the overturning of arbitrary and false rule. The civil rights revolution is clearly faithful to that meaning. But it was the popular will, embodied in the bigotry of the majority, that the civil rights movement had to combat. By planning and good fortune the nation has accumulated in its fundamental law and other institutions certain principles and procedures that, when supplemented by a divided popular conscience, can stand against arbitrary popular rule. But this means that the civil rights movement is as much the story of a restraining as it is the story of a liberation. It was the task of Robert Kennedy's Justice Department to act for that part of the democratic process that is in restraint of an unjust popular will.

The national assault on southern institutions suggests also the continuing conflict in democratic politics between the claims of locality and those of some larger purpose. The defense of local custom and self-determination was, of course, a staple of the segregationist argument. A respect for locality certainly figured in the initial caution of a President whose *Profiles in Courage* reflects the traditional concept of Reconstruction as a brutal assault on regional institutions. It was equally a factor in the thought of his brother the attorney general, who believed that as an imposition upon the South by an alien Reconstruction government, civil rights had withered there for lack of rooting in the local soil. The virtues of locality, of course, appeal to a great variety of political persuasions. Later in the decade, for instance, young radicals attacked the impersonal agencies of the welfare state and became entranced with third world nationalisms combating what the left defined as Western imperialism. But the effect of local autonomy upon the rights of the southern black minority needs no comment here. And in the 1970s the victory, if that is what it was, of autonomy in Vietnam installed a regime that has imprisoned or killed thousands whose thinking might violate the integrity of the new order. So locality, nurturing certain values of community, can also threaten the individual on the one side, as it threatens to rupture the larger human community on the other. The legal assault on southern institutions was both a triumph for individual liberty and a preparation for the national programs of the Johnson years.

Toward the civil rights movement President Kennedy never seized the initiative. Yet the movement has a central place within that public, collective experience that we associate with his presidency. When in 1957, the governor of Arkansas tried to prevent the integration of the Little Rock schools, President Eisenhower had reversed eighty years of executive inactivity by determining that the presidential office would impose its authority and the Constitution upon segregationist states. Never since the end of Reconstruction had the federal government so defied the zealously protected doctrine of states' rights or so directly defied social custom. Had it not been for Eisenhower's assertion of the primacy of the federal will, the civil rights movement might have had a different future. Kennedy's decision to give governmental countenance to the civil rights movement was comparably innovative. The tactics of mass demonstrations, religious witness, and civil disobedience, directed against institutions that embodied deep and traditional popular prejudices, were not the kinds of conduct that governments could ordinarily be expected to deal with even on haltingly friendly terms. In publicly, if cautiously, allying the government with the movement, Kennedy gave the cause a look of legitimacy, of being within the inevitable flow of American history. The general feeling of energy and electricity and challenge that attended the Kennedy presidency made a further, intangible contribution to the struggle for civil rights. The movement, of course, was responsible for a good portion of the feeling, and the presidency may have been as much its beneficiary as its agent. But that is only to say that the relationship of John Kennedy to the Kennedy era is elusive.

The early nonviolent civil rights movement soon died. It would remain the most symbolic of the events of the sixties: a witnessing, a breaking away, charismatic, almost above the political process. But it depended on fragile conditions: keeping the race issue confined to the South; receiving the support of poorer blacks unable to profit immediately from achievement of its goals; and, above all, calling on an extraordinary compound of militancy and nonviolence, celebration and discipline. Ghetto riots and black nationalism soon replaced it in public visibility. And a decade later Senator Edward Kennedy would find how much hostility the war against racism could stir up in the North when its object was the Boston school system and when it applied to a segment of the population that saw itself as being subject to social experiment in compensation for society's failures elsewhere.

In the 1960 campaign John Kennedy had been more insistent about economic issues than about the race question, charging the Eisenhower administration with allowing the national growth rate to fall below that of Western Europe and of the Soviet Union. In office, however, he began by acting cautiously in economics. Against the recession that had begun in 1960 he deployed tactics close to Eisenhower's, which included raising

Social Security payments and the minimum wage. Military spending added jobs; so did a billion-dollar investment tax credit and the Manpower Development and Training Act. The new President faced problems, notably an adverse balance of payments, that discouraged more forthright fiscal or monetary tactics. He insisted that countries getting foreign aid buy more American goods. Until the third quarter of 1962 his prudent policies held the cost of living steady without causing substantial new unemployment.

In May 1962 the stock market dropped sharply. That helped turn Kennedy to a bolder policy to fulfill his campaign promise to get the economy moving again. The patient counsel of Walter Heller, the President's chief economic adviser, had convinced Treasury Secretary Douglas Dillon, a Republican, of the need for more federal action. And as White House conversations make clear, by mid-1962 liberal economists had likewise convinced Kennedy. So for the first time during relative prosperity, an administration was to propose a budget deficit through tax reduction, this despite Kennedy's campaign call for self-sacrifice. The scheme, though widely perceived as radical, was much more acceptable to business than was new spending. In a discussion between the President and his advisers, McNamara voiced the hope that the corporations would recognize the benefits the tax cut would bring them and would "start deviating from the Republican line at this point." When Illinois Senator Paul Douglas had asked for a $6 billion tax cut in 1958, he had been rebuffed by a vote of 65 to 23. In February 1964, 77 senators voted as the slain Kennedy would have wished, favoring a tax cut of more than $10 billion—and at a time when the economy was picking up.

The economy surged forward. Unemployment fell, and prosperity helped fund Lyndon Johnson's Great Society programs. Even before Kennedy's death the economy had achieved a real growth rate of 5.7 percent, unemployment was down to 5 percent, and inflation was 1.3 percent. The growth rate during Eisenhower's presidency had been 2.3 percent. The rate now surpassed that of almost every European economy. The promise of a tax cut probably deserved major credit. Michael Harrington has referred to Kennedy's form of deficit spending as "reactionary Keynesianism." But that was before the Reagan administration came up with a truly reactionary Keynesianism, a deficit spending that favors or spends on everything except the poor. Kennedy's form of Keynesianism stands at midpoint between that and a more generous program that would create its deficits through major spending on social programs.[18]

Like all other Presidents, Kennedy was a friend of business. In 1962 he signed a large depreciation allowance for business, and in 1963 he reduced corporate income taxes by 20 percent. Secretary of Commerce Luther Hodges of North Carolina favored right to work laws, which restricted the power of unions to organize. The Trade Expansion Act of 1962 won some reciprocal tariff reductions from the European Common Market. Yet business never trusted Kennedy, whose administration reminded it more and more of the New Deal. His appointees to the nation's regulatory bodies, among them Newton Minow of the Federal Communications Commission and Joseph Swidler of the Federal Power Commission, usually reflected the public interest. And in the spring of 1962 Kennedy and the steel industry went to war.[19]

Late in the afternoon of April 10 Roger Blough, chairman of the board of United States Steel, arrived at the White House to tell the President that as they spoke, press releases announcing a rise in the price of steel were being issued. The President was outraged at what seemed both a deception and an insult. The administration had thought that it had an understanding—there had been no formal agreement—that prices would remain stable, and on this assumption Labor Secretary Arthur Goldberg had persuaded the unions to accept moderate wage raises. The President, like the attorney general on another occasion, privately referred to his father's denunciation of businessmen as sons of bitches and added "pricks"; "robbing bastards" he was to call oil and gasmen that July in a reference preserved on the White House tapes. Agency after federal agency turned on the industry.

The Defense Department threatened to shift steel contracts to small companies that had not yet raised prices; the Justice Department and the Federal Trade Commission threatened to initiate antitrust action and new antitrust laws; the Treasury Department threatened to launch a tax investigation. Kennedy spoke on television: "In this serious hour in our nation's history, when we are confronted with grave crises in Berlin and Southeast Asia . . . [and] asking reservists to leave their homes and families for months on end and servicemen to risk their lives . . . , the American public will find it hard, as I do, to accept a situation in which a tiny handful of steel executives whose pursuit of private power and profit exceeds their sense of public responsibility can show such utter contempt of the interests of 185 million Americans." The presidency was throwing its resources into the service of what Kennedy believed to be the public good. Big Steel, following the lead of Inland Steel and some smaller companies, grudgingly rescinded the increase, then reintroduced it the following year to help the sagging industry.[20]

A month after the clash, when the stock market fell sharply, Sorensen sent a memorandum to the President suggesting that regulatory agencies ease up on business. Also after the crisis Adlai Stevenson, the intellectuals' liberal, advised Kennedy to confront labor in some equally public way. The President, for the moment, had turned angry toward a constituency that he had seldom, if ever, denounced in a liberal's vocabulary. He would not appear again before the United States Chamber of Commerce, he told Stevenson, and he remarked, "I'm beginning to sound like Harry Truman."[21]

By the fall of 1963 Kennedy may have been tightening his grip on domestic problems. Oregon Senator Wayne Morse shepherded through important mental health and education bills. Kennedy and Interior Secretary Udall obtained approval for a Cape Cod National Seashore, and they pushed for more national parks and seashores, particularly in the heavily populated East. Kennedy told Schlesinger in November 1963 that he was planning to put in his State of the Union address a comprehensive scheme for an assault on poverty. The Russian-American détente was under way, the Soviet Union was buying American wheat, technology was grinding out consumer goods, and even the Vietnam War seemed to be going for the better after the removal of Premier Diem. Then, on November 22, Kennedy went to Dallas.

The city has a Texas way of attaining its objectives; the present-day football stadium at Irving and the ultramodern airport shared with Fort Worth are expressions of its will to make for itself, quickly and on a grand scale, the kind of civic life it wants. The confident American energies that the Kennedy administration wished to represent and marshal were a good deal like that, although the Kennedy rhetoric could also emphasize the intractable difficulties of the world toward which those energies were to be directed and the tempering and restraint that had to qualify their exercise. The speech the President had planned to deliver in Dallas celebrated American military might, speaking of the administration's increase in nuclear weapons, but also argued for care in its deployment.

Whether or not he acted alone, Lee Harvey Oswald fits a chilling model of assassins driven by their secret hopes of success: victims of disrupted childhoods; loners having no commitment to an idea or a cause except insofar as it can further aggrandize their own will and their sense of importance. Conspiracy theories deny exactly that uncertainty and chanciness in life that the Oswald story amply illustrates, the uncertainty that he lacked the patience or discipline to accept. Oswald had built a secret world of schemes. According to a schoolmate, he had "seemed to be a boy that was looking for something to belong to, but I don't think anybody was looking for him to belong to them." After a disordered upbringing lacking a spine of principles and goals, he had brief and unsatisfactory careers in the marines, in Russia, and in Mexico. His Marxist politics, from which the assassination sprang, was perhaps an attempt to discover the order behind an existence that he must have perceived as maliciously purposeless.[22]

The flesh-and-blood Oswald, who perhaps could not stand the contrast between himself and the dazzling President, deprives the story of the mystery that a grandiose conspiracy might give it. But Christopher Lasch argues that some liberals in their rejection of conspiracy theories have given to the event another grand meaning it cannot sustain. Liberals, Lasch supposes, have perceived the President as a hero aristocrat, shot down by a psychopath representing the worst of democracy, the hatred that the small and frustrated can feel for intelligence and grace. Conspiracy theories themselves, both right and left, further demonstrate to the liberal mind, as Lasch describes it, the darker side of democracy. Questions about the assassination, at any rate, reflect much in the temperament of the observer. Max Lerner reports that Robert Kennedy did not accept conspiracy explanations of the killing. "The death itself was so shattering that anything that attempted to explain it seemed puny and extraneous." To "raise new theories about the killings," writes Lerner of the death of both brothers, "was a collective way of . . . greening their memories." The Warren Commission report on the assassination, which declared that only a single gunman had been involved, was itself so seriously flawed, factually and logically, that it played to minds haunted by suspicions of conspiracy. The small staff had needed to deal with a tremendous volume of trivia; many witnesses to the event who should have been called were not, and some of those called were not seriously questioned. In the end the report neither put the questions fully to rest nor satisfied those who wanted to believe in a conspiracy.[23]

Jacqueline Kennedy arranged a state funeral for her husband modeled on that of the martyred Lincoln. John Kennedy's mortal remains lie on a hillside of Arlington National Cemetery overlooking the nation's capital; a simple, massive stone and a perpetual flame memorialize him. It took some years after the killing of Lincoln for him to become the martyr and hero that he has been in the twentieth century. John Kennedy at his death was received instantly into the national consciousness as the initiator of something good and promising in American life, and for about a decade public opinion polls ranked him ahead of Franklin D. Roosevelt. One black woman spoke the feelings of many Americans: "Like a good book the life of John F. Kennedy steals inside and has somehow made me different. . . . Everyone I knew loved him with a sort of possessiveness." "Has anybody here seen my old friend Abraham?" asks Dion in a popular song appearing a few years later. "And my old friends Martin and Bobby?—and my old friend John?" The good die young, the song concludes. What had this President done to receive such adulation, leaving so small a legislative achievement and a record, like Lincoln's, of such cautious movement toward some greater measure of racial justice?

What he had done was to be President at a time when the nation collectively felt very good. And he did something toward generating or reflecting that good feeling. In those years before Vietnam, Watergate, and recession, Kennedy's administration made government service appealing to young people. A White House employee has noted that during Kennedy's years the volume of mail to the Executive Mansion leveled off at two and a half times what it had been. He was the first real television President, at a time when television was showing us events as large with promise as the civil rights marches and the space flights, and he had heirs, political heirs in the Democratic administration who would go on, blood heirs in a family that Americans knew they were going to see in the future. How ready the nation seemed to perfect something indefinably great, economic, technological, moral, that had roused and stirred itself at about the beginning of Kennedy's presidency. That was naïve. But what benefits would the disillusionment of the seventies and the early eighties bring us? What could be hoped for from a national mood that fewer than two decades later spent its enthusiasm on a politics hostile to welfare programs? The hopefulness went beyond our borders. In Eisenhower's mild ad-

ministration there had been riots abroad; Eisenhower's more assertive successor was loved. "His actual, tangible impact on history," Louise FitzSimons observes in her unfavorable appraisal
of Kennedy's foreign policy, "was not significant enough to explain his enormous psychological impact, the indefinable way in
which John F. Kennedy touched people throughout the world."
In Indian villages, she notes, photographs of Gandhi, Nehru,
and Kennedy are side by side. "They create illusions and call
them facts," Gore Vidal observed of the Kennedys in 1967. But
the Kennedy myth created illusions and made them facts in the
legislative achievements of Lyndon Johnson's administration.[24]

The Camelot legend has obscured as much of Kennedy as
it has revealed, and in any event it is difficult to measure a presidency that is praised precisely for its intangible merits of style
and purpose or to make conjectures about its unfinished future.
No one can make a clear argument either that Kennedy would
have further increased the American presence in Vietnam or
that he would have moderated it. On domestic issues also it is
difficult to predict what might have happened. Kennedy's record
in managing Congress had not been impressive. The critics of
Kennedy are correct to note his careless administrative practices
and his failure to lobby intensively for such programs as he did
propose. He was, James Reston comments, a good politician for
a campaign but not for working with Congress, and for an example of his lack of a will to lead, Tom Wicker cites his failure
to discipline Democratic Representative James J. Delaney of
Queens, who had introduced an education bill in the interest of
the Catholic Church but embarrassing to the administration.
Yet Kennedy faced obstacles not of his own making.[25]

Congress was run, as it had been since the late 1930s, by a
conservative coalition of Republicans and southern Democrats,
and reapportionment giving liberal metropolitan areas more representation had not yet occurred. In *The Deadlock of Democracy*, published in 1963, James MacGregor Burns gave some definition to the problem. There were four parties in Congress,
Burns argued—southern conservative Democrats, northern liberal

Democrats, Republican conservatives, and Republican liberals, and amid them party discipline did not operate effectively. House committees blocked Kennedy's proposals for public transportation assistance, youth employment aid, programs for migrant workers, Medicare, and a cabinet department of Urban Affairs. House Minority Leader Charles Halleck, instrumental in the passage of civil rights legislation soon after the President's death, was otherwise an effective obstruction to Democratic programs; he exercised over his Republican colleagues the discipline that Burns found lacking elsewhere in Congress. The death of Sam Rayburn in 1961 replaced a forceful speaker of the House with easygoing John McCormack. Senate Democrats, deprived of the leadership of Lyndon Johnson upon his assumption of the vice presidency, acquired in his place the milder Mike Mansfield. The 1962 congressional elections, occurring just after the Cuba missile crisis, opened the national legislature to the possibility of a more ambitious administration program, for it returned a more liberal Congress—four additional Democratic senators and a House membership of a more liberal cast. Some of the congressmen who began their careers that year credit Kennedy with their decisions to enter public service. The results encouraged the President to gain an initiative in Congress, so that in 1963 the congressional jam gave some appearance of breaking up.[26]

At the end of 1962 the President spoke to Walter Heller, chairman of the Council of Economic Advisers, about going beyond what the administration had already done and taking on, for example, the problem of poverty. In 1960 Hubert Humphrey had argued for a youth conservation corps that would provide work for the unskilled and protect natural resources, and Kennedy had opposed it, claiming that it would be wasteful like the Civilian Conservation Corps of the 1930s; speaking in 1963 to a Minnesota audience, he endorsed Humphrey's proposal. He got through Congress an accelerated program of public works that recalls the WPA. Federal aid for building medical schools and for funding mental health programs won easily in both houses. Kennedy got a good housing bill under his presidency. Congress passed the first major law preventing water pollution. Benefits under Social Security expanded, and the retirement age dropped to sixty-two. In 1963, 76 percent of polled voters approved Kennedy's conduct of the presidency. Federal aid to colleges was under consideration in Congress when he was killed. The same was true of civil rights legislation and of the tax cut bill that was to strengthen the economy. Kennedy's tax reforms included a rise in taxes on profits earned from corporate stock options and a reduction in write-offs available to owners of oil wells and real estate. One of Kennedy's favorite economic recommendations was for withholding taxes on interest and dividend income—an innovation that had to wait for action until the Reagan forces passed it in 1982. It was repealed in 1983.[27]

The liberalism of Kennedy's later days responded to utilitarian concerns and never appeared impassioned. His efforts to restrain an unfavorable balance of payments and, through tax concessions, to strengthen American industry signify his caution and his preference for achieving adjustments. Even in foreign policy he was often reactive, and most of the high noons of an administration remembered for its crises—Berlin, steel, Ole Miss, the Cuba missiles—were not at his instigation. If he seemed sometimes on the verge of overreaction, he got through dangerous times with level-headed solutions. Kennedy was puzzled, Schlesinger says, that historians put Woodrow Wilson above James Knox Polk or Harry Truman; it was practical results rather than ideas that he judged. A speech to the American Federation of Labor convention just before his death reflects: "No one gains by being admitted to a lunch counter if he has no money to spend. No one gains from attending a better school if he doesn't have a job after graduation." Civil rights legislation is important, Kennedy told the convention, but the legislation is ineffective without jobs. The speech can be taken to be an expression of the conservative side of Kennedy, of his skepticism about social legislation, but it can also be placed to the left of the conventional liberal concentration during the early sixties on formal acts of desegregation, a foreshadowing of Robert's matured economic progressivism. It is, above all, a lecture in practicality. Kennedy's cool public manner made some liberals, used to the more emotional presence of leaders like Hubert Humphrey, believe he was not interested in reforms. But his record, for the times, is a good one.

Still, there was the aloofness, the critical distance that commentators have described. It has been noted of Kennedy, the product not of an Irish neighborhood but of his father's social aspirations and an upper-class education, that he was something of a snob in his selection of friends. In Wisconsin during the 1960 primary he was asked in effect whether he liked the crowds and the bustle. He hated it, the candidate replied. The dry humor for which Kennedy's press conferences were noted indicated some ease with people, but much humor is also the work of a stepping back from things, of treating existence from the point of view of an observer. While there was something of the Irish in Kennedy, Ralph Martin says, and something of Harvard, "basically, in temperament, he was an English Whig," who believed that perfection is beyond us, that "life was a comedy to those who think, a tragedy to those who feel." Everything in his nation's life, says Richard Rovere, interested and amused Kennedy and invited his criticism. "His zest for simply watching the show was as great as H. L. Mencken's. His curiosity seemed at times not only astonishing in itself but almost frivolous, almost perverse; he would spend time (government time) talking and bothering about . . . the typography of a newspaper, for example." Rovere's comment fits the President who, in the discussions preceding the missile quarantine, kept puzzling over the question, which could have waited, of why the Soviet Union had wanted the missiles emplaced. Kennedy's mentality, Rovere claims, would not let him "think that everything would be Jimdandy if we just had Medicare and stepped up production in our engineer factories and got negroes into nice, clean motels." Rovere's Kennedy was interested not merely in the quantitative strength of American education but in its character and direction. Is Rovere describing an extraordinarily engaged President, alive to every detail and implication of the American life he had to make policy for, or an ironic spectator wishing for excellence in the things he carefully perceived and knowing that excellence would probably elude them? Kennedy may have been both, and simultaneously.[28]

The most loyal and affectionate liberal partisan of John Kennedy cannot make him into a dedicated, consistent, and impassioned champion of a leftward movement in American politics. Yet much happened during the Kennedy administration that foreshadowed or gave energy to that era remembered as the sixties and to many of the social, cultural, and political changes shaping American civilization since.

There were the beginnings of détente. Even the war in Vietnam would not go frontally against the shift in American policy and perceptions that came with the Kennedy years. For the defenders of that war would struggle to explain the Western interests in Vietnam more technically in geopolitical terms and with less recourse to the warnings of worldwide Communist expansion than had been the staple of political rhetoric in the 1950s. It was during the Kennedy administration that the federal government first clearly sided with the civil rights demonstrators, and it was then that the government began its commitment and lent its prestige to the end of segregation. By the finish of Kennedy's life or just afterward the civil rights movement had taken his photograph into black homes as an emblem. It was to remain there as black liberation awakened the other liberation movements of the late sixties and beyond. During Kennedy's presidency, and with the help of government spending, recession ended and unemployment lessened, and while the national economy by the end of the sixties was slumping badly, the prosperity of the early sixties nourished the social movements of the decade. The administration, especially in the Department of the Interior and in the person of its secretary, Stewart Udall, stood at the beginning of the recent federal involvement in environmentalism. As for the cultural revolutions of the late sixties and early seventies that have left a mark on American mores, something even of that was suggested in the Kennedy years.[29]

Those who are old enough to remember the 1960s as one experience passed into another will recall the styles of the young Kennedy liberals: Peace Corpsmen, their sleeves rolled up, their hair slightly lengthened and slightly disheveled; shorter skirts and a somewhat franker sexuality; men who went to restaurants without neckties and women who went there in slacks. Even during Kennedy's lifetime hints of the future could be heard in the harsh harmonica of Bob Dylan. And then in two or three years after Kennedy's death the hair of many young males went to shoulder length, and people in San Francisco and Berkeley and across the country experimented in every variant of living arrangement and sensual experience. Put a photograph of President Kennedy, clean-shaven, business-suited, side by side with a photograph of a bearded communard of 1968, and you will think you are looking at two eras; travel in recollection through that time, and you will recapture the connection. But this is to speak of the surfaces of style. Far deeper was that sudden freedom that happened not in Washington but at some southern lunch counter on a sticky, hot summer afternoon.

6

Robert Kennedy: The Leftward Journey

ROBERT FRANCIS KENNEDY HAD A SOMEWHAT DIFFERENT UPBRING-
ing from that of Joe, Jr., or Jack. His family did not prepare
him specifically and intensively for public life. He received a
more intensively Catholic upbringing than his brothers. Perhaps
that is a reason why there was always something of the driven
moralist about Robert Kennedy, whose stern Catholicism contrasted with Jack's easy observance; he had the moralist's capacity for arrogant, overbearing anger and for self-criticism and
growth. His temperament, aggressive in politics and sports, could
be mild in other circumstances. He had the Kennedy ruthlessness, but that ruthlessness was both tempered and made all the
more efficient by an absence in him of the assertive virility that
drew Joe, Jr., into barroom brawls and, in the midst of war and
government, distracted John into womanizing.[1]

Robert Kennedy, born on November 20, 1925, was the seventh Kennedy child, the third son, and the first boy after four

girls. The family, long to remain the most important consideration in his life, left Massachusetts for New York City's northern suburbs the next year, and at the end of his life he was to be New York's United States senator. "What I remember most vividly about growing up," he would remark, "was going to a lot of different schools, always having to make new friends, and that I was very awkward. I dropped things and fell down. I was pretty quiet most of the time. And I didn't mind being alone."[2]

When Robert was fourteen, his mother took advantage of her husband's absence in London to send her son for three years to Portsmouth Priory, a Benedictine school with morning and evening prayers, along with mass three times during the week and on Sunday. His grades were low, sinking to 50 in history. Like many other boys, he found consolation in sports. He served as an altar boy and prayed often. To improve his chances of getting into Harvard, Robert's family moved him to Milton Academy, a Protestant school where, a female acquaintance has remembered, "He used to walk with his head way down, buried in his neck, like a bird in a storm." But soon he became friends with the school's star athlete; that increased his self-confidence.

In late 1943, after entering Harvard, Robert went into the naval reserve. "We haven't really had too much action here in Harvard Square," he wrote home, "but we're on the alert at every moment for an attack." He offered self-analysis from the Maine woods in 1944: "My usual moody self. I get very sad at times." Eventually he went into the navy, serving as a second-class seaman on a cruise of the *Joseph P. Kennedy, Jr.* to Guantánamo. After his discharge he worked in his brother's first congressional campaign, improving the Democratic vote in three Italian wards of Cambridge, but he returned in September 1946 to Harvard, where he did poorly in his courses, played football, and, like Jack, made athletes his friends. (He later commented on his school days, "I spent ten years learning second-year French.") After graduation in 1948 at the height of the cold war, Kennedy traveled through Europe as a newspaper correspondent as Jack had done earlier. Robert, who joined any number of conservatives and right-wingers in opining that the government had exercised poor judgment at Yalta and Potsdam, was the most fastidiously conservative of the brothers. In law school at the University of Virginia, he wrote a term paper, "The Reserve Powers of the Constitution," calling on the American conservative tradition for "effective control of the federal government." Head of the student law forum, Robert brought to the campus his father's friends—Joe McCarthy, Arthur Krock, William O. Douglas—and the elder Kennedy himself, whose argument against the Democratic policies of confronting communism throughout the world contemplated a contraction of American power abroad, as his son argued for a check on federal power at home. Herbert Hoover gave a similar talk at the university soon after, and then Senator Robert A. Taft made a blistering attack on Truman for committing troops abroad without congressional approval.

Robert Kennedy also proposed that Ralph Bunche of the United Nations be invited to speak in conservative Charlottesville. Bunche responded to his invitation by stipulating that he would address only an integrated group. Virginia law, however, forbade racially mixed audiences. Kennedy's anger flared, and a strong letter with his signature went to the university president. Thereupon a technicality was devised that would allow for an integrated audience.

While still in law school, Robert married the vivacious Ethel Skakel, who came from a conservative Republican family of Greenwich, Connecticut. Her athletic brothers and Robert's athletic friends wrecked part of New York's Harvard Club at a memorable bachelor's dinner. Ethel had social gifts that offset Robert's blunt ways. They were to have eleven children, therein living by a traditional concept of family in an age that was beginning to define large families as quaint and Catholic.

Late in 1951, after a trip through Asia with his congressman brother, which included an audience with Nehru, Robert went to work in the internal security division of the Department of Justice. He aided in the investigation of alleged Soviet spies, much to his father's approval. He next moved to the criminal division, where he helped prepare a corruption case against some Truman administration officials, and then went to Boston to help Jack in his 1952 senatorial campaign. After the election he got a job of assistant counsel on the infamous Permanent Senate Subcommittee on Investigations. Joe McCarthy's slashing tactics, fully demonstrated at this late date, had apparently not repelled Robert.[3]

Kennedy's first assignment for McCarthy was to monitor trade between allied countries and Communist China during the Korean War. McCarthy used the issue in inimitable fashion. "We should keep in mind the American boys . . . who had their hands wired behind their backs and their faces shot off with [Communist] machine guns . . . supplied by those flag vessels of our allies," ranted the senator from Wisconsin. The State Department had already negotiated an agreement by which the owners of 300 Greek ships promised to stop the trade. But Japanese and British commerce with China, involving local interests in Hong Kong and Malaya, was more complicated. Eisenhower was bristling at McCarthy when Kennedy drafted and personally delivered to the White House a letter asking for information on British strategic goods being shipped to China. The President was annoyed at what he considered a rude intrusion on his staff, and Vice President Nixon persuaded McCarthy to withdraw the letter. Kennedy, his literal mind transfixed by the trade, barely suppressed his moral outrage at the administration.

In August 1953 Kennedy undertook the less controversial role of staff assistant to his father on the first Hoover Commission, which was to design a reorganization of the government. The job left him unsatisfied and quarrelsome. Ted Sorensen has described the Bobby of those days as shallow, opinionated, intolerant. Early the next year he found another outlet for his restless intensity. He rejoined the McCarthy committee, this time as counsel to the three-member Democratic minority, which included John L. McClellan of Arkansas. During the Army-

McCarthy hearings of April 1954 Kennedy and McCarthy's assistant Roy Cohn became embroiled in a furious argument that almost ended in a fistfight. Yet in January 1955 he walked out during a talk by Edward R. Murrow to the United States Junior Chamber of Commerce honoring Kennedy and nine other "outstanding young men of 1954," in protest against Murrow's recent television demolition job on McCarthy.

When Congress, now wrested from Republican control, convened early in 1955, Senator McClellan became subcommittee chairman, and Robert Kennedy majority counsel. They continued the investigations of alleged Communists but did so with more care and greater skepticism than McCarthy had done. The Democrats, anxious to appear at least as anti-Communist as the Republicans, resurrected the old case of Irving Peress, a dentist promoted from captain to major who had tenuous associations with the Communist party. Kennedy found the army guilty of dozens of errors in handling Peress but not that of encouraging subversion. The anti-Communist investigations were running down.

Robert Kennedy never during McCarthy's lifetime publicly turned from him. He visited the Wisconsin senator when others deserted him. In 1957 he would cry at the news of McCarthy's death, writing in his journal: "I dismissed the office for the day. It was all very difficult for me as I felt that I had lost an important part of my life." He attended the state funeral in the Senate chamber and the graveside ceremonies in Appleton, Wisconsin; but the reporter Edwin R. Bayley notes that at the funeral Robert asked the press not to say that he was there. Perhaps both Robert and John Kennedy had found it difficult to leave behind them an Irish anti-Communist whose downfall seemed somehow the work of the WASP establishment. Robert Kennedy's most satisfactory comment is his simple statement "I thought there was a serious internal security threat to the United States; I felt at the time that Joe McCarthy seemed to be the only one who was doing anything about it—I was wrong."[4]

At the other end of politics from McCarthy among Robert's acquaintances was his father's old New Deal friend William O. Douglas. In 1955 Bobby went on a trip through Asia with Douglas. He subsisted principally on watermelon, refusing caviar and what he called dirty Russian food. But meeting the Russian people got through to the crusty young man, and Douglas and his wife were to call the trip "the final undoing of McCarthyism."[5]

Back at work in 1955 on the investigations subcommittee, Kennedy revived the stale topic of trade between the Soviet bloc and the West. Soon, though, he found an enemy tough enough to accommodate his intensity. Mobsters had moved in on some trade unions, using them as covers for various illegal activities and corrupting their pension funds. Picking up on the earlier televised hearings of Senator Estes Kefauver, who had beaten Jack for the 1956 vice presidential nomination, Robert targeted the International Brotherhood of Teamsters and its Republican president, Dave Beck. The teamsters were the largest, richest, and most corrupt union in the country.[6]

In 1957 a select Senate committee chaired by McClellan launched an investigation of labor. Robert Kennedy became majority counsel to the committee. It was a gamble. The family could expect that some voters would confuse the two Kennedys while others would assume that John thought like his brother, and in either case the investigation could darken John's political fortunes among Americans sensitive to any attack on labor unions. The rank-and-file teamsters respected Beck and his successor, Jimmy Hoffa, for their aggressiveness in organizing, and the trucking industry appreciated the ability of the union to prevent wildcat strikes. But Robert saw his work as a moral fight and counted on the kind of public reaction that had reelected Robert Taft in Ohio. On the committee Joe McCarthy, Barry Goldwater, Homer Capehart, Karl Mundt, and one liberal, Irving Ives, represented the Republicans. Had not John Kennedy signed on, Strom Thurmond would have joined Sam Ervin and McClellan and made it a committee exceptionally hostile to labor. Pierre Salinger and Kenneth O'Donnell came on the staff that was to become a presidential campaign corps for the Kennedys, and Robert's work aided in keeping the family visible.

Robert Kennedy did his job thoroughly. He asked direct, pertinent questions, some of which recall McCarthy's browbeating techniques. Dave Beck, who enjoyed a luxurious standard of living that infuriated the puritanical Bobby, was to go to prison for grand larceny and income tax evasion. Jimmy Hoffa, who may have shuffled some evidence toward Kennedy to help convict Beck, bribed a lawyer to infiltrate the McClellan committee, but the man went straight to Kennedy, who set a trap for Hoffa. A superb lawyer in the District of Columbia won him an acquittal in a jury trial. But Kennedy was relentless. A story has it that driving home from his office at 1:00 A.M., he saw the lights on in Hoffa's office and went back to his to work for two more hours. (Hoffa heard the story and thereafter let his lights burn all night.) Kennedy subpoenaed teamster records and forced Hoffa to submit to long examinations, informed by Kennedy's transparent assumption of his quarry's guilt. "Mr. Kennedy appears to find congenial the role of prosecutor, judge and jury," observed the constitutional lawyer Alexander Bickel. The AFL-CIO, alleging that Hoffa had used union funds for personal enrichment, expelled the teamsters. Hoffa managed to get a hung jury in another indictment, for wiretapping, and two dismissals of a charge of perjury. The teamsters answered Kennedy by electing Hoffa their president and awarding Beck a $50,000-a-year pension. Kennedy responded—without compunction since he was combating Evil—that Hoffa's chosen associates were "convicted killers, robbers, extortionists, perjurers, blackmailers, safe crackers, dope peddlers, white slavers, and sodomists."[7]

What would Robert Kennedy have been like had he been forced to claw his way up from the bottom? "You take any industry," Hoffa related, "and look at the problems they ran into while they were building up—how they did it, who they associated with, how they cut corners. The best example is Kennedy's old man." Perhaps the aggressively single-minded Robert would have built an industry or a union by like methods. But his ancestors had done the building, and he was a moral, perhaps morally simplistic young man. His aggressions were a function of whatever moral idea held him at a given moment. So far it had been first anticommunism and then the putting down of labor corruption. Kennedy had not publicly condemned the methods of the Redbaiters, and as a committee lawyer and later as attorney general he was prepared to pursue and hound in ways that trouble scrupulous liberals. In the 1960s his zeal was to find its final object in a progressivism more morally urgent and more convincing than the anticommunism of the McCarthy years. His service on the Senate Labor Committee, however, invited from him anything but a liberal animus. Peter Lisagor among others has recalled his blanket condemnations of labor at the time.[8]

The efforts of Kennedy and the committee led to dozens of changes in union leadership and, in the wake of Walter Reuther's appearance before the senators, to the strengthening of that honest union leader. The investigations also brought the problem of union corruption to public attention and increased the awareness of it on the part of people like labor leader George Meany. The AFL-CIO Ethical Practices Committee praised Kennedy and noted the usefulness of the powerful weapon of the government subpoena. A bill cosponsored by John Kennedy and Irving Ives required financial reports by unions to the Labor Department and regular elections with secret ballots. It passed the Senate, but the House substituted the harsher Landrum-Griffin bill. A combination of the two bills became law. Robert Kennedy resigned from the Labor Committee in September 1959 and published a book about union corruption, *The Enemy Within*, written largely by his assistant John Seigenthaler. The title brings to mind the theme of *Why England Slept*, the internal sapping of a democracy's strength. By the late 1950s Robert was troubled that the FBI was more energetically hunting Communists than pursuing gangsters.

Bobby's first venture into presidential politics had not brought out the aggressive moralism characteristic of him. After

working for Jack's 1956 vice presidential bid, he had joined
Adlai Stevenson's campaign party, at least in part to gain knowledge about presidential campaigning. He despaired of Stevenson,
who spoke from prepared texts even at whistle stops; he could
never get it clear, observed the Kennedy who could move from
moralist to politico, that it was not so much what he said as how
he said it that counted. "This is the most disastrous operation
you ever saw," Robert complained. Stevenson "gives an eloquent
speech on world affairs to a group of twenty-five coal miners
standing on a railroad track in West Virginia." Kennedy quietly
voted for Eisenhower.

At the end of 1959 Robert began work on his brother's
presidential campaign, displacing Theodore Sorensen as manager. Decisions were made ably by a staff chosen on the basis of
experience and loyalty to the Kennedys. The family, Hubert
Humphrey complained in the important Wisconsin primary,
made him feel like an independent merchant competing against
a chain store. He spoke of "ruthlessness": easy money, dirty
rumors, a manipulating of the anti-Catholic issue. Robert, for
example, repeatedly said that Jimmy Hoffa would do anything
to beat Jack Kennedy in Wisconsin, as though Hoffa were somehow in Humphrey's camp. A journalist remarked of Robert's
role in the 1960 campaign, during which he often played the
heavy to deflect criticism from his brother, "He has all the patience of a vulture without any of the dripping sentimentality."[9]

Schlesinger, in his biography of Robert Kennedy, stands by
his earlier portrayal of the Kennedys as underdogs, victims of
religious prejudice. The liberal Humphrey had reason to think
otherwise, for in West Virginia he became the real victim of the
religion issue. John and Robert Kennedy were the first national
politicians to turn religious bigotry into a weapon against itself.
Drawing on the reservoir of tolerance created during World
War II in comics, on the radio, on posters, in government pronouncements, John Kennedy declared, "Nobody asked me if I
was a Catholic when I joined the United States Navy." It was
a gamble, but it turned out that the West Virginia voter was

not going to be cast in the national media as a prejudiced hick. It was Robert Kennedy's touch to persuade Franklin D. Roosevelt, Jr., to contrast John's war record with Humphrey's absence of one. Roosevelt was later to blame his descent into the mud on Bobby's determination to win at any cost.

At the Los Angeles convention Robert figured notably in the drama of Lyndon Johnson and the vice presidency. It seems a good guess that his opposition to Johnson was intended partially to appease liberals. But their further conciliation was in order. Robert had to offset the southern strategy that he and his brother had played at the 1956 convention and as recently as 1959 in dealings with southern governors. Robert told Jack's campaign adviser on civil rights, Harris Wofford, "We really don't know much about the whole thing. . . . I haven't known many Negroes in my life." Then he surprised Wofford by accepting a strong civil rights plank.

Had Jack seen the explosiveness of the racial issue more clearly, he might not have appointed his brother attorney general, for much of the hostility of segregationist whites was to be directed at that office. But the idea of making Bobby attorney general was several years old. Joe is quoted in the *Saturday Evening Post* of September 7, 1957, as saying that Bobby would hold that office, and Ted the Senate seat from Massachusetts. Robert was barely thirty-five when he was appointed attorney general, taking charge of 30,000 employees and a $30 million budget.[10]

In his early days in his brother's cabinet Bobby could direct his aggressiveness toward foreign policy. He went along with the invasion of Cuba, and he called Undersecretary of State Chester Bowles a "gutless bastard" for not wanting to send troops to the Dominican Republic during an alleged crisis there in 1961. Throughout his brother's administration Robert aided in the development of the Special Forces, and he was involved in a program, applying particularly to Vietnam, for training foreign police forces in such activities as crowd control.

As attorney general, meanwhile, he first pursued not the

violators of civil rights but an old prey: organized crime. Appalled by its infiltration of legitimate business and by the FBI's disproportionate attention to communism, he enlisted his own Narcotics Bureau and the Internal Revenue Service in the fray. Justice's organized crime section quadrupled in size and coordinated the fight. Kennedy was being obtuse if he did not recognize that the rich information the FBI was supplying him by 1962 had to be coming in part through extensive wiretapping, much of it illegal. The result of the drive against crime was, however, impressive. Convictions by the department's organized crime section went from 96 in 1961 to 373 in 1963. American justice had gained some victories, but it had paid for them. The cost was in the use of laws and government agencies to punish behavior that was outside their province. Louis Gallo was convicted for false statements on an application for a Veterans Administration mortgage. Another conviction of a suspected racketeer, later overturned on a technicality, was for possession of dead fowl in violation of the Migratory Bird Act. Wherever these ideas were spawned, their adoption was in the spirit of the Justice Department under its unresting new chief. Robert Kennedy, in pursuit of a goal to which ambition or morality directed him, was not cautious.

He was cautious when as attorney general he first encountered the race issue. His prudence accorded with that of the administration as a whole and with his own political past, in which the race question had not been important. The chronology of Robert's growth in commitment to racial justice belongs with the story of his brother's administration, and much of it concerns the forces that pressed upon the government: the black congregations and the northern white freedom riders who made sure the issue would not conveniently recede and the southern white mobs and law officers who had the misfortune to receive national news coverage, so pulling down the old system over their own heads. All this contributed to the political transformation of Robert Kennedy. His transformation was sharper and faster than that of others in the administration. He retained enough of conventional Democratic politics to be able to boast to an interviewer in 1963 that more had been done for business in the last three years than ever before, but by then Robert had put the rights issue ahead of economics. When the President, the Vice President, and adviser Lawrence O'Brien wished rights legislation to go after tax reduction, the attorney general and his Justice Department did not want to wait.[11]

In civil rights Robert Kennedy's driven moralism, once preoccupied with anticommunism and racket busting, was finding a new cause. And here his conscience was vulnerable to the Catholicism that he had taken more strictly than Jack had, for the church was pressing for integration.

The church of the Kennedys, in fact, had many elements of teaching and tradition that should have contributed to the emergent progressivism of the brothers. Catholicism in this century has probably preached a greater respect for the state than have the Protestant sects, presenting it as one of the foundations of the moral order; historically the church has been less militantly individualistic than Protestantism. And Catholicism has gathered much more in the way of a communal life than has been the case for either main-line or evangelical Protestantism. The feeling for the community within Catholic culture has expressed itself in any number of ways, from saloons to ward politics to the communion service itself. Catholicism has looked to shelter the individual within its charitable organizations, its religious orders, its services, and its sacraments. Such social and religious practices perceive society as being richer than the collection of wealth-seeking individuals that the ideology of the American right depicts and the elder Kennedy had embodied. It is unlikely that this particular side of the Catholic experience did much to shape the politics of any of the Kennedy brothers. The church in this country had for years been more vocal in its anticommunism than in its quest for social justice, and in Europe much of the communal implication of Catholicism had gone to a corporatist philosophy not capable of translation into an American democratic idiom. Much of what the church here had to offer Bobby, insofar as it was a central influence, was the inculcation in him of a conscience as demanding as it was abrasive. Beyond that, during his career the church acted increasingly as a social critic, was beginning to press during the late fifties for integration and not many years afterward becoming one of the most progressive of major American institutions, a champion of migrant workers, welfare programs, and disarmament.

At least once during his first years in office Robert Kennedy turned to the left of his preoccupation with organized crime. Under his direction a 1962 conference considered differences between the effect of the justice system on the poor and its workings for the rest of society. Afterward he instituted an office of criminal justice to see to such equitable provisions as free counsel for poor defendants. By 1962 Kennedy's angry energy was pouring itself into the race issue. A year earlier he had turned it on "gutless bastards" who did not want to invade the Dominican Republic; now he targeted whomever was not up to his standards, at the moment, on integration. On May 29, 1963, he interrupted a meeting of Lyndon Johnson's committee against racial discrimination, angry at what he took to be an inadequate effort to reform a government agency. "You mean," he shouted to James Webb of NASA, that "you have 40,000 employees and one-and-one-half men working on this?" He swore at Webb, glared at Johnson, and departed as abruptly as he had come.

Kennedy might act the bully. But his irritability could easily flare at others who acted so, if he detected anything that smacked of moral self-indulgence or emotional excess. Five days before his display of anger to Johnson's committee he had met in New York City with James Baldwin and other black artists and intellectuals. He was astonished when Jerome Smith, a CORE worker who had been beaten in a southern jail, denounced the administration for failing to protect civil rights workers and said that he did not feel obliged to fight for the United States while discrimination continued. Kennedy made the point that his grandparents had encountered discrimination. Baldwin adequately replied, "Your family has been here for three generations. My family has been here far longer than that. Why is your brother at the top while we are still far away? That's the heart of the problem." The gathering offered a foretaste of the verbal manners of the late sixties, the rhetorical violence—"being at this meeting makes me want to throw up"—that would pass for honesty. Anthony Lewis records Kennedy's recollections: "James Baldwin couldn't discuss any legislation. . . . He didn't know anything." The verbal anger, in Kennedy's doubtless unfair opinion, was the way a black achiever could compensate for his distance from the ghetto, and the abrupt young Kennedy would not have wished to be ensnared in anyone's strategies of compensation. But what of his display of temper in front of the Johnson committee shortly afterward: was that his compensation for his own chastisement less than a week before?[12]

After Jack's death Robert remained as attorney general, giving legitimacy to the new Johnson government and working hard on the civil rights legislation of 1964. But deprived of a beloved brother and a nearly certain route to political greatness, he took some months to recover his bearings. The situation was unique. A popular President assassinated in his prime had left an heir. Sooner or later, many people thought, Robert Kennedy would be President. Teddy, too, some believed. The phrase "Kennedy dynasty," spoken frequently enough during John's presidency, now became a commonplace. The 1964 Democratic Convention showed a film on the life and death of John Kennedy. The applause that followed went on for almost half an hour; then Robert, in one of the most moving appearances of his life, evoked his brother's memory in an address that swelled to a familiar passage from *Romeo and Juliet*:

> . . . *when he shall die*
> *Take him and cut him out in little stars,*
> *And he will make the face of heav'n so fine*
> *That all the world will be in love with night*
> *And pay no worship to the garish sun.*

But Lyndon Johnson, living now in the shadow of the martyred President, had no use for Robert Kennedy, who wanted to be his Vice President and successor. Each wished to inherit the Kennedy dream. The device the new President chose to rid himself of Robert Kennedy was to eliminate the cabinet from consideration in choosing a vice presidential candidate. Robert soon resigned to run against the liberal New York Republican Kenneth Keating for Keating's Senate seat.

Robert's political candidacy seemed a ruthless invasion of the state, and it expressed the aggressiveness that made him stand out even within this most aggressive of callings. The *New York Times* endorsed Keating, saying that Kennedy aroused "an uneasiness that is no less real because it is difficult to define"—a statement eloquent of the pained sensitivity that liberalism can employ on the attack. But Robert Kennedy had spent his boyhood in New York State, not in Massachusetts, and the Democratic leadership had been looking for a strong candidate to oppose the popular incumbent Keating. He was an appropriate senator, along with Jacob Javits (and for that matter Keating), for the state that had long distinguished itself for progressive political leadership. He could hardly lose in that year of Republican catastrophe with candidates scurrying from Barry Goldwater. Kennedy money again flowed, paying for extensive footage of the candidate that was made available to television stations across the state. While Robert did not do impressively among white liberals, more than ninety percent of New York's black vote went to him. Though smaller than Johnson's triumph in the state, his overwhelming victory gave him an independent power base for 1968 or 1972. Thereafter he espoused a politics of dissent and reformation that, along with his name and past, gave him a fully distinct liberal political identity.[13]

Kennedy's years in the office of attorney general had done much to prepare him for that identity. Nothing indicates that he would have discovered the race issue on his own or felt deeply about it, but dealing with the assaults on freedom riders and the integration of southern universities forced him to recognize the moral significance of the events. That both black Americans and segregationists perceived him and his office as a source of the assault on white supremacy must have contributed to his perception of himself as irrevocably a figure in the civil rights movement. Particularly through the influence of David Hackett, his friend from childhood and now head of a federal agency on juvenile delinquency, Robert became especially concerned with the problems of the young poor, touring Harlem, pushing legislation on youth delinquency through the House, beginning to think about poverty in the ways that he would be doing a few years later, when the issue of civil rights and the issue of social and economic justice merged. Allen Matusow, a sharp progressive critic of the decade and its central figures, finds Kennedy as attorney general to have been entirely genuine in this. It is evidence that on poverty, the most difficult and telling of concerns, his leftward progress was beginning well before his brother's death, well before opportunism might have tempted him in search of presidential constituencies. At least one other social program, now known as Volunteers in Service to America (VISTA), is traceable in part to the attorney general, who headed a study group that worked out a plan for a national service corps. Robert Kennedy was among the least hawkish administration advisers during the missile crisis. And disillusionment over Vietnam came more swiftly to him than to most Americans. As early as September 1963 he suggested that it might be time to withdraw. Once, when Dean Rusk said that our enemy in Vietnam was China—in effect, that we needed to teach China proper international behavior—Kennedy with his taste for censorious moral expression responded, "So we can blow women and children apart in somebody's else's backyard."

The new senator's championing of domestic reform could appear to be an extension of his work in the Justice Department and of the promise that his brother's administration had been lucky enough to become identified with. But his repudiation of the war was, not by intention but by its effect, a break with the foreign policy of the Kennedy troops and a violation of the Kennedy way of publicly closed ranks. In 1967 Robert McNamara also made the break, quietly, resigning from the office of secretary of defense and becoming head of the World Bank.

Meanwhile, Robert, as his brother's heir, was a political presence and an international figure. On a trip in 1965 to Latin America, where he spoke the sentiments of advanced liberalism, crowds greeted him as a statesman. The next year he was in South Africa, defiantly talking about the civil rights movement in the United States. Black Americans trusted the Kennedy family. A youth was asked why Kennedy's visit to his neighborhood could make for such excitement. "His brother, the President, was like a father to me" came the answer, in tribute to a President who had taken so long to assume fatherhood of a civil rights bill. And from the beginning of his senatorial career Robert Kennedy was staking out visible ground on the left of conventional politics.[14]

Kennedy's first senatorial speech in 1965 was one of many warnings against the spread of nuclear weapons. The same year he was horrified at the slaying of 100,000 alleged Communists in Indonesia when the rest of the nation was ignoring the event or taking silent satisfaction at Indonesia's turn rightward. He harshly criticized our military intervention of that year in the Dominican Republic. In February 1966 he urged bringing the National Liberation Front into the Vietnamese political process. In a Senate address of May 9 and 10 on the Alliance for Progress and our proper role in Latin America, he argued that the United States should press for such programs as land reform: "Large-scale land redistribution necessarily implies major changes in the internal political balance of many Latin American countries—away from oligarchy and privilege, toward more popular governments." And that summer Kennedy talked with Schlesinger about setting up a Washington information center that could propose standards for elections in Vietnam, investigate whether the military gains of defoliation were worth the violence to the Vietnamese people, and look into the practice of turning over prisoners to the South Vietnamese, who employed torture.[15]

The problems of poverty and discrimination he addressed in a way that combined left liberal concern with tough-mindedness. He disliked welfare for reasons that conservatives could share: it breaks up families, weakens self-respect, and puts the poor under the scrutiny of a middle-class bureaucracy. He advocated replacing welfare with jobs at public or business expense and bringing the affected communities into the decision-making process.

Data gathered by the President's Committee on Juvenile Delinquency, with Attorney General Kennedy at its helm, had contributed to the War on Poverty, particularly the community action component. Schlesinger writes that it was Robert who induced Sargent Shriver to add community action to the program. After walking through New York City's afflicted Bedford-Stuyvesant section on February 4, 1966, Kennedy persuaded businesses to invest in the area with community control over allocations. He spoke in July 1967 for a bill giving businesses tax incentives for providing jobs in poor neighborhoods. The Kennedy-Clark bill aimed to create two million public service jobs. Kennedy had observed while attorney general that employment would reach beyond civil rights legislation as the solution to racial problems. That does not set him far from his antagonist Lyndon Johnson; Burke Marshall had remarked at about the same time that Johnson, thinking back to his early days and his leadership of the Texas branch of FDR's National Youth Administration, treated the race issue as a poverty issue to be addressed with jobs.[16]

Pressing for a left liberal social program, the former counsel for the McCarthy committee was also now a civil libertarian. As attorney general he had not so begun. He had authorized, condoned, or overlooked numerous wiretaps. To the FBI, suspicious that Martin Luther King, Jr., had connections with communism, he gave permission to tap some of King's phones. Victor Navasky in a careful examination of the event suggests the attorney general's desire to placate the FBI. Robert's account in an oral history he and Burke Marshall provided in 1964 is that he initiated the tap, concerned about King's possible associations with Communists. A reasonable conjecture is that Robert, protective as always of the Kennedy name and political fortunes, wanted to see whether the civil rights leader was someone from whom the administration would have to distance itself. The language of Robert Kennedy and Burke Marshall is remarkable for its preoccupation with Communists; it is straight out of the fifties. But Kennedy had also removed cold war restrictions against travel to Communist countries and concurred in his brother's commutation of the sentence for convicted Communist Junius Scales, who had refused to give the names of his associates as the act of penitence the American right demanded of former Communists. As a senator Kennedy stood against Redbaiting. He insisted that the Marxist historian Eugene Genovese, a teacher in the New Jersey state university system and therefore a public employee, had the right to express his hope for a victory for his nation's battlefield opponents in Vietnam. At a press conference in 1965 Kennedy made a stir by defending peace advocates for their gift of blood plasma to North Vietnam. In 1966 he publicly criticized Attorney General Nicholas Katzenbach for refusing to permit the burial in Arlington National Cemetery of the World War II hero and Communist party leader Robert Thompson. He told Schlesinger that if the people at rest there—his brother, of course, was among them—could know of the burial, they would not mind. And in 1967 he was one of only two senators to vote against extending the life of the Subversive Activities Control Board.[17]

Now the acerbic moralist was no longer wielding the instrument of federal law but lecturing the community at large from the posture of angry virtue. He told a group of midwestern businessmen that New York City was populated by more rats than people. "Don't laugh," he said in cold, even tones to his audience when it seemed amused. At the University of Oklahoma early in 1967 he asked how many in the assembly favored draft deferments for students. The audience was a forest of upraised arms. How many favor an escalation of the war? he asked. Either exceptionally honest or exceptionally weak in survival skills, his victims again raised their hands. How many had voted for both? was his next and inevitable question. The same year he polled a group of students at his wife's alma mater and discovered that the women of Marymount favored increasing, not lessening, the bombing in Vietnam. "Do you understand what this means?" he demanded. "It means you are voting to send people, Americans and Vietnamese, to die. . . . Don't you understand that what we are doing to the Vietnamese is not very different [from] what Hitler did to the Jews?" Later Kennedy told a group of college students in Omaha, "You're the most exclusive minority in the world. . . . Look around you. How many black faces do you see here, how many American Indians, how many Mexican Americans? The fact is, if you look at any regiment or division of paratroopers in Vietnam, 45 percent of them are black. How can you accept this?" And at the University of Indiana Medical School after a talk about programs for the poor Kennedy was asked where the money would come from to pay for the programs. He stared at his well-to-do audience and answered ruthlessly, "From you."[18]

Robert Kennedy was a passionate man in an impassioned time, as his brother had been cool, in public style at least, in a time that favored coolness. John Kennedy had seen poverty in Cambridge slums when he ran for Congress in 1946, and he had seen it, so it has often been remarked, when he campaigned across West Virginia in 1960. But while his sympathetic feelings were visible, he did not transform them into political passion. Robert Kennedy, to the contrary, was angry at a migrant camp owner who kept his employees in filth. Speaking of his tour into the Mississippi delta in the spring of 1967, the black lawyer Marian Wright later remarked to Roy Wilkins of the NAACP, Robert "went into the dirtiest, filthiest, poorest black homes, and he would sit with a baby who had open sores and whose belly was bloated from malnutrition, and he'd sit and touch and hold those babies." His concerns ranged far: he tried to get airlines to stop giving away free samples of cigarettes ("Our customers like them," Delta replied).[19]

Robert Kennedy made his leftward journey in a large company. A portion of educated liberalism, continuing its adherence to effective big government and the premises of the cold war, was sounding increasingly conservative both in its support of the war in Vietnam and in its scorn of the New Leftist idea of dismantling central government institutions. But some of the academic community, hitherto loyal to traditional liberalism, was moving to the left in varying degrees. Radicals and the youth culture, notably the young so self-congratulatory about their dates of birth, which freed them from responsibility for the world's perversities, were rejecting the limits of political possibility that American liberals had long trusted in. A portion of young radicals, some of them conventional in conduct and others adopting the hair, clothes, and drugs of Haight-Ashbury, accepted the disciplines of political militancy, which can range from the drudgery of leafleting and phone banks within the system to a night or a year in jail for acts of resistance. Others of the newly liberated young ventured into hippie communes, convinced of their right to experience freedom and pleasure in its totality, right now and at no price. The race issue—which, with the discrediting of segregation, had seemed the one subject to be moving to a new consensual understanding—was producing an unexpected factionalism as black and white radicals rejected integration and called for black separatism.

Robert Kennedy was not to be an Eisenhower or John Kennedy or Lyndon Johnson, appearing to represent that amorphous and, in fact, mythic entity, the collective interest. He and his supporters were more explicit in naming injustice and suffering, more passionate and insurgent, than was to the taste of conventional politicians. It was appropriate to a Kennedy whose personality was sharper and more acrid than Jack's. Robert came, for example, to regard the NAACP and the Urban League as insufficiently militant and lacking bases in the urban ghettos. Even King's Southern Christian Leadership Conference was at once too evangelically traditional and too middle-class. Kennedy preferred Floyd McKissick's Congress of Racial Equality. Yet he was perhaps the last politician in the late sixties who could salvage a coalition between blacks and whites and the last liberal who could communicate with white working-class voters.[20]

By the time Robert Kennedy became a presidential candidate there was a clear sense of living in the sixties, a notion that there was something unique about that fact. People thought and talked about the decade. Thinking and talking are themselves cultural events, the most interesting of events, and they can reflect and evoke modes of feeling and behavior. By whatever other measures we may call the sixties a legitimately separate period, we can certainly do so by the measure of its own self-consciousness.

What was the effect upon contemporaries of the sixties, of the very notion that they were living in a distinctive period? There was undoubtedly something like a surrender of judgment and will on the part of a few cultural radicals by late in the decade. The conviction was abroad that history was meaningless, that the times could dictate their own terms, that the new American must be in a demonstration, or on drugs, or in a commune, or be irrelevant. But coexisting was a rational belief that the times did demand a reformation in racial relations and in the most intimate connections among people. Americans knew what they have almost forgotten: that quick change is possible. Perhaps what was most noticeable about the mentality of the 1960s was the sense that private lives were partaking of something of the energy and direction of public events. If the decade did not draw so large a portion of the population so forcibly together around a single event as had the Great Depression, it related a larger range of private considerations to public events. There were, of course, the great public happenings that cut deeply into lives: the civil rights movement, the Vietnam War, the assassinations, the beginnings of the women's movement. And along with these was the remarkable proliferation of public gatherings: the sit-ins, the March on Washington, the campus demonstrations, the rock concerts, the folk masses, and the national gatherings that took place whenever the country watched a speech or an event over the almost new medium of television. The events that swirled about President Kennedy had offered, along with his own figure, early foci for a public consciousness as Americans watched their TVs. And Robert Kennedy late in his career seemed always to be in the center of a crowd, the core of an instant community.

Like his brother, Robert was the personification of young maturity, and the young surrounded him. It has been the conviction of psychotherapy since the days of Freud that youth is something faintly pathological to be gotten over as quickly as possible, with maturity being a state of conquest over wayward and agonized adolescence. That belief has more truth than does the mindless celebration of adolescence that this country can indulge in. The decade of the sixties learned to respect not the Pepsodent prettiness that advertising equates with beauty and youth but the rawer emotions of that youthful cadre angry and confused at the war or the more introspective confusions explored in a few youth-centered movies. But the 1960s, which displayed a richer, more various, more discordant presence of youth in American society than the television commercials would ever choose to do, did not know how to deal with the passing of youth into later life. So by the early 1970s confident rebels were changing into slightly aging hippies who wanted the sixties to be forever. Some beneficiaries of the youth rebellions were so in love with their own liberation from middle-class concerns that on principle they would refuse to limit their freedom with children of their own. Still others went straight from long hair into three-piece suits and money and conservatism, as though if youth is a fling of ideals and temper tantrums, maturity must properly be a time of sensible Republicanism and bank accounts.

Among the more established groups that did not take to

the political manners of an assertively young radicalism was the Americans for Democratic Action. In the autumn of 1967 the organization voted emphatically against dumping Johnson. Then it fervently applauded Professor Daniel Patrick Moynihan's plea that it ally with conservatives to save society from being torn apart by campus radicals. The attitude of the ADA liberals is explainable. First in the dangerous times of Redbaiting and then in the placidly conservative mid-1950s, they had been instrumental in keeping liberalism alive. Now their brand of liberalism was under attack by young people who had no memory of the Great Depression, no adult memories of the second Red scare, no great respect for the structures of the welfare state that had brought some measure of relief, if not full economic justice, to the impoverished. Recalling the times when triumphant rightwingers had denounced progressive teachers and threatened the freedom of the campuses, they now watched in rage as students shouted down professors who were not impeccably radical. Their anticommunism was in a fine liberal antitotalitarian tradition that abhorred the one-party militancy of North Vietnam. Such were the polarizations of the times that the fury of the ADA liberals at the young radicals placed them in the company of right-wingers. Still, in 1967 the ADA gave Kennedy and only one other senator a rating of 100 percent.

Robert Kennedy, who had detested Adlai Stevenson's indecisiveness, was thrust into the role of a veritable Hamlet as the 1968 primaries approached. He must have had a party loyalist's traditional hesitancy to challenge an incumbent President belonging to his own party. That was the kind of consideration that Eugene McCarthy, establishing an identity outside party and nearly outside politics, would be less susceptible to. Most Democratic bosses believed that Johnson would be a strong candidate against the likely Republican nominee, Richard Nixon. Robert and the President were known to be cool to each other, moreover, and Kennedy would not want to appear to be seeking a grudge match. By this time it was plain that racial conflict, disgust with young radicals, and further alienation of the South from the Democratic party were moving the country to the right. Kennedy was out of step when, for instance, he called for an expansion of Great Society poverty programs. Nor was it yet apparent that the peace movement was in the political mainstream. The Tet offensive, a propaganda though not a military victory for the Vietcong, had not yet occurred, and most of the peace candidates Kennedy had backed in the fall 1966 congressional elections had lost. It could be presumed that Johnson was in command of the war issue and could make gestures of scaling down the conflict as the elections approached.

Nevertheless, a meeting of Kennedy people on October 9, 1967, determined that Robert should be more active politically and more in touch with party leaders and that a poll should test his strength in New Hampshire. The poll, which registered a two-to-one margin for Johnson over Kennedy, confirmed his advisers in their caution. But Kennedy knew that the country was off its moral course, just as his brother's presidential advisers had been in October 1962, when he told them an attack on Cuba would be reminiscent of Pearl Harbor. Vietnam was inexorably pushing Kennedy into a race he did not want to make even as it was bringing about the fall of the Johnson government.[21]

Within three days after Eugene McCarthy's near victory in New Hampshire had made the Democratic primaries of 1968 an open contest, Robert Kennedy entered the field against him. Even now as he sought to win the peace movement that McCarthy commanded, he could still exhibit a Kennedy's somewhat presumptuous idea of his country's place in the world. "At stake," he said in his statement, ". . . is our right to the moral leadership of this planet." University liberals were horrified at the brutal opportunism of his late candidacy. Of all that can be said of the Kennedy ruthlessness in politics, this is one accusation that will not stick. Eugene McCarthy did not like the grubby realities of politics. He had neither the appeal nor the will to shape a wide coalition among electoral groups, bringing blacks, labor unions, and cities into the same camp with those university activists and suburban liberals whom he attracted.

Later in the spring he would disastrously slacken the pace of his campaigning. It was not the obligation of a more aggressive politician and a more politically promising standard-bearer for the peace forces to remain outside the campaign as an act of courtesy to McCarthy. Once McCarthy by his courageous bid in New Hampshire had demonstrated the vulnerability of Johnson, he had done precisely the service to the peace movement which he was capable of. It was now legitimate for Robert Kennedy to do what he was capable of: to lessen the possibility that the Johnson forces, working for the President himself or for Humphrey, would carry the popular primaries.[22]

Johnson, faced with the formidable candidacy of Kennedy as well as with the considerable threat of McCarthy, declared on March 31 that he would not seek reelection. His withdrawal from the race did not undermine the platform of the Johnson Democrats, who had Hubert Humphrey as their candidate. It did potentially threaten Kennedy, for McCarthy was likely to gain the credit for it. Humphrey did not enter the open primaries. There the contest was between McCarthy and Kennedy.

McCarthy was perfectly suited to represent a liberalism alternative to Kennedy's. Among the first to suggest McCarthy's candidacy had been some of the Stevenson people. They were grateful for his speech nominating Stevenson at the convention of 1960, and they doubtless saw the two to be alike in their almost deliberately unpolitical manner, their air of conversationally addressing an audience on some point of curiosity: more alike than either Stevenson or McCarthy and a Kennedy who was comfortable with the ways and machineries of mass politics. McCarthy embraced the peace movement, or, rather, let its collegiate wing embrace him. Kennedy worked with the peace movement since he agreed with its objective of disengagement from Vietnam, but for all his moralistic abruptness, so akin to the angered idealism of the peace forces, he was not really of their persuasion or temper. He referred to one peace group as "Adlai's people." He was not in agreement with the belief, popular among the more committed of McCarthy's supporters, that we should withdraw from Vietnam at any or almost any cost. He thought that the United States should use its military presence to get a satisfactory compromise settlement there. As for McCarthy's sense of politics or of rapport with the public, he spoke of blacks early in his campaign as "those people"—not disrespectfully, but as people out there somewhere, with the rest of the population, to be dealt with because it had to be done. If McCarthy's campaign had a central theme to reinforce his attack on American involvement in Vietnam, it was a criticism of the overgrown and misapplied powers of the presidency that he was at least ostensibly seeking to occupy. That theme signifies McCarthy's detachment from democratic politics. The presidency in all its power has been popular in this century, for the social programs it has organized and for its charismatic stature. An assault on a wayward presidency may not be politically offensive, but neither is it likely to touch vital public beliefs or interests—which is not to say that it is an illegitimate political act: democracy will never have more critics than it needs.[23]

The first encounter between Kennedy and McCarthy came in Indiana. The Kennedy camp had expected to win in that state, with its concentrations of blue-collar and black voters, a vote so large as to give him the remaining primaries. Kennedy did win and by 42 percent to McCarthy's 26, with the state's governor taking the residue. Kennedy won by a substantial margin in Nebraska as well. In Oregon McCarthy could draw on a suburban population that was an exceptionally large percentage of the state's electorate, a group of voters especially susceptible to a candidate who offered not hard-edged economic and social programs but skepticism and dry wit. John Kennedy in 1960 had purposely stayed out of Oregon, which his polls showed could be lost to a write-in vote for Adlai Stevenson, the intellectuals' candidate, and Robert, it is apparent, was still having the difficulties with middle-class white liberals that had given much of New York's liberal vote to Keating in 1964. Oregon delivered to Robert Kennedy an experience none of the brothers had ever undergone: a defeat in a popular vote.[24]

California, too, contained many liberals uneasy at Robert Kennedy's reputation for ruthlessness and power seeking, and like Oregon, it had a party organization inheriting Stevensonian sympathies. On that state's television talk shows Kennedy had to soften his image, while McCarthy found this medium a perfect forum for addressing liberals. In a TV debate the night before the election, when McCarthy spoke for integration, Kennedy argued that the more important solution to the troubles of the black residents of Los Angeles was not integration into the white neighborhoods of Orange County but the economic development of their own communities. He thereby combined his idea of community action with his willingness to go after the blue-collar electorate that seems to have interested McCarthy so little. California provided Kennedy with large black and Hispanic populations. On the night of his California victory, the night of his assassination by the Jordanian Sirhan Sirhan, he also beat McCarthy and Humphrey in South Dakota, next door to their own Minnesota. Had he lived and gone on to win in the New York primary, Chicago's Mayor Daley and other politicos might have swung behind him.[25]

Kennedy's campaign had much in common with the campaigns of the two other most visible dissidents, McCarthy and George Wallace, in that year of the New Politics. Each candidate was characterized, more so than most politicians, by some particularity of style: McCarthy's dryness; Kennedy's energy, candor, and craggy looks; Wallace's friendly pugnacity. Each was distinctive in his ability not merely to gain the support of a portion of the populace but to speak to it in its own style. Each challenged regular party structures and leaders and built his power on direct appeal to voters. But here Kennedy differed from the other two rebels, a difference in degree that was also a difference in kind. While McCarthy kept to his middle-class peace constituency and Wallace's American party reached for the blue-collar vote, Kennedy addressed a wide range of people: politicos, liberals, working-class Democrats who might have followed Hubert Humphrey; antiwar leftists and intellectuals who did not turn to McCarthy; and, of course, the black and Hispanic voters. He had not been so captivated by the anger and rhetoric of the New Left as to turn his attention from the traditional New Deal constituencies. His scolding of middle-class audiences, for all its irritability, suggests an implicit assumption that his listeners shared his moral vocabulary and could be won not by self-interest alone but by moral suasion. His popularity among the minorities, moreover, obliged liberals even of the McCarthy stripe to take him seriously. In the breadth of his reach toward the electorate, Kennedy was more in the tradition of political insurgency than were the New Leftists who wished to speak for the People but not for the people.

There is no evidence that Robert Kennedy, the candidate who wanted his nation to be fit to assume "the moral leadership of the planet," ever abandoned the Wilsonian and the techno-cratic ideals of his brother's administration. During John's presi-dency Robert had been a strenuous advocate of counterinsur-gency techniques; in *To Seek a Newer World*, published in 1967, he argued that counterinsurgency is a preventive against massive military involvement and described it as a program not merely for training local police forces but for land reform, schools, clinics, roads, unions, and "a share for all men in the decisions that shape their lives"—a program of winning the allegiance of the people. Counterinsurgency, then, means, on the one side, a trained expertise in the spirit of John Kennedy's presidency and, on the other, the nurturing of local participatory communities, in the spirit of the community action that Robert Kennedy wanted at home. It was in the tradition of cold warriors who even in the late 1940s had wished for alternatives to reaction and to Communist totalitarianism; its operatives would be as skilled and workmanlike as a Green Beret officer or a Peace Corpsman; its product would be a participatory democracy tougher than the communities of feeling that cultural radicals romantically con-ceived.

Like his brother the President, Robert became the political figure to whom the civil rights movement looked, but unlike

John, he would finally embrace the movement with full awareness of its force and meaning. He came to speak for a peace movement more far-reaching than the politics of partial détente that had triumphed in John Kennedy's test ban treaty. And the extension of the welfare state for which John had mildly spoken had in Robert an articulate and insistent advocate. Still, without John Kennedy the civil rights movement might never have become identified with the entire federal government and so might not have prepared the way for the great civil rights laws for which Lyndon Johnson did the work and the memory of John Kennedy received much of the credit. Without John and all the trappings of Camelot, American progressivism might not have felt the stirring that resulted in the Great Society legislation. In his absence the federal government might not have taken on both that new militancy in international relations and that new commitment to détente that together would confuse the course of American diplomacy for years to come. By the time that Robert Kennedy became a politician of presidential stature almost all the political vocabulary of the 1960s, that which had come of the hopeful John Kennedy years along with the more radical varieties, was in circulation. Robert Kennedy's task was to know that vocabulary and to speak for as large a number of concerns as could possibly find alliance with one another. Neither his upbringing nor his temperament had equipped him for the new political movements that found him attractive. Nor did his mind and presence create ideologies or politics; both he and his brothers, it is said, hated abstract ideas. What he did form was a fleeting coalition of admirers.[26]

Robert Kennedy's constituency, along with those forces that were on its left or beyond, represented a fragile moment in the history of American progressivism. Shortly after his death its ideological components would be spinning farther apart. The celebration of feeling and the project of self-discovery that had given their energy to radical politics in the late sixties spawned cults of therapeutic self-development that had nothing to offer to a cooperative politics. Other persuasions with far more to say struggled with their separate concerns and vocabularies. Some liberals turned to an ecology movement that would mistrust the whole scientific and technological apparatus that both old liberals and old leftists had believed in. While the political wing of the women's movement began winning victories in the courts and legislatures, some feminist rhetoric encouraged resentment and a cultivation of an angry independence. The labor movement drifted, unsure of what it wanted or how much it could effectively demand. Still unattended to was a program for a politics that could bring such separate languages together as components of American progressivism.

7

Edward Moore Kennedy: The Heir

EDWARD KENNEDY WAS IN HIS SHIRT SLEEVES, AN ARM AROUND A Kennedy child, raising the other hand to the knots of people from the rear platform of Robert Kennedy's funeral train in its progress from New York City to Washington, D.C. Edward alone now represented the family that had come to stand collectively for the progressive wing of American establishment politics. His visible presence on the train was a way of announcing that the Kennedy public need not feel robbed of its hopes.

As the heir to the politics of his brothers Edward is the most philosophically complete of the three, the most consistent from year to year. He is also the repository for the idealism of the 1960s. The youngest of the Kennedy children, he has nothing in his past like that early monomaniacal anticommunism of the fifties that liberals find repugnant in his brothers John and Robert. He encompasses the potentially conflicting strains in the politics of his brothers, having Robert's vocabulary of social justice and both elder brothers' familiarity with the politicos. If Edward Kennedy has profited by inheriting Kennedy liberalism instead of having to devise or to stumble upon it, coming after his brothers has also diminished his stature. However harshly some academic liberals have turned against the memory of John Kennedy, there remain in the press and elsewhere recollections of a more vigorous and hopeful time when the nation was challenged and drawn together for common purposes and of a President whom the nation was grief-stricken to lose. And Edward Kennedy is faulted for lacking the rigid integrity of Robert. He is, in fact, a harder legislative worker and a better orator than Jack, and his graciousness contrasts with Bobby's moral bullying. But he does not have the energy of the 1960s to draw on, or the glamour of two brothers who suddenly emerged as national figures. Whatever success he can win comes in good part from his ability to labor hard and skillfully at conventional political tasks: devising legislation; working on committees; answering the needs of a nation of constituents.[1]

Of Edward Moore Kennedy, born on Washington's Birthday, 1932, his mother has recalled: "You wonder if the mother and father aren't quite tired when the ninth one comes along. You have to make more of an effort to tell bedtime stories and be interested in swimming matches." Older brothers and sisters, Rose Kennedy has explained, "seem to be more important in a family and always get the best rooms, but Ted never seemed to resent it." As the ninth and last child Ted was perhaps not subject to the full force of his father's ambitions. He turned to his brothers and sisters for parenting, learning harsh lessons from the competitive Joe, Jr. When he was just seven, his eldest brother took him sailing for the first time. It was a race. What followed is recorded in a simple tribute composed by Teddy not long after Joe's death: "We were going along very nicely when he suddenly told me to pull in the jib. I had no idea what he was talking about. He repeated the command again in a little louder tone, meanwhile we were slowly getting further and further away from the other boats. Joe suddenly leaped up and crabed the jib. I was a little scared, but suddenly he zeized me by the pant and through me into the cold water." Teddy was "scared to death practully . . . and then he lifted me into the boat. . . . One felt . . . he got very easily mad in a race as you have witnessed." When the family was reminiscing about the lost brother and someone spoke of his calm, Edward demurred: "He threw me in the ocean." While studying at a British school, Edward once received from his father, the ambassador, a lesson in a more equitable application of Kennedy self-assertiveness. Could he punch back a fellow student who had punched him? Teddy asked. "Of course" was the answer, more entrepreneurial than ambassadorial.[2]

Ted was a chubby, happy, healthy little boy who wanted to please and had many older brothers and sisters to please. "Dear Daddy," he wrote, "I have been to the Worlds Fair today with Jimmy Murphy. I went into the swimming pool with my clothes on but the pool was empty. Love from Teddy." Gregarious and likable, he accepted innocently his family's glittering life. During his first day in the ambassador's thirty-eight-room mansion on London's Grosvenor Square he corraled several servants to play "department store." The staff rode floor by floor in the embassy's elevator, as Teddy gravely announced each stop. After receiving communion from Pope Pius XII—the first American child so honored—Teddy charmed the press. "I wasn't frightened at all. . . . He told me I was a smart little fellow." That he was forever falling down at dancing school must have won him further good will, if not from his dancing partners. At a birthday party for Jack in 1946 fourteen-year-old Ted, after many toasts had been drunk, stunned the festivities with a toast of his own to Joe, Jr., already dead for three years: "To our brother who is not here." The good nature endured. Meyer Feldman, a former aide to John Kennedy, has commented that as a tennis player "Teddy bends over backward to be fair, is scrupulous about the calls, always giving the advantage to his opponent—and I haven't seen that in any other Kennedy."[3]

Like his brothers before him, Ted boarded at an early age in prestigious New England preparatory schools. He attended eleven different private academies during his elementary grades, and friends attribute his affability to a childhood of constant friend making. He once told a reporter, "I don't have any complexes about it, that school-changing." It seems not to have been so easy as that. When Edward was eight years old, Rose put him in Robert's school, Portsmouth Priory, a Benedictine institution in Rhode Island, so that the two could be together. The school normally took in boys from the seventh grade up, so Teddy found himself among older boys who could be unfriendly. While he was on his back taking a pummeling from a bigger boy, reports his biographer James MacGregor Burns, Bobby came along but refrained from interfering, reasoning that Edward should learn to take care of himself. After three months, however, Edward was transferred. Among his unhappier periods was his time at Cranwell, a Jesuit school in the Berkshires, where he felt lonesome. More settled, at any rate, was his four-year stay at Milton Academy, the boarding school not far from Boston that Robert had also attended. His teachers there have remembered that he participated in many extracurricular activities, particularly debate and football. Physically courageous like his brothers, but stronger than Jack and Bobby, he played varsity end during his junior and senior years. His debate coach considered him precise in thought, good at rebuttal, and well versed in issues. He was on a team that defeated the Harvard freshmen.[4]

In the autumn of 1950 Edward Kennedy entered Harvard, though he had finished thirty-sixth in a class of fifty-six. By his college days he was well over six feet tall and weighed 200 pounds. His brothers had gamely, dutifully run up and down the Cambridge gridiron, but they had never exhibited Teddy's verve, and John and Joe, Jr., had never lettered in the sport. The prospect of bettering his older brothers beckoned. Then, in the spring of 1951, he put a blot on his career. Though he was not flunking Spanish, he worried that his grade in the introductory course might not be high enough to exempt him from future language classes and could keep him from varsity football the following fall. He or some fellow athletes suggested that his roommate's brother take the exam for him. Kennedy went along with the scheme; this most easygoing of the brothers was none-theless a Kennedy opportunist. "It was an easy test," Kennedy's substitute reported, "and I think you did very well. But I think we're caught." The teaching fellow proctoring the exam had recognized Kennedy's cohort; within hours a dean expelled them both. Disgraced, Teddy enlisted in the army and served in Europe as a private. "Sixteen of the most worthwhile months of my life," he wrote his former headmaster at Milton, "but an experience I never want to duplicate." Harvard deans readmitted him in the fall of 1953.[5]

The GI newly mustered out did better in Cambridge than the preppie from Milton. A more subdued Kennedy buckled down to his studies. He also made the varsity football team. His coach recalls, "Teddy was good at everything. If you gave him a job to do, he'd do it, exactly as you asked." Kennedy's grand-standing plays in two Harvard-Yale games earned him hero status among peers on the team and the varsity letters that had eluded his brothers. Shunning the programmed summer vacations at Hyannis Port, he adventured on a trans-Pacific yacht race one year, taught water skiing at Acapulco another, and once worked as a forest ranger. Edward's studies at Harvard ended creditably, with honors in history and government. His teacher Arthur Holcombe has commented that while young Kennedy had the ability, he had no ambition to do more than keep in good standing. It had become, it appears, a tradition for Kennedys to be competitive in everything except studies.[6]

Disappointed when Harvard Law School rejected his application for admission, Kennedy traveled for a year in Europe and North Africa, occasionally gathering items for the International News Service, owned by his father's famous friend William Randolph Hearst. Family connections had again served the Kennedys. And Edward's experience served his brother; he has suggested that his conversation with John about Algeria sparked the Senate speech critical of French policy in that country. Upon his return home he followed the path of another brother, entering the University of Virginia Law School in the fall of 1957. Of

Edward at Virginia, a friend noted, "Teddy takes in everything you tell him and gives it back exactly." But his grades averaged C. Besides being chairman of the student law forum, he won the school's prestigious moot court competition, overwhelming his opponents with careful research and forensic ability. The final case, which he won in partnership with his housemate John Tunney, later a senator from California, was argued before a panel that included Justice Stanley Reed of the Supreme Court. Ted was graduated from law school in 1959.

In Teddy's student years another quality had revealed itself alongside the good fellowship: the peculiar Kennedy aggressiveness, the pursuit of success as something to be won again and again. Beneath the affability, suggests Burns, there was rage. At Virginia Edward ran red lights and sped through the streets of Charlottesville. During a game of rugby he lost his temper so often that the referee threw him out of the game. In a sport that prides itself upon self-control Kennedy three times fought with opponents. "I never kicked anyone out of a game in thirty years," the official said later, "except him."[7]

Public life, the pursuit and use of power, gripped Edward Kennedy even before he left law school. During 1958 he worked eagerly in his brother's campaign for reelection to the Senate. His father financed and finagled behind the scenes, but Teddy proved no mere ornament. He toured Massachusetts constantly, sometimes filling in for Jack. Campaigning absorbed him. "I remember once we got stalled in a traffic jam," a friend recalls, "so he jumped out and started going from car to car shaking hands and attaching bumper stickers."

After a brief honeymoon trip to South America with his new wife, Joan Bennett, Teddy labored hard for John in the presidential campaign that followed the senatorial victory. In West Virginia the friendly Ted was a success at addressing working-class crowds. In Montana he rode a bronco in a rodeo; in Wisconsin he skied off a formidable 180-foot snow ramp. He had a penchant for frankness in public life that kept him from a major policy role, and his inexperience often showed. In 1960 he wasted time in Wyoming and Colorado and Utah while avoiding the critical state of California. Politics there defied an old-fashioned schooling in the ethnic and class maneuvers of Massachusetts. No entrenched Democratic machines called out voters in the big cities. Nixon narrowly carried California and nine other western states. "Can I come back home," Teddy wired the President-elect, "if I promise to carry the Western States in 1964?"

The indefatigable Joe Kennedy had now scouted Ted's own future. The former ambassador is supposed to have said of Jack's Massachusetts Senate seat, "Look, I paid for [it]. It belongs in the family." Jack had persuaded the outgoing Massachusetts governor, Democrat Foster Furcolo, to appoint the President's former college roommate Benjamin Smith to the vacant seat. Smith could be counted on to bow out gracefully in 1962, when Edward would be thirty years old, the age of eligibility for the Senate. The standby Senator Smith even used John Kennedy's former senatorial staff on Capitol Hill. Teddy came back to Boston, rented a town house on Beacon Hill, and went to work in the district attorney's office as an assistant prosecutor. Soon afterward the twenty-eight-year-old lawyer plunged into a campaign of sorts. "I know he is running for something," a family friend confided to a reporter. Kennedy spoke dozens of times each month at PTA meetings and charity groups, in front of the Sons of Italy or the Kiwanis. At staff headquarters in Jack's former office pins on a huge map of Massachusetts marked the cities and hamlets Ted had visited. He traveled to South America, Africa, Italy, and Ireland to broaden his credentials. A bevy of ward politicians flocked around the latest Kennedy. When asked what problems his son might encounter in a premature candidacy, Joe Kennedy snapped, "None."[8]

That estimate was optimistic. Ted's drive for the 1962 Senate nomination required more than revving up the well-proved Kennedy machine: again a Kennedy was in trouble with liberals. Professors at Harvard and MIT openly opposed Edward's candidacy as contrived. The liberal National Committee for an Effective Congress attacked him. Old-line Irish politicians thought him presumptuous. He had not worked his way up, and besides, one politician grumbled, "The Kennedys always run solo," ignoring the rest of the ticket. James Reston of the *New York Times* wrote that voters would perceive three political Kennedys as an invasion of Washington. A powerful opponent also appeared. Edward McCormack, nephew of Speaker John McCormack, first in his class at Boston University Law School and editor of its law review, had built a record as one of the state's chief prosecutors, and he aspired to the Senate. If the Kennedys pushed Teddy, the speaker might damage the President's program on Capitol Hill. Nonetheless, Edward, just after his thirtieth birthday, told Benjamin Smith of his intentions. Smith stepped aside.

Edward McCormack did not. Opinion polls, however, showed Kennedy the favorite among Democrats and the winner, unlike McCormack, against any Republican in the fall election. Politicians and voters could remind themselves of what the brother of a President could mean for their state in federal money and patronage. Kennedy organization and Kennedy money blitzed delegates. At the state convention in Springfield McCormack had one phone line, while Kennedy forces had a twelve-line switchboard in addition to people on the floor with walkie-talkies. Kennedy swept the convention and became the state party's choice in the primary election. But the popular vote was still to come, and McCormack continued his fight.

It was a contest between liberals: McCormack strong on questions of civil rights and civil liberties; Kennedy advocating federal aid to education, federally assisted medical insurance, and repeal of discriminatory quotas in immigration. So McCormack made Kennedy himself the issue. "You never worked for a living," he taunted his opponent during a debate. The "office of United States Senator," he observed, "should be merited, not inherited." At least once he mocked Kennedy viciously: "If his name was [only] Edward Moore, with his qualifications, with your qualifications, Teddy . . . , your candidacy would be a joke." But attacks were fruitless in the prosecutor's faltering campaign.

There was a supposed exchange between Teddy and a factory worker: "I hear you never worked a day in your life," said the worker; "well, you haven't missed a thing." It is superfluous to say that the Kennedy machine was relentless. "He can do more for Massachusetts," correctly proclaimed the billboards in support of the President's brother, and bumper stickers were issued in typical Kennedy profusion. Edward, like his maternal grandfather, repeatedly sang "Sweet Adeline," a brand of politicking inconceivable of the aloof Jack or the tense, earnest Bobby. Kennedy's increasingly professional style, the barnstorming of a glamorous family, his easy access to the White House—all added up to an outstanding victory. The newest Kennedy won 64 percent of the vote in the primary, and McCormack retired permanently from politics.[9]

Kennedy's fall campaign against the Republican nominee, George Cabot Lodge, was anticlimactic. The White House dispatched advisers to drill Kennedy on facts, write speeches, and hone his political skills. Again money gushed out of Kennedy bank accounts. Teddy's speeches convinced audiences that young as he was, he understood the issues. His voice and his looks reminded everyone of the President. His opponent, the son of the man Jack Kennedy had beaten in his 1952 Senate race, was himself only thirty-four and had worked only briefly in a federal post, serving in the Department of Labor. Experience, then, was not a large issue. Kennedy and Lodge debated in a desultory way, both ignoring the gadfly candidacy of H. Stuart Hughes, a Harvard professor running on a peace platform. The gentlemanly campaign— "Ivy League all the way," one reporter wrote—ended predictably: Kennedy swamped Lodge in the November election. At the age of thirty the last Kennedy became the junior senator from Massachusetts. He would serve out the last two remaining years of Jack's term before coming up again for reelection.[10]

After the President's death in 1963 Edward Kennedy found solace in an extraordinarily busy reelection campaign. He visited Massachusetts every weekend for nearly seven months, talking with local party leaders and appearing at hundreds of meetings around the state. It was clear that he would again win handily, but he kept driving himself. Then, on the evening of June 22, 1964, after voting for a strong civil rights bill, he left Washington on a private plane. The pilot headed toward West Springfield, where a Democratic convention had just renominated Kennedy for a full term in the Senate. In an attempt to land at the local airport despite heavy fog, the plane crashed into an orchard three miles from the runway. One passenger died instantly; two others, Senator Birch Bayh of Indiana and his wife, Marvella, stumbled out of the remains of the plane with minor injuries. Kennedy lay in the wreckage, his back broken. The Bayhs pulled him from the plane. Surgeons at a local hospital worried about possible paralysis. Doctors wrapped him in a canvas cocoon, and he lay suspended from a metal frame for nearly six months. Kennedy made use of his recuperation to learn economics, history, and related fields from visiting members of liberal academia that his family had been turning to. Serious campaigning ended. Joan Kennedy made a remarkable stand-in that fall, appearing all over the state and reporting to crowds on her husband's medical progress. Sympathetic voters, moved by his misfortunes and his brother's death, reelected Ted in November over Republican Howard Whitmore by the greatest plurality in Massachusetts history, seventy-four percent, a margin of some 1.2 million votes.

Joan Kennedy, who adapted so rapidly to the demands of public life, had not been trained for it. Born in 1936 and reared in Bronxville, New York, Joan Bennett had lived a childhood different from the purposeful, urgent existence of her future husband. Life at undemanding preparatory schools and four years at Manhattanville College, a strict Catholic school favored by socialites, insulated her from the world. She floated through a brief but successful modeling career and at a summer party in 1957 met Ted Kennedy. Fifteen months later they married. A cardinal officiated at the wedding; wire services telegraphed pictures of the two throughout the United States. Two years later Joan's brother-in-law was President. Two years after that her husband was a senator.[11]

It was Joan's fate that instead of sharing in the public glamour of a glittering Kennedy career, she was forced for years to guard her privacy while her husband's fortunes and the public perception of him fluctuated. An attractive woman with an ingratiating shyness, she had to cope late in the 1960s with the public knowledge that her marriage was widely discussed. At twelve her son Teddy developed a rare bone cancer in his leg, which had to be amputated, and like the wife of President Gerald Ford, she had to struggle with alcoholism. Joan's life mirrors the fortunes of the Kennedy family. After three brothers had died, one as a war hero and two others at moments of charismatic success, the family was destined to a grimmer public existence. It is as though the Kennedys had become expressive of a time confronting more stubborn problems requiring a more private courage, with less visible economic and political energy to draw upon—a time more aware of the intractabilities of day-to-day life.

As if in preparation for that unhopeful period, Edward Kennedy from early in his senatorial career had worked to be a success at the undramatic strategies of legislation. In this he could be contrasted with both his brothers. John Kennedy had never appeared to be centrally a senator rather than a politician using the Senate as a convenient vehicle. Robert Kennedy lacked the manners or patience to work congenially in the Senate. Teddy, the friendly youngest child, quickly won over the older Senate leadership. In the years to come he was to be a superior senatorial and political technician, maintaining a large staff, employing specialists for specific issues, doing favors for constituents and fellow senators, which included making campaign speeches for Democratic colleagues, and securing for liberals strategic spots on the party's senatorial committees. His office has been described as resembling an Irish political machine. In his earlier years in the upper house, moreover, Edward Kennedy was already pressing for major liberal legislation, the kinds of legislation that later, after liberals had lost the presidency and the mood of the mid-sixties, would be a remaining instrument of progressivism. He attempted to add to the civil rights bill of 1965 a provision banning the poll tax. It was an admirable measure within the liberal tradition, but its application was limited. It would have affected only four states, and even there only contests for state and local offices, for constitutional interpretation had already effectually banished the poll tax from federal election. Many liberals supported the amendment, but President Johnson, Vice President Humphrey, and Eugene McCarthy were among the opponents. Some liberals feared that the addition would endanger passage of the bill; for once a Kennedy, possibly out of self-aggrandizement, had chosen a course less tactically cautious than fellow liberals preferred. The Senate did not adopt the ban, but in 1966 the Supreme Court found the poll tax unconstitutional. Whether Kennedy was wise in wishing the provision added to the rights bill, the skill with which he had managed the fight won praise from *Newsweek*, which also lauded his craftsmanship in getting through the Senate a bill easing restrictions on immigration. And the next year he led a successful assault against Senate passage of a measure delaying implementation of the Supreme Court decision requiring equal apportionment in voting districts.[12]

In 1966 Kennedy had committed an act of no political shrewdness but considerable loyalty to a Kennedy family friend when he proposed and Johnson nominated Boston Municipal Judge Francis X. Morrissey for a federal judgeship. The candidate was considered lacking in the experience requisite for the job, and the business looked like a favor to old-fashioned machine politics. When it became apparent that the selection was going nowhere in the Senate, Edward withdrew Morrissey's name. In his service to Boston politics and a friend, a Kennedy had yet again set himself apart from those liberals whose quest is for an immaculate politics.

As chairman of a Senate subcommittee on refugees and escapees Kennedy made an inspection tour of South Vietnam in 1965. Perhaps in loyalty to John Kennedy and to the President who had succeeded him, and certainly out of an obligation to Saigon that few major political figures would have scorned in 1966, he spoke that year of the strength of our commitment to South Vietnam. The chairmanship, though, was revealing to him and gave him a chance to reveal to the Senate and the public what the war was doing to the Vietnamese people. He commented that military victories would be meaningless unless the Vietnamese could be brought to hope for a better life. That sounds like the beginning of a break with the administration's war. But it could also represent the thinking of a cold war liberalism that, in reaching its most progressive implication, was about to pass beyond its own earlier premises. By 1967 Edward was using the committee to assault the American failure to provide adequately for Vietnamese victims of the war. Another visit to Vietnam confirmed him in his criticism of the war effort for its effect on civilians.[13]

Kennedy unsuccessfully worked in subcommittee hearings and on the floor to effect a reform of the selective service system. He favored a scheme abolishing student deferments and a conscription by a national lottery. The 1967 plan had the good liberal objective of eliminating the privileged status of the student population, which was also on the whole an economically favored class. Equally liberal in its concern was Kennedy's opposition to an all-volunteer army, which he feared would be divided on class and race lines between enlistees and officers. But his support of conscription, so modified, in fact, as to draw more extensively on that part of the nation that contained the most vocal opponents of the war, separated him as a traditional liberal from the radicals who would have discarded the draft and the war together.

Kennedy was doubting the wisdom of our policy in Vietnam, although he was for a time on agreeable terms with the President. But he worked for Robert's presidential nomination in 1968 after first advising him against the politically risky at-

tempt. Upon Robert's death some liberals, discouraged at Mc-
Carthy's air of detachment from campaigning, became interested
in Edward. Mayor Daley, recognizing the plight of the party,
turned to him as a popular and unifying figure. He proposed
that Kennedy offer himself as vice presidential candidate; after
Edward's unequivocal rejection of that idea the mayor suggested
to him that he head the ticket. (McCarthy also explored the notion of Kennedy's heading the ticket but would not agree to
nominate him.) Edward, for personal reasons, thought himself
unready to be President and refused to oppose Hubert Humphrey. During the convention he was in Hyannis Port, spending
much of his time on a sailboat.

He nevertheless inherited the family ambitions. His own career proceeded as it had, with a diligent application to the work
of the Senate. So thoroughly had the Senate become his forum
that to the surprise of political observers, he sought out one of
the most politically charged and surely one of the most irritating
of legislative positions. In January 1969 he defeated Russell Long
of Louisiana for the post of whip to the majority party, which
obligated him to pursue his fellow Democrats one by one whenever the occasion should arise and shepherd them to a floor
vote or otherwise to the support of Democratic legislation. Self-
advancement; a resolve to promote the kinds of programs he was
dedicated to; perhaps even a craftsmanlike appetite for the legislative and political process: these are motives that suggest themselves. In March 1969 Kennedy proposed replacing nationalist
China in the United Nations with Communist China. He waged
a fight against President Nixon's plan for developing the anti-
ballistic missile (ABM) system. Then, on July 18, came Chappaquiddick.[14]

The day began happily. Garry Wills, who has few friendly
things to say about the Kennedys, points out that the party at
Chappaquiddick Island was not a planned tryst but was rather
the reward to a hard-working political staff originally devoted to
Robert Kennedy and that Mary Jo Kopechne attended it in that
spirit. Afterward she and Kennedy drove down a dirt road in

place of the public highway he was to claim he had been seeking. The car slipped off a bridge into a body of water; Mary Jo Kopechne died, and Kennedy escaped, later explaining that he had dived many times trying to save her. What followed has raised questions that bear not so much on Kennedy's private life as on his ability to act in a crisis. That he waited eight hours before he reported the accident, meanwhile talking to a large corps of advisers, has suggested panic and indecision. It was possibly just the opposite. Kennedy behaved as Kennedys behave: measuring each action and consulting the extended family of Kennedy associates. His first call was to Burke Marshall. Among the others summoned to consultation was Robert McNamara, to whom Kennedys had customarily turned. A young woman had died, and we have no way to gauge the depth of Kennedy's private grief. But he meanwhile had a political career to which he was devoted, and he acted with a calculation that we normally expect and want from public figures in crisis. Mary Jo's mother simply observes of the accident, "It doesn't mean he won't be a good President."[15]

Seven days later Kennedy spoke to a television audience. A comment, perhaps entirely sincere, came across to many critics as self-serving, bathetic, tasteless: "I wondered whether some awful curse did actually hang over all the Kennedys." Edward's call for Massachusetts voters to advise him whether to resign from the Senate reminded liberals of their arch foe, Richard Nixon, and his Checkers speech in the 1952 vice presidential campaign. After a cursory local investigation Kennedy was permitted to plead guilty to a minor charge of leaving the scene of an accident. The state district attorney and his staff opened their own investigation, but Kennedy's lawyers used legal tactics to delay it. Six months later a state judge presided over a private inquest. He issued a strongly worded report: "I . . . believe that Edward Kennedy operated his motor vehicle negligently . . . and such operation appears to have contributed to the death of Mary Jo Kopechne." But nothing came of it. Critics see in the ease with which Kennedy escaped the possible legal consequences of the evening the power of the Kennedy family so to manipulate events as to survive political danger. But that is not a revelation. The family has been manifestly aggressive and manifestly willing to put anything it can to its service, and in this case it would have been logical for the Kennedy people to plead with authorities not to drag on an investigation of an incident that was damaging a promising career. Still, it was not in the best form for Edward to say, in September 1973 with reference to Watergate, that this country "stands for the principle that no man is above the law."

William Buckley soon after observed that the event had broken the "dynastic claims" of Edward Kennedy, forcing him to get by on his own. It was a brilliant guess, and if not quite true—Kennedy has continued to be known, and will continue to be, as a Kennedy—it does point up the violence of the rupture that Chappaquiddick effected between Edward's future and his past. Yet the ways in which he set about rebuilding his career involved the same methodical, programmatic activities that had marked his senatorial behavior for years.

In the late summer of 1969 Kennedy continued his attack on the ABM with a Senate speech against it, and while the Senate failed by one vote to reject funding for it, his effort is credited with Nixon's reduction in the proposed number of missile sites. Kennedy called for a firm minimum tax on the wealthy. He also worked for legislation insuring the vote to eighteen-year-olds. During the American incursion into Cambodia in 1970 he called for his nation's withdrawal from that country and Vietnam. Kennedy conducted his reelection campaign that year with the aggressiveness of a confident politician, and in a civilized contest with Republican Josiah Spaulding, who did not make use of Chappaquiddick, won 63 percent of the vote. Kennedy, however, was not managing the range of his activities so successfully as his outward achievements would indicate. Burns describes months of relative inactivity after Chappaquiddick; that, added to the death of his father and the demands of his Massachusetts campaign, made him less than effective as Senate whip.

While Kennedy was out of town, Robert Byrd of West Virginia was collecting votes, and in January 1972 the party caucus chose him to replace Kennedy. For once Edward had faltered in the senatorial process that he has usually employed so skillfully in the fashioning of liberal policy and of his own career. But the defeat freed him from the time-consuming Senate floor, which the position required him to police.[16]

Just afterward Kennedy became chairman of a Senate subcommittee on health policy, therein regaining a specific hold on the legislative system. In the Senate he pressed for cancer research, whereupon President Nixon declared war on cancer. But his particular interest has been in the staggering uncovered costs of medical care that the majority of Americans face. In 1971 he introduced a bill for a national health insurance program. His effort to get the controversial measure through Congress, during which he published his polemic *In Critical Condition* for the cause of health insurance, led him to work out a compromise involving more deductibles with Arkansas Representative Wilbur Mills, chairman of the House Ways and Means Committee. Again a Kennedy was under attack from liberals, and the resentment on the part of his staff at this liberal passion for perfection is reminiscent of Robert's anger at the legislators who had wanted a civil rights bill more rigorous than President Kennedy's. The attempt at a compromise fell apart, and Edward Kennedy continued to press for a comprehensive plan. Like Bobby and unlike John in the directness with which he could confront an issue of the maldistribution of wealth, he spoke of the need "to counterbalance the magnetic medical drawing power of our rich suburban areas." A bill Kennedy championed in 1974 would have required all medical students supported with federal financial aid to serve for two years after graduation in communities having inadequate medical staffing.[17]

For years Edward Kennedy had been chairman of the subcommittee investigating the plight of refugees and escapees, and this assignment, too, became an instrument for articulating his own policies. After the military coup that overthrew the leftist

Allende government in Chile, he held hearings that detailed torture in that country, and he denounced violations of human rights there. As a senator and a Kennedy he had also to address himself to the biggest question in foreign policy: the war in Vietnam. He had now come around to full opposition. In 1973, while his country was still at war, he suggested that it aid both North and South Vietnam with postwar reconstruction. Kennedy joined a majority of his Democratic colleagues in opposing the saturation bombing of Cambodia and Laos begun in the spring of 1973, and he denounced the compromise that allowed bombing for another forty-five days. He also led the opposition in the Senate to further American aid to the South Vietnamese police. Yet Kennedy has been identified less than either of his brothers with questions of American policy abroad. It is principally on domestic issues that he has built his politics.[18]

The most politically desirable issues, of course, are those promising an eventual consensus. National health insurance, whatever it might do to spread medical care more evenly, is an issue that could draw wide agreement. Medical bills threaten the white middle class along with the black poor. The elderly, the politically important constituency that Medicare directly addresses, have needs we all respect if only because those needs may someday be ours. And however indifferent the nation might have appeared to be on the question of campaign financing, a national consensus might take shape on the good liberal program, for which Kennedy worked, of public financing of federal election campaigns and limitation of private funding of congressional candidates. (The political history of his family, of course, is a study in why that reform is needed.)

Busing had an entirely different political prospect. By the mid-seventies Kennedy was mildly in favor of busing, perceiving it as a means of last resort in compensation for de facto segregation and recognizing as well that at least among white opponents of busing, the opposition conveyed a racism that needed to be confronted. But on this question his Boston constituents would not allow even a modestly affirmative position. When he supported the court order of W. Arthur Garrity, a federal judge appointed by his brother, requiring a racial mix in Boston's schools, many of the Irish of the city along with Councilwoman Louise Day Hicks turned on Kennedy angrily. In the fall of 1974 he attempted to speak in a rally called by ROAR (Restore Our Alienated Rights). The mob silenced him with tomatoes and eggs, ugly epithets, and shoving and kicking. The following April a crowd in North Quincy verbally assaulted him. John and even Robert Kennedy had hesitated to commit themselves to what are today seen as the minimal essentials of the civil rights revolution. Now a Kennedy was speaking for one of the most unpopular of rights measures.

Edward Kennedy has been capable of supporting other politically risky causes: amnesty for Vietnam era draft evaders and gun control, a measure apparently commanding a plurality of popular sentiment but unpopular among Americans who have strong feelings about it. He has told a hostile audience in Alabama that Lieutenant William Calley of the My Lai massacre got justice from his court-martial, and an audience of American Legionnaires that war resisters who left the country should get full amnesty because "if the war was wrong . . . , they were right." But in a speech before the Chicago Crime Commission in October 1975, several months after the incident in North Quincy, Kennedy advocated mandatory minimum sentences for serious street crimes. With a conservative, John L. McClellan of Arkansas, he sponsored tough crime legislation. This hard line on crime, which the American Civil Liberties Union condemned, was of a kind to win the approval of the Boston white constituency that Kennedy had angered. But it was also consistent with the mentality of a family that had never been completely at home with the social and cultural liberalism of the intellectuals. After the nuclear accident at Three Mile Island Edward called for a two-year moratorium on constructing further nuclear plants, along with a separate agency to investigate mishaps so that the Nuclear Regulatory Agency would not be the sole investigator of the application of its own rules. But he has not shared in the suspicion of economic and technological growth that now animates some liberals. Favoring deregulation of airlines and trucks, though not of oil and gas, he cosponsored a deregulation bill with conservative James Buckley of New York, and he proposed tax incentives for business.[19]

Kennedy has also shown some care to keep up contact with social forces that liberals of a more puristic strain abhor. In 1973 he went to Decatur, Alabama, to be Governor George Wallace's guest at a July 4 banquet. Praising the courage of the governor, who had been confined to a wheelchair since being shot during his presidential primary campaign a year before, Kennedy criticized the people of both Wallace's state and his own for failing to provide blacks with equal access to education and jobs. In October 1983 Kennedy took seriously Jerry Falwell's accidental invitation to speak at Falwell's fundamentalist and right-wing Liberty Baptist College in Lynchburg, Virginia. He argued there against bringing religious intolerance into politics. At Harvard Falwell had been booed; Kennedy remarked on the contrast between that behavior and the courtesy accorded him by Falwell's students.

This maintenance of connections with conservative forces puts Edward Kennedy where his family has located itself and, through all its leftward shifts, has attempted to remain: within the Democratic coalition politics that goes back to the New Deal and earlier. And of the three brothers he has maintained for the longest time and with the greatest consistency the reach that Robert's presidential candidacy was beginning to achieve between popular social elements within the party and liberals who veer to the left.

Kennedy speaks to a national rather than to a statewide constituency, and he has been doing so for more than a decade. It was taken as completely natural, for example, that his Chappaquiddick address should be nationally televised. Yet he has been the most cautious of the three brothers to campaign actively for the presidency. In 1972 he decided that he would not run unless the convention were stymied or Wallace were nominated; even so, the delegates treated his stunning late-night speech as an event. He did not stay long in the 1976 presidential contest and that fall won reelection with 77 percent of the vote. In 1980 at last he became a persistent presidential campaigner. Even then, however, he did something uncharacteristic of a Kennedy: he entered the race without successfully massive preparation.

The decision to open his campaign with an interview by Roger Mudd on November 4, 1979, it seems, was based on Mudd's fairness to Robert in 1968. But in his questioning of Edward, Mudd set John and Robert at their best against Teddy's vulnerabilities, dwelling on Chappaquiddick and his marriage. John Kennedy had used television; Edward allowed it to use him. Edward Kennedy, the less manufactured and posed of the two brothers, had begun his campaign by submitting to an interview of unexpected aggressiveness, edited to his further detriment. The most famous segment was the stuttering response to Mudd's query about why the senator wanted to be President. The reaction to the reply among commentators and the public marks the decline in the fortunes of the Kennedys as a media family. No unfavorable publicity had followed the blank stare James Reston received on asking the newly elected John Kennedy what his philosophy was, what vision he had of the good life, and no derision had followed when Robert, asked by a Canadian television interviewer what his values were, snapped, "I can't answer questions like that. Ask me something specific." The whole incident nevertheless brings to mind Feldman's description of Edward at tennis: that he is the least competitive Kennedy.[20]

Kennedy did go on to conduct a vigorous campaign, but the Mudd interview was a foretaste of its ill fortune. President Jimmy Carter had the advantages of an incumbent seeking renomination by his own party. Simply being President put him forever before the public; not until March did he leave the White House for an explicitly political event. His effective explanation for why he was ignoring the campaign was that he needed to be in Washington to monitor the hostage situation in Iran. Kennedy was beaten by two to one in the January Iowa party caucuses. The hostage crisis and the Soviet invasion of Afghanistan were in progress, and the presidency was enjoying the enhancement in the public eye that times of international drama bring it. The *New Yorker*, interpreting the Iowa result, observed that the party had been troubled by Kennedy's insurgency. Always shadowing Kennedy was the notion that he had not yet proved himself, had not fully matured. Before he announced his candidacy, to be sure, polls had indicated that he was the most powerful of possible contenders. That, however, had been before the hostage taking. Besides, Kennedy in the months of the primaries became defined as not quite an adequate candidate, as the contestant who had started out badly. Putting himself to the left of Carter on questions of public spending, Kennedy won a number of important states, Pennsylvania, Michigan, New York, and New Jersey among them. Yet long before the convention he was effectively out of the race. The convention was the best thing that happened to him. His speech there, a moving appeal to the party to be faithful to its past dedication to social justice, identified him with those Democrats who disliked the party's drift to the right or to a cautious ideological neutrality, and perhaps he gave some articulateness and cohesion to their cause. Beyond that, his speech contained enough rousing rhetoric to move any good Democrat. The address demonstrated that he could be a powerful speaker, not the unsure contender of the Mudd interview.[21]

In his 1982 reelection campaign Kennedy maintained a devotion to the New Deal tradition within a party that had been scrambling to prove that it, too, hated government spending. He differed with President Reagan on national health care, on the financing of programs aiding the handicapped and offering legal services to the poor, and on the administration's tolerance of repression in nations like El Salvador. He attacked the failure of the free market administration to drop subsidies for tobacco growers and to abolish regulations of the trucking industry. A leading target of the New Right, Kennedy won reelection to the Senate by 65 percent. This loyalty to a practical liberalism of social programs identifies, as much as anything else about his political style, the public character of Edward Kennedy. That liberalism is now in opposition to the dominant politics. Edward's "generation of the Kennedys can never command again," wrote Murray Kempton in November 1983; "it endures in him only to oppose, the most elevated of all political functions." That describes only the present position of those Democrats who have not allowed their politics to shrivel to the size and shape of the neoconservative times.[22]

On December 1, 1982, Kennedy removed himself from consideration for the 1984 presidential campaign, and he did so with a candor that betokens the slight ironic apartness from the conventions of politics that had also marked John: "I don't think it's any mystery that I want to be President." As if to accentuate the public and journalistic curiosity with which, largely through his own indiscretions, Kennedy has had to deal, Ted Koppel on an ABC-TV's "Nightline" at the time concentrated on the stories of cheating and infidelity. It can be assumed that in 1984 Kennedy will at least be a power broker. And beyond 1984—Edward is a Kennedy in ambitions and one of a number of Democratic politicians able to attract many of the scattered, quarreling elements of liberalism in a small cold time of an ascendant political right.

To speak of the public that John and Robert represented, the public for which Edward Kennedy has reached, is to refer to two entities. There are the groups that have contributed to the solid basis of the family's power: blue-collar Democrats, liberal professionals, Catholic ethnics, blacks, Hispanics, democratic leftists, and a good number of Democratic politicians who recognize the Kennedys as politicos. But the Kennedys are associated also with a tone and persuasion that do not define any set of interest groups. A Kennedy could appeal both to the New Deal labor tradition in liberalism and to a newer cultural politics; a Kennedy could capture much of Gene McCarthy's constituency but give it a less elitist articulation; a Kennedy could appeal to a range of Americans looking for something more visionary than conventional Democratic machine politicians could offer yet more solidly grounded in questions of labor and economics and even military preparedness than, say, the ecology movement habitually considers.

Often Kennedy liberalism has been presented here as something that came upon the family. Certainly two of the brothers, Jack and Robert, began their careers looking much like conservatives, Jack talking about the sellout at Yalta and Robert working on the McCarthy committee. Both of them were pulled into the civil rights issue by the events of their times and by their membership in the Democratic party. And John, who by the end of his tenure was an architect of détente, had made the missile gap one of his major issues and had conducted his presidency with assertive displays of American power, which marks the difference between midcentury liberalism and that of the 1980s. Yet this is to be said of the earlier John and the earlier Robert: their rhetoric had seldom narrowed to the pinched tenets of American economic conservatism, and there was a certain largeness and style even to the early Jack Kennedy. It was appropriate that in the 1960s the Kennedys fastened on to the largest, most energetic, most liberating of events, the civil rights movement, and that, as much as anything else, defines their liberalism.

All this is to say that in our Republic without titles of nobility, family does mean something. Perhaps family means all that aristocracies have ever needed to mean: the maintenance of continuity from one time or project to another. The concept of "Kennedy liberalism" is a composite, but it is capable of bringing about the phenomenon that it defines, capable of drawing to the Kennedys those forces that had begun to discover themselves in the presidency of one brother and had acquired an articulate voice in the brief presidential candidacy of another and a persistent legislative artisan of progressive politics in a third. The continuance of family from one generation to another has survived longer in Irish culture than in much of the rest of Western civilization, and the continuance of the Kennedy politics, and through it the sustaining of the New Deal strain in Democratic party politics, represent a conservatism, like that of Irish and other traditional cultures, far more profound than the thin economic doctrine that today passes for conservatism.

The political right adheres to a definable ideology capable of simple explication. Its adherents dislike governmental centralization and spending, and they have a fairly clear conviction that every dollar that comes to you by the workings of the market economy is yours by right, the earnings of your labor, to be surrendered reluctantly, if at all, to social needs. Neither Edward Kennedy nor his brothers have presented a philosophy as simple or explicit as that, answering it point for point. They have spoken for another persuasion that presumes the fortunes of the individual to be more closely dependent on the efforts of the rest of society and believes that it is morally right that those fortunes be so joined.

It is appropriate to Kennedy liberalism that John Kennedy was something of a technocrat, enthusiastic about the space program and using the Peace Corps to solve problems of world poverty through skill and expert knowledge. For modern technology has been the collectivizing enterprise of recent times, bringing together the skills of a Detroit welder and a Mississippi farmer and an Arab oil worker into a world workplace more visible than was any regional economy of premodern times. Liberals today are more skeptical of twentieth-century technology than they were in 1960, and some of them would like a dismantling of it that would probably result in far more decentralization than any Reaganite's dismembering of the federal government. But the liberal internationalist position militates against any return to economic parochialism. The commitment of the federal government to the breakup of segregation, by now a central tenet of Kennedy liberalism, constitutes the largest political acknowledgment in our times that private customs are not merely private.

There is nothing especially new in this awareness of interdependence; it has animated much of American politics of the twentieth century. But Kennedy liberalism, from the first tentative response to the civil rights movement to Edward Kennedy's espousal of a comprehensive national health plan, has given it some of the more vigorous expressions in recent times. That the Kennedy public is, and was from the beginning, a coalition of interests, any one of which might turn against the others if private profit beckoned, is a comment on human nature and also on the ways that American society has always pieced itself together. In our times it has been the destiny of a family rooted once in the squabbling ward politics of the immigrant experience and more recently in the larger coalition politics of the Democratic party to continue in the tradition of putting society together as a cooperative, if only barely cooperative, community.

Epilogue: A Note on Liberal Ideology

The Grapes of Wrath, PUBLISHED IN 1939, IS THE QUINTESSEN-
tial novel of its time. It speaks so surely of a virtuous American folk dwelling on a young, clean land and puts its characters
through dislocation and hardship having enormous political implications—only to give the Joad family no definite politics at
all. In this the novel is like the New Deal itself as a popular political event: an event that was energetic, hopeful, self-conscious,
and in the end, like other American political projects, so lacking
in a finished program that historians labor to figure out what
kinds of philosophical or programmatic schemes guided it. It is
also appropriate, and something of an epilogue to the thirties,
that John Steinbeck in his last days supported with reservations
the American cause in Vietnam. For *The Grapes of Wrath* cele-
brates the nation, attempts to make of the Joads and their desperate westward trek a mythic representation of their country.
And while the most fervent patriotism does not demand uncritical support for every one of a nation's wars, the patriotism that
is implicit in the novel would at least have put a distance be-

tween Steinbeck and an antiwar movement marked at times by flag burnings and a rhetoric of hostility and contempt.

To speak of the New Deal as amorphous is not to say that nothing definite determined its policies. Many interests crowded their imperatives into the federal programs of the 1930s. The most easily recallable of these interests were big business, which got the National Recovery Administration; big labor, which got the Wagner Act; and big agriculture, which got the price support programs. But if interest groups have figured prominently in twentieth-century American politics, it is not because the public has been cynical or selfish but because of a widespread assumption that the nation does not have to do any fundamental political thinking, that there is an American way of some sort that is already doing very nicely, even in the midst of the Great Depression or social strife, needing only to be better supplemented and articulated through particular governmental programs.

Americans in this century have thought that they knew what the word "liberal" means, not as it applies to classical nineteenth-century economics but in reference to the collection of policies and the outlook that have attended the country's transformation into a moderate welfare state. The word by mid-century meant a number of measures alleviating poverty or regulating the economy or integrating the armed forces and an attendant enlargement of the federal government. It meant a greater tolerance for forms of political dissent or of personal conduct than has been common among people calling themselves conservatives. And it meant a diplomatic and military containment of the Soviet empire that leftist critics defined as aggression, along with a degree of diplomatic and rhetorical restraint that right-wingers defined as appeasement.

Expressive of this liberalism was a kind of historiography that Arthur M. Schlesinger, Jr., has spoken for in his studies of American politics. It assumes that it has been the American enterprise since the early days of the Republic to rewin amid changing conditions and reactionary resistance the nation's original promise of freedom and equality. This interpretation in effect substitutes for revolutionist ideologies an assumption that the American experience itself will carry us through. Thomas Jefferson, as Schlesinger has presented him, stood for agrarian democracy; the Jacksonians transferred Jefferson's egalitarianism to the nineteenth-century farm and urban workplace; the New Deal rescued a primal American equality from the hands of twentieth-century reactionaries. In 1965 Schlesinger produced A Thousand Days, his comprehensive study of the Kennedy administration. Written with an inside knowledge of the administration, in which Schlesinger had served as an adviser, the work presents Kennedy liberalism as another instance of progressive politics.

The elements of liberalism as Americans commonly identify them are not bound together by absolute laws of logic. Liberals, for example, have been as little suspicious of the expansion of governmental economic powers as they have been fearful of government restrictions of unpopular political ideas or social practices, and a number of conservatives have been strict constitutional libertarians for good conservative reasons. About the only constant within the mix of policies and ideas that Americans have come to define as liberal is an attitude that a liberal will perceive as compassionate and a conservative will dismiss as irresponsibly soft-minded—toward the poor, toward minorities, toward the victims of Red scares. Even the politics of the early cold war that made liberals ready to confront Soviet ambitions in Europe at a time when many conservatives were still isolationists, and then ready to negotiate when conservatives dismissed negotiation as appeasement, has a common source in what conservatives have found to be a compulsion to do good. Yet if liberals have seemed more tender-hearted than conservatives, liberal intellectuals have taken more quickly than their conservative counterparts to the drier regions of the twentieth-century mind: scientific inquiry, behaviorist psychology, administrative expertise. And in their conduct of the cold war, liberals have exalted the virtues of strategy and coolness, while impassioned right-wingers chafe.

Energetically pursuing the public good in its detail, American liberals have not stopped very often to think what the public good or the public or the human community really is. Neither have American conservatives of the same era. The word "conservative" implies a sense of community or continuity among generations and among individuals, but the twentieth-century politics that goes by the name of conservatism favors a less communal economics than liberals do and is not very useful on the subject of community. Americans as a whole, in fact, have for much of their history taken in bulk and without sorting much of the heritage of the Reformation and of the social contract theories. Americans expect people to organize themselves by contract—a political constitution or a business agreement. They also believe in that community—in part biological, partly contractual, in part conventional—that is the nuclear family. Americans believe in private property, and they do not discriminate among the morally contradictory justifications for property, allowing it to come by inheritance, or by the good fortune of a happily placed investment, or by a salary that may happen to be twice as large as that earned by an equally industrious neighbor down the street. Americans believe in the work ethic, but they are not sure whether they mean by this that work is a virtue and a way to self-identity and is therefore beyond exterior reward or whether they mean that you are a fool to do something for nothing. Some of this constitutes not much more than an excuse for barricading yourself and your family behind whatever property the market has bestowed on you.

Liberals have not made an explicit attack on these more anticommunal American traditions or to affirm the more communal traditions. They have instead acted in very particular and often almost unrelated ways that duplicate the tactics of early twentieth-century reformers. Ralph Nader's detailed assaults on shoddy products are in the spirit of the muckraking journalists of the turn of the century. Liberal sociology, with its self-deluding faith in dispassionate research, continues the work of such scholars as flourished at the University of Wisconsin in the days of Robert La Follette. Liberals who wish to subject industry to constantly administered regulation are akin to the progressives whom Robert Wiebe has described in *The Search for Order*, published in 1967. The welfare system that liberalism has created is infinitely better than an unmodified free market. But that system lacks the philosophical articulateness to affirm that a welfare mother on food stamps or a starving East African rescued by American surplus grain is not the recipient of somebody else's property but is receiving what human beings have a right to receive of the world's goods. In the New Deal, when much of the nation was suffering from the Depression and a populist rhetoric prevailed, the concept of a roughly egalitarian commonweal of middle classes and blue-collar classes, of migrants and small entrepreneurs, made its appearance. By the 1960s that vision had faded.

So while there was among liberals in the sixties a certain optimism and an ambition for social justice that reached beyond the immediate objectives of the New Deal, the presidential programs of those later years proceeded in the absence of some one confident concept of the American public. The most vocal segments of that public during the years of Johnson's Great Society were in varying degrees disaffected from the government and at odds with one another: the civil rights movement, black power, the antiwar students, the blue-collar backlash. The designers of the Great Society, however, did proceed according to an idea of sorts, or so says Theodore Lowi in his 1969 study *The End of Liberalism*, one of the most suggestive of recent interpretations of the politics of American liberalism.[1]

Lowi works from the assumption that the self-regulating mechanisms of capitalism and technology will not perform automatically for the social good. At the same time, he contends, capitalism, along with the rest of modern technological civilization, embodies the urge to impose order and rationality, an urge that will not tolerate the irrationalities of an unregulated market. But Lowi will not endorse the Kennedy-Johnson form of liberalism that is the most recent assault on the inequities of capitalism; his book is an attack on that thinking. Will Lowi, then, elect for a mild welfare state that goes about as far as the New Deal went with a few improvements—the kind of welfare state that even right-wingers today accept? Much of the book does argue in that direction. But the most interesting thing about Lowi's work is his liking for government that can make clear laws and declare them with moral authority, a government that could pursue justice and the common good more vigorously than any recent federal administration has done.

Lowi's disagreement is with the differing ideologies that look to some process outside of government as a self-regulating source of public good. It is easy enough to see therefore that he will not call for a return to pure capitalist ideology. More surprising is that he describes modern liberalism as a variant of the philosophy of self-regulation. Modern social science, according to Lowi, dismisses government as an "epiphenomenon," a mere shadow or reflection of real social forces; and liberals suspect the government's laws of trying to freeze and shape what should be a perpetual flow of social energies. Yet liberalism, having the most compassionate of objectives, does have to turn to government to implement its attack on poverty and injustice. The solution that this interest-group liberalism has hit upon is to make governmental programs so vague in their objects, and to delegate so much power to localities and groups for the spending of public money, that government will be merely servicing rather than controlling the competitive social process.

That solution, Lowi says, amounts to a new welfare system. Old welfare, essentially the welfare measures of the New Deal, began by being good legislation: recognizing that capitalism produces poverty, it specifically defined certain categories of poverty or disability and supplied for each some form of relief. Old welfare did not go far enough, but it proceeded from the right premises. New welfare defines the poor as an interest among other interests, encourages the poor to organize, and supplies them with government funds. Such appropriations can get into the wrong hands and, for example, make it possible for a city government to construct housing units so as to reinstate segregation. But the deeper fault of new welfare is that it collapses the differences between right and wrong. If, say, the segregated black urban poor are simply one interest among others, then the racial injustices that got them into their present fix cannot necessarily be defined as injustices that the government is free to address on its own authority.

This commentary is directed specifically to the phenomenon Lowi calls interest-group liberalism, a liberalism that conceives of politics not as the pursuit of a common good defined by universal principles but as the clash of social interests. Whether or not he is right in his appraisal of the rationale of recent welfare programs, the mind that he describes is familiar in other expressions of liberal distaste for authority and standards, whether in obscenity laws or in the teaching of grammatical English. But perhaps Lowi's thesis is applicable most broadly to democracy itself, with which liberals should not be on easy terms. It is not so much liberalism as democracy that, in theory at least, refuses to recognize any authority outside of the popular will and its political process. In the absence of that authority democracy can behave in every defiance of the liberal ethos, turning viciously against minorities or minority beliefs, resenting the outside world. To believe that democracy has at least one self-policing mechanism, the mutual checks that its competition of interests provides, is not unsophisticated. It comes close to that conviction asserted in *The Federalist Papers* that an enlargement in the size of a republic gathers in a greater diversity of interests and so decreases the possibility that any one interest will tyrannize the rest. But this competition comes at the expense of a concept of the common good to which individuals and particular interests should in conscience submit themselves.

The exercise by government of that authority which Lowi champions is a way of asserting the primacy of moral objects and the general good. Within a few years after the Supreme Court's school desegregation decision of 1954, even racists were according it some measure of obedience. That was partly because citizens do acknowledge that law and government possess authority and in part because even racists could know in some corner of their minds that the authority was being exercised for moral ends. When President Gerald Ford, at a time of public bitterness and hostility, decided to admit the first wave of Indochinese refugees, the government was acting once more on its authority and in the service of a morality that in much of the population had temporarily lapsed. From time to time, in fact, liberals have used government to achieve a welfare measure, the modification of a social custom, or some other object in the face of public indifference or resentment. But that puts liberals into a precarious relationship with the public.

The practical politics of liberalism, then, will be piecemeal. Closer to the core of the liberal intelligence are a style and taste that refer to much more than politics narrowly defined: a skepticism, a distrust of force, a habit of self-criticism. Lionel Trilling's *The Middle of the Journey*, a 1947 novel reflecting on the confusions within the American left in the era of Stalin and the Great Depression, offers in its protagonist John Laskell a representation of the type.[2]

Laskell is a diffident liberal, more like the worried and apologetic whites who sometimes appeared at the edges of the civil rights movement of the sixties than like the self-assured political and military strategists of the Kennedy administration, who is nearly convinced at one point that not being a revolutionist consigns him to the sidelines of history. To his left is Nancy Croom, so innocent that she imagines a neighborhood ne'er-do-well to be a personification of the people, yet merciless in the revolutionary beliefs born of her innocence. To Laskell's right is Gifford Maxim, a character modeled in part on Whittaker Chambers, already well known among New York intellectuals even before his public identification of Alger Hiss as a Communist. Maxim has a ruthless intellect unmodified by the compassion that informs *Witness*, Chambers' eloquent recollections and commentary published in 1952. After achieving an important place in the party, Maxim has recoiled from its absolutist logic, which points to the liquidation of its enemies. He has turned to a philosophical conservatism complete and unyielding, like the party ideology, but denying any human force for progress. Against the shallow fierce certainties of the revolutionary left and the dark certainties of the philosophical right, the unassertive Laskell moves tentatively toward a faith affirming the range of capacities that Maxim the ex-revolutionist rejects, but suspicious of the arrogant virtue that revolution manifests. Rejecting the revolutionary confidence in direct, unrestrained action, he argues for a sensibility that he likens to poetry, in which the triumph is to set rigorous forms, adhere to them, and overcome the difficulties they create.

The skepticism and the hesitancies of the liberals can put them at a disadvantage in the presence of more assertively complete persuasions but can also provide subtle and vigorous social and intellectual criticism. In 1949 Arthur Schlesinger published *The Vital Center*, an early articulation of cold war thinking and a liberal's attack on a liberalism that gets by on sentimentality or fails to recognize savagery when it appears on the left. Schlesinger in 1963 brought out *The Politics of Hope*, a collection of his essays dating from 1949 through 1960. One piece after another reflects the discontent of a liberal intellectual with what he sees as the state of the nation at midcentury: the complacency, the mediocrity of standards, the distrust of thought. The introduction, written during the Kennedy administration when Schlesinger was a presidential adviser, rejoices at the new spirit abroad in the country, the ascendancy of style and adventurous intellect—so this critic of liberal sentimentality somewhat sentimentally perceived the time of the Kennedy presidency. The collection therefore indicates not only how a partisan could retrospectively view the victory of John Kennedy but also what a liberal could have been looking for in the years preceding 1961.[3]

Schlesinger's liberalism had much of its founding in the optimistic, relativist New Deal reformism that today can appear facile in its hope and in its perceptions of the people. It is therefore something of a surprise to find him detecting the presence in humankind of what would once have been identified as original sin. Schlesinger writes a respectful review of Chambers' *Witness*, an account of a tortured childhood, years in the Communist party, and a spiritually profound break with the party. Yet he warns against Chambers' pronouncements that communism, as an arrogant assertion of the unchecked will to remake the world, is the logical expression of a time that has abandoned the absolute values that tame arrogance. Human will is tempted to arrogance, Schlesinger agrees; but it can quickly seize on absolute values as ways of asserting itself, and a critical pluralism may be a good discipline for it. So strong, in fact, is Schlesinger's taste for invention and criticism as goods in themselves, apart from their social and economic results, that he would probably prefer an unfinished and corruptible human nature, if only because its manifestations would be more various and because coping with its willfulness would bring forth a more active political intelligence and moral strategy.

Schlesinger's essays reflect a preoccupation with every variety of cultural and social failing of his time and nation—except poverty. The omission is not complete. Some poverty remains, Schlesinger remarks in a 1960 essay. But he predicts that the problem the individual will now have to face more and more is that of preserving identity and dignity in a culture of mass affluence. Schlesinger along with many of his fellow citizens believed that the nation had passed permanently from an economy of scarcity to an economy of surplus, and perhaps he thought that the rest of the world was not very far from making that transition.

The argument can be taken beyond the point at which Schlesinger leaves it. If the most generous hopes of the past century for the benefits of technology and democracy ever come true, it will become a serious question what forms courage, fortitude, and common dignity can take in a world without war, poverty, and the other conditions under which the traditional virtues once gained simple definition. Romantics of the left who talk of the heroic struggles of the oppressed peoples of the third world and despise bourgeois softness, romantics of the right who follow Aleksandr Solzhenitsyn in the conviction that the West has had it too easy and that only the oppressed in Communist lands can know the enemy and confront it are not much help. For both sets of enthusiasts proceed with their projects for an end to oppression and therefore, or so an innocent observer might suppose, for an end to what both define as the basis of heroism and endurance. An answer will have to be sought elsewhere to the question of what strength and authenticity of character might remain in a safe and prosperous future. Schlesinger suggests that freedom itself can demand so vigorous a political, artistic, and critical life that the individual will be invited to traverse a difficult course of introspection and self-identification. A free and egalitarian society, he comments—and, he could have added, an affluent society, insofar as affluence is a foundation for modern freedoms—does not provide the corners and crannies in which the individual could once be safe. If Schlesinger, like other social commentators at midcentury, assumed too quickly that the future of universal plenty was near, he at least knew what to ask of that future.

Schlesinger's relish for energy and innovation calls to mind another characteristic of liberalism: the tendency to view society and politics as being in an incessant process of problem solving. That is one of the many resonances between liberalism and modern technology. There would be exuberance in the energies the author of *The Politics of Hope* wanted released, but it is customary of liberals to be guilt-haunted in their social objectives. Here liberalism differs both from the left with its concentration on larger historical forces and from the traditional philosophical right, which inclines to limit the duties of the individual to those that tradition and place define. Laissez-faire liberals sent the individual into the open market to hunger or prosper. Twentieth-century liberals send at least themselves, if not the rest of society, into a lifetime project of self-questioning and of anxious social endeavor. They, like their earlier namesakes, act as though the human enterprise were mostly a matter of will and decision, although as students of the behavioral sciences they recognize all kinds of social conditionings by which they will explain away everyone's failings except, perhaps, their own.

Convinced that society ought to be forever at work on its own imperfections, liberalism can be hard on the conscience of the individual, as long as that individual is liberal or of the prosperous classes. Yet it can also be so solicitous of the rights of the person, so entranced at the possibilities of the expressive, emotive, self-actualizing individual, as to be unsure in the presence of anything like permanent, restrictive responsibilities. That has been a prominent character especially of liberalism in the Kennedy era.

Liberals went into the Kennedy presidency believing in form and structure. They believed in legal procedures, in scientific and technological endeavor, in vigorous education. Under the leadership of Martin Luther King, Jr., the civil rights movement revealed to them another discipline: that of nonviolence. Much of the source of that ethic of self-restraint was evangelical and must have puzzled many of its liberal admirers. But they saw its power. Then something happened to liberalism, something besides though in conjunction with the Vietnam War. Liberalism lost its ability to speak convincingly for the civic virtues.

Part of the loss and much of the explanation are to be found in the liberal view of the schools. Conservatives had complained for decades about progressive education and the decline of classroom discipline, but much of this expressed the conservatives' confusion of rigidity with good performance and of innovation with decadence. The essentials of conventional schooling—in exact language, in the impersonality of scientific inquiry, in humanistic balanced against technical learning—liberals did not question. They were no more interested in the free expressiveness than in the conventional academic achievement of their own children. But liberals are afraid of being intolerant and of being unreceptive to experiment. The political movements of the sixties brought with them the exhilarating notion that feeling, and perhaps knowledge itself, were more quickly available than middle-class culture had thought—that encounter sessions, for example, could bring knowledge because whatever is most angrily blurted out must be most authentic. Many liberals hesitated to disagree. Some college students insisted that the only questions worth asking about were this year's revolutions. Some liberals joined them. Ghetto schools envisioned by militants would consider street English good enough, with no introduction to the English of Shakespeare or of Stephen Crane. Guilt and cultural relativism silenced numbers of liberals.

Liberals have become uncertain of what to teach the nation's students; more broadly they have spoken increasingly for the claims of privacy as opposed to the claims of community. The civil rights movement demanded that black Americans gain full participation in citizenship. Black nationalism demanded separation, and while some liberals remained true to their earlier convictions and opposed it, others were acquiescent or consenting. The women's movement can be equally contradictory on whether the individual is to join in the social enterprise or to remain unburdened by it; one feminist will argue that fathers should share more equally in parenthood, while another will argue for the freedom of either parent to leave the family. All this liberalism now adds to its long-standing unwillingness fully to subordinate to the public interest the privileges of private ownership. Theodore Lowi is close to describing the present condition of liberalism when he speaks of the distaste for clear, authoritative laws that tell citizens what they must do for the public welfare. It is through the waywardness of history that a liberalism increasingly fearful of limits and demands should have joined forces with a President irritated at liberal indecisiveness and a brother who was forever lecturing people on their moral imperfections.

How had it happened years before then that liberals, already

self-doubting in their more reflective moods and uneasy about
the exercise of authority, came to design the massive military
and diplomatic power structures of the cold war? A commonsense answer would be that there are liberals and liberals. Combative Harry Truman and the crusty patrician Dean Acheson
had no inhibitions to overcome. Much in the containment policy attracted academic and journalist liberals as well. They were
drawn to the conviction that the country has global duties, to
the balancing of military with economic aid, and to the ongoing
argument with political rightists who wanted an emotionally satisfying simplification of policy. By the late sixties, however, numbers of liberals were recoiling from the power that liberalism had
wrought, recoiling particularly from the memory of the Kennedy
presidency, which seemed in retrospect the most urgent cele-
brant of power.

A graceful early assault on the Kennedy presidency is Henry
Fairlie's *The Kennedy Promise*. The work, published in 1973,
does not rant about American imperialism. It speaks admiringly
of the American aid following the Second World War that
saved Western Europe from the Soviet Union, and its criticism
of the Kennedy administration makes a complex argument. Kennedy and his advisers craved energy and action for their own
sake. The argument, at least by extension, would hold that whatever might have been Kennedy's practical contribution to the
build-up in Vietnam, he was spiritually responsible for an American adventurism that did not know how to stop short of engagement in Vietnam. The United States since 1945, says Fairlie,
had put its power to upholding a "legitimate world order" against
the Communist nations; the Kennedy presidency, with its ambitions about waging guerrilla warfare against communism, undermined that concept of legitimacy. And it failed adequately to
realize that power demands not merely action but patience.[4]

The Kennedy Neurosis is the title of Nancy Gager Clinch's
study of the family, also published in 1973, and the neurosis she
defines within the family is, she thinks, only an accentuation of
that of the country as a whole. Driven by Joe, Sr., to an obses-

sive commitment to competitive achievement, constantly confronted with their failure perfectly to answer to their father's
expectations and demands—which, of course, had become fixed
in their own psyches—the Kennedy brothers have exhibited apparently contradictory drives—toward success and toward self-
punishment—along with an inability to experience the full range
of emotions. The Kennedy neurosis, Nancy Clinch argues, has
stood in the way of a healthier employment of remarkable virtues—among them energy, wit, intelligence, and physical courage—that distinguish the family. The author employs all this to
explain what she, along with other recent critics, perceives as
failings of John Kennedy's administration—adventurism combined with an inability to recognize, for instance, the sufferings
of poverty. That, *The Kennedy Neurosis* says, is the American
story: competitiveness and self-punishment in place of cultivation of a full personality.[5]

Much of what Nancy Clinch says consists of clinical interpretation—that, for instance, repeatedly speeding through red
lights at night can signify compulsiveness, rage, and self-hatred.
Such a study cannot have the authority of a therapist's private,
continuing, and unpolemical discovery of a patient. Nor will it
allow its subjects what people are generally granted when they
step before a public: to be accepted, hated, liked for the public
self they construct. But the author's comments fix suggestively
on policy as the expression of a national mind and personality.
Perhaps her most interesting political criticism is of the commitment to economic growth, a policy that assumes in effect
that the answer to economic ills is not a major redistribution
of wealth but the production of more of it. It is certainly true
that John Kennedy talked more insistently about stimulating
the economy than about a more equitable sharing of its fruits.
And if public policy does manifest the character not only of its
architects but of a nation, then the growth philosophy surely
could reflect a national neurosis that, as Nancy Clinch perceives
it, includes a suppression of the human capacity for cooperation.
A country can pursue growth as an impersonal, technical achieve-

ment. *The Kennedy Neurosis* is right to define in the national character and politics the absence of a larger imagination.

Toward the beginning of his 1982 commentary *The Kennedy Imprisonment*, Garry Wills recalls the admiration that even women liberals could once have for the machismo of John Kennedy and the New Frontiersmen. Wills comments on the fortunes of the sexual revolution of recent years, which began in the liberated expression of prowling masculinity and has proceeded to the feminist rejection of that kind of malehood. The Kennedys, their close associates, and at least some of the liberals who hoped for much from the Kennedy presidency, Wills contends, expected the new administration to bring to politics a power to act and a charismatic leadership that would cut through bureaucratic procedures and make of government itself a continual assertion of masculine will. John Kennedy was supposed to embody power and will, manifest in his sexuality, his PT exploit, his style and rhetoric. He would rescue the nation from the inertia of the 1950s and lead it on to—what? Wills's Kennedy is not specific here, and the author quotes the British essayist and novelist G. K. Chesterton to the effect that if you admire sheer will, you have nothing in particular that you want and are therefore without will. Garry Wills does find in Robert Kennedy's later positions on civil rights and the war in Vietnam a genuine and growing moral sensitivity, and he discusses Edward Kennedy with considerable sympathy not only as a good senator but as the Kennedy least reflective of the family's power mania.[6]

The subtitle of *The Kennedy Imprisonment* is *A Meditation on Power*, and the relentless attention that Wills devotes, page after page, to the public and private doings of the family takes its intellectual form not as an attack on the Kennedys but as an essay on the folly of exalting power and will into a principle of politics and personal behavior. He presents the obsession with power as resulting in a series of imprisonments, committing its practitioner victims to acting out roles and policies that take on a life force of their own. This was, for example, the course of

President Kennedy's determination to have a foreign policy that would be an assertion of the will of the United States; it turned him feverish in his efforts to confront or undo Castro, and it portended the nation's deeper involvement in Vietnam. The Kennedy people trusted above all in the charisma of a leader as the way to swift and effective government, and they wished to bypass the regular bureaucracy and agencies of law, to establish or encourage special units—within the CIA, for instance—that could operate a good deal like Green Berets in the forest. It is here that Wills's work is most directly the meditation on power that the title announces and most directly expressive of the conservatism that the author has never deserted in the last two decades even as he has moved leftward on specific issues. He argues that government must achieve the continuity, the spread of responsibility, the decentralization of power that regular bureaus and procedures provide.

You do not have to be as unfriendly an observer of the Kennedy liberals as Garry Wills to recognize that he has fairly described one facet of the liberal mentality of the early sixties. The exaltation of will, indeed, constitutes a good deal of what, in the way of a foreign policy, twentieth-century American liberalism has both fostered and warned against. Its Wilsonian heritage once made liberalism far more prepared than either responsible conservatism or the far right to commit the country to a purposeful and unresting global role. But the suspicion among liberals, nourished by their quarrel with the right, of anything like self-gratification as an objective of foreign policy must have as its logical end a distrust of any evocation of a national will, even a will as resolute in restraint as in readiness to act. It tempts too much of posturing; it hints of calisthenics and distance running in the cold.

These three works do not together represent precisely a liberal or left liberal view of the Kennedy family. The British-born Fairlie is something of a Tory intellectual in his published comments on twentieth-century mores, though his politics have been closer to those of democratic socialism, and Wills has retained much of the philosophical conservatism that once made him a writer for the *National Review*. But these studies offer a sampling of what much of the professional classes once so encouraged by the Kennedy presidency were later coming to think.

The critics have done their work with eloquence and often with research. There is sufficient consistency among their presentations to make a collectively plausible case that before the late 1960s the Kennedy family lacked an articulate set of principles and goals, acting instead out of the elder Kennedy's ambitions programmed into the brothers, and that the Kennedy presidency was a peculiar combination of purposelessness and excessive assertion of national power. And still this preoccupation with the smallest detail of conduct that could reveal the family's unfitness for office is a puzzling development. John Kennedy, for all his slowness to press for domestic reform, presided over a progressive administration that led into the extensive social legislation of Lyndon Johnson's presidency, and already textbooks treat the two presidencies almost as a unit. Robert Kennedy, for all his driven aggressiveness, spent his last years speaking for social reform and an end to the war in Vietnam. Edward Kennedy, for all his private problems, has been a hard-working senator and a persistent spokesman for liberalism in its lean years. Yet critics who might find the Kennedys creditable, if imperfect, instruments of progressivism search relentlessly beyond or beneath all this to construct devastating, and in some degree plausible, indictments. A specific reason, of course, was the Vietnam War. It is unlikely that without the war there would have been much retrospective repudiation of the Kennedy presidency; the assassination had replaced with grief the considerable impatience among liberals during the later days of the presidency. But while the war explains much of the shift in informed opinion, it is also in the character of American liberalism to be critical of its own past. It is particularly appropriate for liberalism, which has sought so hard to expand the power of the state, to turn to doubting power—not as a conservative doubts power, because it may disrupt a settled social order, but for the arrogant and absolute voice in which power speaks.

Liberalism has lost confidence in its past, which includes its recent past in the early sixties. It is at contraries with itself. Its driven conscience is irreconcilable with its permissiveness; its wish for a more cooperative social order is mocked by its fascination with the claims of privacy and self-cultivation. Present-day conservatism is similarly contradictory when it furnishes an individualist economics with the vocabulary of an older ideology of order, place, and hierarchy. Conservatism can do better. An illustration is George F. Will's *Statecraft as Soulcraft,* published in 1983. Against a modern presupposition that self-interest is the basic and legitimate motive of conduct, Will seeks to recall conservatism to Western political traditions that define the health of a community and its government as depending on civic morality, which in turn needs laws that will actively nourish it.[7]

Will intends his book as a rebuke equally to modern liberalism, which claims that government must not legislate morality, and to modern conservatism, which denounces governmental legislation of economic morality in the form of the welfare state. Government cannot act without imposing a morality of some sort or another, he says to liberals, and it did so correctly when civil rights legislation during the sixties encouraged people away from racism toward civility. Government can and should impose economic morality, Will says to conservatives, promoting an "ethic of common provision" that will draw the community more tightly together. But in one way this commentary by a conservative columnist unintentionally lends itself to a liberal's modernism, while in another it more closely follows a conservative sensibility; and in both ways it invites some reflections on American liberalism.

Will's doubtless unconscious alliance with liberalism consists of his willingness to think outside of the concept of human nature as it is now in frequent use among the opponents of liberalism. Will himself stands by the good conservative conviction that there is a human nature that it is the business of government to preserve and cultivate; he does not like the modernist reduction of human beings to a flux of sensations and possibilities. But again as a good conservative he insists that government must impose a second nature, a set of civic virtues, that will recover the buried best in our innate nature. In so arguing he is putting himself at a farther distance than he may have planned from a strategy not uncommon among a brand of conservatives today, which is to center human nature in the appetite for property, the passion for public vengeance against criminals, and whatever other clamorous desires reinforce a conservative agenda. Even a philosophical conservatism more benign than this can be solicitous of the world as it is, and of human inclinations in their normal, fairly selfish state, lest our attempts to reshape them violate human nature. Will's conservatism is more austere and demanding. And in extraordinary defiance of the individualist economics that has taken to itself the title of conservatism, he observes that there is no "natural" economic system, no economic arrangements that happen outside of human will, decision, and law. The polity that he would design, then, is deliberate, ambitious, prepared to bend raw human nature to codes and virtues; it would have the contrived forms that Trilling elects for in *The Middle of the Journey*. Above all else, it would provide an education in civic conduct, as much at odds with popular prejudices and traditions as the civil rights laws. It would have something in common with the national renovation that the rhetoric of John Kennedy promised.

But in another respect, and more deeply than in its pronouncements of conservative philosophy, *Statecraft as Soulcraft* is conservative. It displays a traditionalist preference for the particular, limited, and concrete as opposed to the universal. It describes not a morality that will direct the individual toward the rest of humankind but a specific civic morality, sustaining and getting its sustenance from a specific body politic. In *Statecraft as Soulcraft* Will calls for the restraint of self-interest within a political community, but in his newspaper and television commentaries he is a partisan of a hard-line foreign policy which generally presumes that, for example, the interest of the United States should dictate which Central American governments we shall tolerate. A specific set of civic habits, just demanding enough to give continuance to the polity, can make for more congenial neighbors than a morality restlessly determined to do good. But anyone who is not a neighbor—a Nicaraguan, perhaps, who is about to be fitted into the interest of the northern republic— will not profit from the most refined civility among the inhabitants of the United States. The liberal moralism of the Bay of Pigs offers a threat of another kind; self-contained citizens would not be seized with a notion of going off and liberating somebody. But liberal morality is not particularistic, not preoccupied with the harmony of a specific community, and so, while it can produce a Bay of Pigs, it can also produce a Robert Kennedy critical of his nation's adventures abroad.

The tentativeness, the habit of self-criticism, the fear of ideological certitude that are among the strengths of liberalism have contributed to a signal failure: the inability to think beyond the nation's hesitant welfare state. From the point of view of a thorough social democracy, there is little to choose between the center conservatism of the Republicans and the center liberalism of the Democrats. Both of them accept a radical inequality, with no moral foundation, that defines the domestic clients of welfare and the hungry clients of foreign aid as recipients of middle-class charity administered by the government. From the viewpoint of a welfare mother whose family needs government aid to get by, the difference between a conservative and a liberal administration may be extreme. To argue merely for the quantitative extension of welfare capitalism is to leave the poor at the fringes of society. To despise the welfare state, as left ideologues do, is to be loftily superior to its small concrete easements of poverty. So serious liberal and left critics of the American center may need to sustain an argumentative good will toward the politics of the Kennedy and Johnson administrations, respecting them as progressivism in a common American idiom and probing beyond their limits.

As a way of looking at social and moral problems liberalism will doubtless continue in its contradictory habits: seeking power but suspicious of it; affirmative and distrustful of democracy; sternly evoking a social conscience yet critical of the moral programs that the conscience devises; respectful of every variety of hedonistic self-expression and equally respectful of the severe impersonality of science and technology. It is almost circular to say that liberalism will continue in those habits; the very term "liberalism" in its present usage refers to movements that encompass them. The administration of John Kennedy, which in the public memory still dominates and gives meaning to the more articulate politics of his brothers, was at once so energetic in appearance and so vague in its goals that liberals could believe that their cause had unity and direction. The splintering of liberalism afterward means really that the elements within the liberal mind have become more distinct, the argument within that mind more pronounced. Perhaps no more than the accidents of history have brought together the components of what today is generally called liberalism. Yet they have had this, at least, in common: they manifest a critical mentality so restless, and so dissatisfied with any one completed ideological system, that it is bound to generate contradictions. And in association with politicians as effective as the Kennedys, liberalism has achieved the most vigorous American politics of the century.

Notes

This book is not intended as an exhaustive scholarly work, and footnoting has purposely been very selective. Footnotes here are for materials that are fresh or only recently released, for important quotations, and for core sections in the Kennedy literature. There are several useful Kennedy bibliographies: Dorothy Ryan, *The Kennedy Family of Massachusetts: A Bibliography* (Westport: Greenwood Press, 1981); Joan I. Newcomb, *John F. Kennedy: An Annotated Bibliography* (Metuchen: Scarecrow Press, 1977); Ralph A. Stone, ed. *John F. Kennedy, 1917–1962: Chronology—Documents—Bibliographical Aids* (Dobbs Ferry: Oceana Publications, 1971); James Tracy Crown, *The Kennedy Literature: A Bibliographical Essay on John F. Kennedy* (New York: New York University Press, 1968).

Abbreviations used include:

CUOH	Columbia University Oral History
FDRL	Franklin D. Roosevelt Library
JFKL	John F. Kennedy Library
JFKL-OH	John F. Kennedy Library Oral History
LC	Library of Congress
NA	National Archives
NYT	*New York Times*
RFK	Robert F. Kennedy Papers, JFKL

Chapter 2
STRIVE AND SUCCEED

1. Early biographical material on the Kennedy family used in this chapter is compactly available in Boxes 1 and 2 of the John F.

Kennedy Personal Papers and in Box 1 of the Robert F. Kennedy Personal Papers, JFKL. Doris Kearns has sole access to the Joseph P. Kennedy Papers until she publishes a book. In the meantime, two good biographies of the elder Kennedy are the highly critical David E. Koskoff, *Joseph P. Kennedy* (Englewood Cliffs: Prentice-Hall, 1974), and Richard Whalen, *The Founding Father* (New York: New American Library, 1964). Rose Kennedy has supplied her own excellent reminiscences, *Time to Remember* (Garden City: Doubleday, 1974).

2. Handlin, *Boston's Immigrants*, rev. and enlarged (Cambridge: Belknap Press, 1979).

3. John Davis, *The Kennedys* (New York: McGraw-Hill, 1984).

4. Edward Martin, JFKL-OH.

5. Biographical fact sheet (undated), Box 1, Joseph P. Kennedy Papers, JFKL.

6. James MacGregor Burns, in his able campaign-year biography of John Kennedy, quotes a Republican newspaper's remark that Honey Fitz was the only man who could get away with singing "Sweet Adeline" while sober: *John Kennedy: A Political Profile* (New York: Harcourt, Brace, 1960), p. 10.

7. Gail Cameron, *Rose* (New York: G. P. Putnam's, 1971).

8. This paragraph and the next two are based largely on material in Joseph McCarthy, *The Remarkable Kennedys* (New York: Popular Library, 1960), especially pp. 33ff.

9. Gloria Swanson, *Swanson on Swanson* (New York: Random House, 1980), has the last word.

10. Arthur Sylvester, JFKL-OH; Burns, *John Kennedy*, p. 26; Victor Lasky, *J.F.K.: The Man and the Myth* (New Rochelle: Arlington House, 1963), p. 71.

11. Ralph G. Martin, *JFK: A Hero for Our Times* (New York: Macmillan, 1983), p. 27.

12. Rose Kennedy, *Time to Remember*, p. 168.

13. The Kennedy parents, who followed the standard psychiatric advice of their day in treating Rosemary, deserve credit for keeping her within the family setting. Indeed, during her stay in London she was presented at court.

14. The standard source is Michael R. Beschloss, *Kennedy and Roosevelt: The Uneasy Alliance* (New York: W. W. Norton, 1980).

15. William O. Douglas remembers stimulating intellectual "seminars" at the Marwood dinner table, noting that he and Joe, Sr., became "warm friends": *Go East, Young Man* (New York: Random House, 1974), p. 264.

16. John T. Flynn believes Kennedy crippled the SEC: "Other People's Money," *New Republic*, Vol. 84 (October 9, 1935), p. 244; cf. Flynn, *Country Squire in the White House* (New York: Doubleday, Doran, 1940), pp. 84, 121.

17. Joseph P. Kennedy to Franklin Roosevelt, September 6, 1935, President's personal file, FDRL; Arthur Krock, *Memoirs* (New York: Funk & Wagnalls, 1968), p. 322.

18. McCarthy, *The Remarkable Kennedys*, pp. 80–81; *NYT*, October 20, 1938.

19. Beschloss, *Kennedy and Roosevelt, passim*.

20. James M. Landis to Joseph P. Kennedy, February 8, 1952, Box 51, LC.

21. Koskoff, *Joseph P. Kennedy, passim*.

22. Joseph Kennedy wired FDR on October 9, 1940, "Request you instruct me come Washington for consultations *before end of October*." Thomas M. C. Johnston Papers, JFKL; Felix Sper to Franklin D. Roosevelt, PPF file, FDRL.

23. John F. Kennedy, "My Brother Joe," in John F. Kennedy, ed., *As We Remember Joe* (Cambridge, Mass.: privately printed at the university press, 1945), pp. 1–5.

24. John F. Kennedy's European diary (especially August 21, 1937) and letters to his parents and others, Box 1, Personal Papers, JFKL.

25. Kennedy, *As We Remember Joe*; Maurice Shea, JFKL-OH.

26. "Though I may not be able to remember material things such as tickets, gloves and so on," Jack wrote to his father, "I can remember things like Ivanhoe and the last time we had an exam on it I got a ninety eight": Box 1, Personal Papers, JFKL. Ralph Horton, JFKL-OH.

27. Box 51, Landis Papers, LC.

28. Payson Wild, one of Kennedy's professors at Harvard, said in an oral history, "I am positive that the first book was his own because he would come in with sections of it. He would write it during the week, and we would talk about it. He was pretty thorough on some things and would have to be prodded on others": JFKL-OH. Box 2, Personal Papers, JFKL. John F. Kennedy, *Why England Slept* (New York: Wilfred Funk, 1940).

29. Boxes 1 and 2, Personal Papers, JFKL; Kennedy to Blair Moody, March 10, 1942, Box 75, Prepresidential Papers, JFKL; Charles Bohlen, *Witness to History* (New York: W. W. Norton, 1973); Bohlen, JFKL-OH.

30. The FBI dossier on Jack and Inga and on Jack and numerous other women was released in 1983 to a researcher.

31. The best source on JFK in the South Pacific is Joan and Clay Blair, *The Search for JFK* (New York: Berkeley, 1976).

32. Hank Searls, *The Lost Prince* (Cleveland: World, 1969); Jack Olsen, *Aphrodite: Desperate Mission* (New York: G. P. Putnam's, 1970), pp. 270–74. Also, an unidentified caller from the Hamptons on Long Island told Professor Burner, after a program on the Kennedys had aired over the SUNY at Stony Brook radio station, that Joe's had not been the first such flight and that the caller had been stationed on the base at the time. See also Raynes Minns, *Bombers and Mash* (London: Vintage, 1980).

33. Kennedy, *As We Remember Joe*.

34. Lynne McTaggart, *Kathleen Kennedy* (Garden City: Dial, 1983); the author interviewed more than 100 titled Britons. See also the Duchess of Devonshire, *The House* (London: Macmillan, 1982).

35. Arthur M. Schlesinger, Jr., *A Thousand Days* (Boston: Houghton Mifflin, 1965), p. 31.

36. Peter D. Garvan, North American Newspaper Alliance memorandum, Box 51, James M. Landis Papers, LC.

37. Peter Lisagor, JFKL-OH.

38. Barbara Ward, JFKL-OH.

39. David F. Powers Papers, Box 1, JFKL; Kenneth P. O'Donnell and David F. Powers with Joe McCarthy, *"Johnny, We Hardly Knew Ye"* (Boston: Little, Brown, 1972), p. 59; Alec Barbrook, *God Save the Commonwealth* (Amherst: The University of Massachusetts Press, 1973), p. 110.

40. Barbara Ward, JFKL-OH.

41. The Harvard seminar was Arthur Holcombe's, and the incident is discussed at length in his papers. James D. Mallan wrote Holcombe on October 15, 1952, complaining that the *New Republic* had chosen the title "Massachusetts: Liberal and Corrupt" for the article he wrote about the seminar, Vol. 127 (October 13, 1952), pp. 10–11: Holcombe Papers, JFKL. The incident further soured John Kennedy on liberals. Barbara Ward, JFKL-OH.

42. Box 5, John F. Kennedy Personal Papers, JFKL; Martin, *JFK*, p. 36.

43. Arthur Krock told a friend, "Don't you know he is going to die? . . . His father told me he had only four years to live," Margaret Coit, JFKL-OH; "Management of Adrenocortical Insufficiency During Surgery," AMA *Archives of Surgery* (November 1955), pp. 737–42; Janet Travell, JFKL-OH.

44. Boxes 6–10, John F. Kennedy Personal Papers, JFKL; Martin, *JFK*, p. 58.

45. Herbert S. Parmet, *JFK: The Presidency of John F. Kennedy* (New York: Dial, 1983), p. 110; Parmet's two-volume life of Kennedy is now the standard scholarly biography. Some critics judge that the earlier volume is of greater quality: *Jack: The Struggles of John F. Kennedy* (New York: Dial, 1980).

46. George Smathers in his oral history reports that Jack thought Joe McCarthy "a pretty good guy," his loyalty being, however, more personal than anything else: JFKL-OH. There is a Columbia University master's essay on the Kennedy-McCarthy connection: Jeanne M. Luboja, "John F. Kennedy and the McCarthy Issue: A Study in the Politics of Liberalism (1925–1960)," 1974, p. 30. William Benton, JFKL-OH.

47. Kennedy to Mona Pendergast, April 15, 1958, Box 12, John F. Kennedy Prepresidential Papers, JFKL; Robert Amory, JFKL-OH.

48. Lasky, *J.F.K.*, p. 111.

49. Tyler Abell, ed., *Drew Pearson Diaries, 1949–1959* (New York: Holt, Rinehart & Winston, 1974), p. 420; Burns, JFKL-OH; James Landis, CUOH.

50. John F. Kennedy, *Profiles in Courage* (New York: Harper & Brothers, 1956); Margaret Coit reports that Kennedy told her in reference to her own reception of that honor, "I would rather win a Pulitzer Prize than be President of the United States." Margaret Coit, JFKL-OH.

51. Carl Brauer argues that the act would not have passed without the jury trial amendment: *John F. Kennedy and the Second Reconstruction* (New York: Columbia University Press, 1977), p. 21. Box 108, Prepresidential Papers, JFKL.

52. Kennedy to Clifford Lamar of Birmingham, Alabama, August 1, 1957, Box 664, Prepresidential Papers, JFKL.

53. Stevenson to Kennedy, August 26, 1956, Box 434, "Selected Pre-Election Name Files (K)," Firestone Library, Princeton University.

Chapter 3
THE CANDIDATE DISCOVERS THE LIBERALS

1. David W. Reinhard touches at various points on the isolationist strain in *The Republican Right Since 1945* (Lexington: University Press of Kentucky, 1983), especially pp. 74ff. Various biographies of Senate and House Republicans tell other parts of the

story. An outstanding biography is James T. Patterson, *Mr. Republican: A Biography of Robert Taft* (Boston: Houghton Mifflin, 1972). A good survey of foreign policy in the postwar years is Seyom Brown, *The Faces of Power*, rev. ed. (New York: Columbia University Press, 1983). More central to this study is John Gaddis' excellent *Strategies of Containment* (New York: Oxford University Press, 1982), particularly pp. 198–236, 237ff. Rostow's magnum opus is *The Diffusion of Power* (New York: Macmillan, 1972). Schlesinger, "The New Isolationists," *Atlantic*, Vol. 189 (May 1952), pp. 34–38; W. Reed West, "Senator Taft's Foreign Policy," *Atlantic*, Vol. 189 (June 1952), pp. 50–52.

2. This and subsequent paragraphs are based in part on David Burner, Robert D. Marcus, and Thomas R. West, *A Giant's Strength: America in the 1960s* (New York: Holt, Rinehart & Winston, 1971).

3. The latest revisionist view of Eisenhower is Fred Greenstein, *The Hidden-Hand Presidency: Eisenhower as Leader* (New York: Basic Books, 1982). The Eisenhower response to William McGaffin is in the *Chicago Daily News*, January 26, 1960.

4. A most suggestive book, used here extensively, is Richard A. Aliano, *American Defense Policy from Eisenhower to Kennedy* (Athens: Ohio University Press, 1975); Aliano is particularly strong on the role of the press, pp. 146–74, and on that of academia, pp. 175–99. Until work in progress is published, Edgar M. Bottome is standard on *The Missile Gap* (Rutherford: Fairleigh Dickinson University Press, 1971). That topic also concerns Stewart Alsop, *The Center* (New York: Harper & Row, 1968). *New Republic*, Vol. 144 January 30, 1961), pp. 62–68; *U.S. News & World Report*, Vol. 50 (January 23, 1961), pp. 25–28. Henry Kissinger, *The Necessity for Choice* (New York: Harper & Brothers, 1961); Rockefeller Brothers Fund, *Prospects for America* (I, 1958; II, 1961).

5. Louise FitzSimons, *The Kennedy Doctrine* (New York: Random House, 1972).

6. Rovere's article is one in an important early compilation edited by Aïda DePace Donald, *John F. Kennedy and the New Frontier* (New York: Hill & Wang, 1966).

7. Box 151, Prepresidential Papers, JFKL.

8. Victor Lasky, *J.F.K.: The Man and the Myth* (New Rochelle: Arlington House, 1963), p. 100; Jeanne M. Luboja, "John F. Kennedy and the McCarthy Issue: A Study in the Politics of Liberalism (1925–1960)," unpublished master's essay, Columbia University, p. 37.

9. Douglas is quoted in the oral history of Paul Dixon, JFKL-OH.

10. Quoted in Kenneth P. O'Donnell and David F. Powers with Joe McCarthy, *"Johnny, We Hardly Knew Ye"* (Boston: Little, Brown, 1972), p. 127.

11. The Wayne Morse Papers at the University of Oregon are replete with denunciations of Kennedy as unfriendly toward labor; see, for example, Morse to Charles Brooks, telegram, November 10, 1959. Samuel Merrick, JFKL-OH.

12. Eleanor Roosevelt to Kennedy, December 18, 1958, January 6, 1959, and January 20, 1959, and Kennedy to Mrs. Roosevelt, various drafts and letters, Box 32, Prepresidential Papers, JFKL; Box 18, Sorensen Papers, JFKL.

13. Humphrey writes of FDR, Jr.: "He labeled me a draft dodger . . . , and he continued to do so even after we had made repeated contacts with the Kennedys demonstrating the untruth of the allegations. They believed me, but never shut FDR, Jr., up, as they easily could have." *The Education of a Public Man* (Garden City: Doubleday, 1976), p. 475. Standard on the 1960 campaign is Theodore H. White, *The Making of the President 1960* (New York: Atheneum, 1961).

14. Sorensen to Kennedy, memorandum, n.d., Box 25, Sorensen Papers, JFKL.

15. O'Donnell *et al.* describe the DiSalle incident perceptively, *"Johnny,"* pp. 148–52.

16. Guy Emerson, *The New Frontier* (New York: H. Holt and Co., 1920), epilogue.

17. After the West Virginia primary Kennedy told Chester Bowles that Johnson would be the "wisest" choice for Vice President. *Promises to Keep: My Years in Public Life, 1941–1969* (New York: Harper & Row, 1971), p. 297. Burke Marshall, Meyer Feldman, Charles Bartlett, JFKL-OH.

18. Peter Lisagor, JFKL-OH; Victor Lasky, *It Didn't Start with Watergate* (New York: Dial, 1976), p. 30.

19. *New Republic*, Vol. 110 (May 10, 1959), p. 97.

20. Lawrence H. Fuchs wrote the standard study, *John F. Kennedy and American Catholicism* (New York: Meredith Press, 1967).

21. Tyler Abell, ed., *Drew Pearson Diaries, 1949–1959* (New York: Holt, Rinehart & Winston, 1974), p. 30.

22. Robert Kennedy echoed the Sorensen strategy. See, for example, Robert Kennedy to Senator Frank E. Moss, August 31, 1960, Special Collection, University of Utah Library. Boxes 18 and 19 of

the Sorensen Papers are excellent as a source of Kennedy strategy on the religious issue, JFKL; David Burner, *The Politics of Provincialism: The Democratic Party in Transition, 1918–1932* (New York: Alfred A. Knopf, 1968), chapter seven.

23. Harris Wofford gives the most recent account of the famous phone calls: *Of Kennedys and Kings* (New York: Farrar, Straus, Giroux, 1980), chapter I. See his oral history on the disseminating of the Nixon lease, JFKL-OH.

24. The *New York Herald Tribune* alleged that the stuffing of ballot boxes in Cook County and elsewhere—while dozens of election machines in Republican precincts jammed mysteriously—had resulted in the counting of at least 100,000 phantom votes for Kennedy. The November 1960 columns on the topic were somewhat mysteriously aborted.

25. Roger Kent, commenting on the situation in southern California, is one of many who argue that Kennedy's religion lost him important states outside the South, JFKL-OH.

26. The mood was not Kennedy's alone. Even so prudent a participant as Senator J. William Fulbright wrote, "I do not believe that the problems inherited by Roosevelt in 1933 were anything like as ominous and difficult as the ones now confronting Kennedy." And Eleanor Roosevelt remarked late in 1958 that the next President will "have some of the toughest decisions that any President has ever had." Fulbright to R. B. McCallum of Pembroke College, Oxford, January 7, 1961, Fulbright Papers, University of Arkansas; reprinted by permission. Mrs. Roosevelt's observation appears in the typescript of the televised College News Conference, December 7, 1958, Sorensen Papers, Box 25, JFKL.

27. Carol Ann Berthold, "The Image and Character of President John F. Kennedy," unpublished doctoral dissertation, University of Illinois, 1975.

Chapter 4
AN IMPERIAL PRESIDENCY IN FOREIGN POLICY?

1. McGeorge Bundy had been a company commander in Europe, McNamara a lieutenant colonel in the air force, Rostow a picker of targets in Europe for the OSS; and Rusk, McNamara, Schlesinger, Kennedy himself—all had served in World War II. Edwin Guthman, *We Band of Brothers* (New York: Harper & Row, 1971); Gaddis, *Strategies of Containment* (New York: Oxford University Press, 1982). J. Graham Parson, stationed at the Saigon em-

bassy during the presidential transition, said that counterinsurgency plans for Laos and Saigon were already under way when Kennedy came to office, JFKL-OH.

2. Carey McWilliams, *The Education of Carey McWilliams* (New York: Simon & Schuster, 1978); Robin H. Montgomery, "Military Civic Action and Counterinsurgency," unpublished doctoral dissertation, University of Oklahoma, 1971.

3. *Times* of London, April 27, 1961; Theodore Sorensen, *Kennedy* (New York: Harper & Row, 1965), p. 633.

4. Orville Freeman's diary and Arthur Schlesinger's papers are excellent sources on Bowles, JFKL. See the memoranda of June 13, 1962, and July 12, 1962, Bowles Papers, Sterling Library, Yale University. Robert Estabrook, memoranda of conversations, August 28, 1961, Estabrook Papers, JFKL.

5. Warren Cohen, *Dean Rusk* (Totowa, N.J.: Cooper Square Publishers, 1980), p. 167. Rusk Papers, LBJL.

6. Rostow to Kennedy, June 26, 1961, Box 75-81, National Security Files, JFKL.

7. Henry Trewhitt, *McNamara* (New York: Harper & Row, 1971); Berle, *Navigating the Rapids, 1918–1971: From the Papers of Adolf A. Berle*, ed. Beatrice Bishop Berle and Travis Beale Jacobs (New York: Harcourt Brace Jovanovich, 1973), p. 726 (January 6, 1961), p. 755 (November 30, 1961), p. 777 (November 21, 1962).

8. Among the important sources on the Bay of Pigs are Irving Janis, *Victims of Groupthink* (Boston: Houghton Mifflin, 1972), pp. 14–50; Peter Weyden, *Bay of Pigs* (New York: Simon & Schuster, 1979); Haynes Johnson, *The Bay of Pigs* (New York: Simon & Schuster, 1964).

9. Robert Estabrook memoranda of conversations, May 11, 1961, Estabrook Papers, JFKL. Schlesinger calls the speech to the American Newspaper Publishers Association "the worst and most inexplicable speech of [Kennedy's] Presidency." *The Imperial Presidency* (Boston: Houghton Mifflin, 1972), p. 342. Schlesinger opposed the Bay of Pigs invasion, but faced with the consensus that developed for it, he tried to hold it to liberal goals: land reform, better housing, higher wages, improved medical care, and recreational opportunities—anything but tourism. Such suggestions are to be found among the about 20 percent of the National Security Files opened as of 1983 on this subject; see particularly Boxes 35A-36, JFKL. Ronald Radosh has questioned Schlesinger's motives in *The Nation*, Vol. 225 (August 6, 1977), pp. 104–9. Schlesinger's response was printed on August 20, 1977, Vol. 225, pp. 147–48. The most recent account of Kennedy and the press

is Montague Kern, Patricia W. Levering, and Ralph W. Levering, *The Kennedy Crises* (Chapel Hill: University of North Carolina Press, 1984).

10. Wyden concludes: "The Bay of Pigs was a wild gamble. It was not mad"; *The Bay of Pigs*, p. 326. Bundy saw one theme running through all the meetings: Kennedy was "playing for table stakes. He wasn't going to the bank": Wyden, *The Bay of Pigs*, p. 326. Bundy is quoted in Peter Joseph, *Good Times: An Oral History of America in the Nineteen Sixties* (New York: William Morrow, 1974), p. 13. The rolling tanks are in John W. Gardner, ed., *To Turn the Tide* (New York: Harper Brothers, 1962), p. 24.

11. Jack Newfield, *Robert Kennedy: A Memoir* (New York: E. P. Dutton, 1968), pp. 28, 79; Roger Hilsman, *To Move a Nation* (Garden City: Macmillan, 1967), pp. 63–88.

12. Louise FitzSimons, *The Kennedy Doctrine* (New York: Random House, 1972), p. 78.

13. Robert F. Kennedy, JFKL-OH.

14. *New Republic*, Vol. 189 (November 21, 1983), p. 14; White House tapes, April 2, 1963, JFKL.

15. Hilsman, JFKL-OH.

16. Kennedy eventually wrote a preface for a book based on this issue of the *Gazette*: T. N. Greene, ed. *The Guerrilla—and How to Fight Him* (New York: Praeger Publishers, 1962). Hilsman Papers, JFKL; Box 55, NSF, JFKL.

17. The Rusk memorandum is in Box 4, NSF, LBJL.

18. Juan Bosch, JFKL-OH; Hilsman, JFKL-OH.

19. Richard D. Mahoney, *JFK: Ordeal in Africa* (New York: Oxford University Press, 1983); Madeleine G. Kalb, *The Congo Cables* (New York: Macmillan, 1982); John Sherman Cooper OH, University of Kentucky Library; Edwin R. Bayley, JFKL-OH.

20. Khrushchev's probably authentic memoirs are entitled *Khrushchev Remembers: The Last Testament* (New York: Bantam Books, 1976). See also Roy A. and Zhores A. Medvedev, *Khrushchev* (New York: Columbia University Press, 1976).

21. Berlin—apart from the Bay of Pigs, about which almost no author appears to disagree with any other to any considerable extent—is the first occasion for sharply revisionist accounts of John Kennedy and his administration: Richard J. Walton, *Cold War and Counter-Revolution: The Foreign Policy of John F. Kennedy* (Baltimore: Pelican Books, 1973); Henry Fairlie, *The Kennedy Promise* (Garden City: Doubleday, 1973); Louise FitzSimons, *The Kennedy Doctrine* (New York: Random House, 1972); Bruce Miroff, *Pragmatic Illu-*

sions (New York: David McKay, 1976); Nancy Gager Clinch, *The Kennedy Neurosis* (New York: Grosset & Dunlap, 1973); Garry Wills, *The Kennedy Imprisonment* (Boston: Little, Brown, 1982); and Malcolm Smith, *Kennedy's 13 Great Mistakes* (Smithtown, N.Y.: Exposition Press, rev. ed., 1976).

22. The Beer Papers at the Kennedy Library are a study in cold war liberalism. Beer, head of Americans for Democratic Action, was obsessed with the importance of NATO. The main reason to defend Berlin was that NATO had committed itself: "To go back on that commitment would profoundly weaken the alliance." During the missile crisis Beer was to take the irrational position, along with many members of the Kennedy administration, that publicly announcing the withdrawal of the Jupiter missiles from Turkey would be an unacceptable weakening of NATO—this in face of possible world holocaust. The quotation is in Box 3. NEAR is mentioned in the *Kiplinger Washington Letter*, July 29, 1961.

23. Fulbright is quoted in *NYT*, August 3, 1961. The director of the Office of German Affairs in the State Department, Martin J. Hillenbrand—on summer holiday the weekend the wall was built—later observed, "I would never have been away if I had known what was going to happen that weekend": Hillenbrand to Catudal, November 4, 1977, quoted in Honoré Catudal, *Kennedy and the Berlin Wall Crisis* (Berlin: Berlin Verlag, 1980), p. 24; David Halberstam, intro. *The Kennedy Press Conferences* (New York: Carol M. Coleman, 1978), p. 132; Robert Estabrook memoranda, August 28, 1961.

24. Scholars argue the Berlin crisis in Catudal, *Kennedy and the Berlin Wall Crisis*, which does little to confirm a revisionist view of the President; Robert A. Slusser, *The Berlin Crisis of 1961* (Baltimore: Johns Hopkins University Press, 1971); Curtis Cate, *The Ides of August: The Berlin Wall Crisis 1961* (New York: M. Evans, 1978); Eleanor L. Dulles, *The Wall: A Tragedy in Three Acts* (Columbia: University of South Carolina Press, 1972); Willy Brandt—the Mayor of Berlin—*People and Politics: The Years 1960–1975* (Boston: Little, Brown, 1978); Harold Macmillan, *At the End of the Day, 1961–63* (London: Macmillan, 1975). For an unfavorable view, see Thomas G. Paterson, "Bearing the Burden: A Critical Look at JFK's Foreign Policy," *Virginia Quarterly Review*, Vol. 54 (Spring 1978), pp. 193–212.

25. Kenneth P. O'Donnell and David F. Powers with Joe McCarthy, *"Johnny, We Hardly Knew Ye"* (Boston: Little, Brown, 1972), p. 176; Cate, *The Ides of August*, pp. 405–6.

26. Glenn T. Seaborg, *Kennedy and the Test-Ban Treaty* (Berkeley: University of California Press, 1983); Boxes 4 and 5, NSF, LBJL.

27. Lucius D. Clay, JFKL-OH; Walt Whitman Rostow, JFKL-OH; Kennedy to Clay, telegram, March 1, 1962, Box 29, President's Office Files, JFKL. FitzSimons, *The Kennedy Doctrine*, p. 123.

28. Standard works on the Cuba (the missiles were not Cuban) missile crisis abound. There are the fine chapters in Arthur Schlesinger, Jr., *A Thousand Days* (Boston: Houghton Mifflin, 1965) and in *Robert F. Kennedy and His Times* (Boston: Houghton Mifflin, 1978). Other studies include Graham Allison, *Essence of Decision* (Boston: Little, Brown, 1971); Elie Abel, *The Missile Crisis* (Philadelphia: Lippincott, 1968); David Detzer, *The Brink* (New York: Thomas Y. Crowell, 1979); Herbert Dinerstein, *The Making of a Missile Crisis: October 1962* (Baltimore: Johns Hopkins University Press, 1976); and Abram Chayes, *The Cuban Missile Crisis* (New York: Oxford University Press, 1974). Irving L. Janis is perceptive in "The Cuban Missile Crisis," *Victims of Groupthink*, pp. 138–66.

29. Thomas Powers, *The Man Who Kept the Secrets* (New York: Alfred A. Knopf, 1979); Detzer, *The Brink*, p. 31.

30. A striking essay on the missile crisis appeared in the fall 1983 *Political Science Quarterly*: Richard N. Lebow, "The Cuban Missile Crisis: Reading the Lessons Correctly," Vol. 98, pp. 431–58. Barton Bernstein's recent articles on Cuba employ excellent scholarship but make an interpretation different from this book's; according to Bernstein, it was not only Khrushchev but Kennedy who was reckless in the matter of the missiles: "The Cuban Missile Crisis: Trading the Jupiters in Turkey?" *Political Science Quarterly*, Vol. 95 (Spring 1980), pp. 97–125; "Kennedy and Ending the Missile Crisis: Bombers, Inspection, and the No Invasion Pledge," *Foreign Service Journal*, Vol. 56 (July 1979), pp. 8–12; "Their Finest Hour?" *Correspondent*, Vol. 32 (August 1964), pp. 119–21. "The Cuban Missile Crisis," *Reflections on the Cold War*, eds. Lynn Miller and Ronald Pruessen (Philadelphia: Temple University Press, 1974), pp. 111–42; "The Week We Almost Went to War," *Bulletin of the Atomic Scientists*, Vol. 32 (February 1976), pp. 13–21. James Nathan wrote a sharply critical article in the mid-1970s: "The Missile Crisis: His Finest Hour Now?," *World Politics*, Vol. 27 (January 1975), pp. 256–80.

31. White House tapes, October 16, 1962, 11:50 A.M.–12:57 P.M.; October 16, 1962, 630–7:55 P.M. The admirable story of Stevenson's work in the Kennedy administration is told in John Bartlow Martin, *Adlai Stevenson and the World* (Garden City: Doubleday, 1976).

Cuba, Box 36, NSF, JFKL; VP Security files, Cuba, LBJL; Box 42, Sorensen Papers.

32. Lippmann's famous column appeared in the *Washington Post* on October 25, 1962; details on Lippmann's highly independent views of the Kennedy administration may be found in his papers at Yale University and in Ronald Steel, *Walter Lippmann and the American Century* (Boston: Little, Brown, 1980), pp. 521–43.

33. Kennedy was quoted on NBC-TV's excellent but now defunct news program "Overnight," October 27, 1983.

34. The most comprehensive recent book on Vietnam stresses Kennedy's indecisiveness: Stanley Karnow, *Vietnam: A History* (New York: Viking Press, 1983), pp. 247–348. Many of the quotations employed in the next paragraphs are to be found in Karnow's *Vietnam* or in the important, sometimes superb omnibus study on Vietnam, David Halberstam, *The Best and the Brightest* (New York: Random House, 1972). Halberstam is surprisingly gentle with Kennedy, but his account of McNamara is scathing (pp. 214ff.).

35. *The Pentagon Papers* (New York: Bantam Books, 1971), Vol. II, p. 653.

36. Roswell Gilpatric observes about Vietnam in his oral history that Kennedy "evidenced from the beginning a sense of frustration, exasperation about everything that seemed to come up": JFKL-OH; *NYT*, September 6, 1963, April 9, 1963, April 14, 1963; Roger Hilsman, JFKL-OH; O'Donnell, *"Johnny,"* p. 110.

37. A conversation of August 15, 1963, between the President and Lodge is among the five White House tapes lost between the time they left the care of the President's secretary, Evelyn Lincoln (and the custody of the Kennedy family), and the time of their deposit at the Kennedy Presidential Library. The other four missing tapes concern the missile crisis and the test ban negotiations with the Soviet Union in May and June 1963. Lodge gives a simplified version of the story in *The Storm Has Many Eyes* (New York: W. W. Norton, 1973).

38. I. F. Stone, *In a Time of Torment* (New York: Random House, 1967), p. 14.

39. Maxwell Taylor observes in his oral history: "I might say that President Kennedy was very cool on the subject of all nuclear weapons. He felt that we had more than enough of all types," JFKL. Taylor's own account of this period is entitled *Swords and Plowshares* (New York: W. W. Norton, 1972).

Chapter 5
KENNEDY LIBERALISM

1. Tom Wicker, *JFK and LBJ* (New York: William Morrow, 1968), p. 46.

2. Box 1, Arthur Holcombe Papers, JFKL.

3. John Neubauer, "The Camera and JFK," Vol. 61, *Photoplay* (November 1967), pp. 88–104, 144–45; Larry Spruill, "Photojournalism and the Civil Rights Movement," unpublished doctoral dissertation, SUNY at Stony Brook, 1983.

4. Tom Wicker's version of the House Rules fight is useful for suggesting the problems Kennedy had with Congress. *JFK and LBJ*, *passim*. Alan Shank, *Presidential Policy Leadership: Kennedy and Social Welfare* (Lanham: University Press of America, 1980), Daniel Knapp and Kenneth Polk study "reform politics in the Kennedy Administration," in *Scouting the War on Poverty* (Lexington, Mass.: D. C. Heath, 1971). Allen Matusow has an excellent chapter on the origins of the war on poverty in *The Unraveling of America: A History of Liberalism in the 1960s* (New York: Harper & Row, 1984), pp. 97–127.

5. The standard work on Kennedy and civil rights is Carl Brauer, *John F. Kennedy and the Second Reconstruction* (New York: Columbia University Press, 1977); it is a sound, scholarly study that gives the Kennedy brothers every possible consideration. Victor Navasky's *Kennedy Justice* is standard on Robert Kennedy's career in Justice (New York: Atheneum, 1971).

6. Edwin Guthman, *We Band of Brothers* (New York: Harper & Row, 1971), p. 169; Harris Wofford, *Of Kennedys and Kings* (New York: Farrar, Straus, Giroux, 1980), *passim*. An unfriendly source quotes Kennedy as remarking to newsmen in Boston during the 1950s: "It was so hot that even the niggers went to the beach." Victor Lasky, *It Didn't Start with Watergate* (New York: Dial, 1976), p. 14.

7. Marshall, *Federalism and Civil Rights* (New York: Columbia University Press, 1974); Theodore C. Sorensen covers many of Marshall's arguments in *Decision-Making in the White House* (New York: Columbia University Press, 1963). Justice Department attorneys reveal their conservative legal temperament in many places, including the oral histories Marshall made in collaboration with Robert Kennedy. For criticisms of Nicholas Katzenbach, for example,

see Jack T. Conway's oral history (Conway was an aide to Walter Reuther), JFKL-OH.

8. Eugene Rostow of Yale Law School wrote Marshall, "The risk of allowing Patterson or Faubus to seem to have a victory, or a partial victory, is very great": May 25, 1961, Box 4, Marshall Papers, JFKL.

9. Box 319, NSF, JFKL. A good published source on this phase of the civil rights movement is Howell Raines, ed., *My Soul Is Rested* (New York: G. P. Putnam's, 1977).

10. Robert F. Kennedy, JFKL-OH; Wofford, *Of Kennedys and Kings*, p. 156; *The Pentagon Papers* (New York: Bantam Books, 1971), p. 84.

11. The administration received plenty of warnings about appointing segregationist judges. Virginia Durr, Justice Hugo Black's sister, wrote Marshall from Montgomery: "What makes the South so dangerous is that the Law itself has become Lawless. . . . [The] real decision will be made in the nature of the new District Attorney and the new Federal Judges that will be appointed by the Kennedy Administration": April 27, 1961, Box 4, Marshall Papers, JFKL.

12. Kennedy is quoted by Lee G. White, a special counsel in the White House and an old friend of Sorensen, JFKL-OH. Donald Lord points out that when the two most conservative members of the Civil Rights Commission resigned, Kennedy replaced them with two outspoken defenders of civil rights; he also appointed Berl I. Bernard, another advanced liberal, as staff director of the CRC: *John F. Kennedy* (Woodbury: Barron's Educational Series, 1977), pp. 133–72. Wofford, *Of Kennedys and Kings*, p. 163.

13. White House tapes, September 30, 1962, JFKL; Judge J. P. Coleman OH, Mitchell Library, Mississippi State University.

14. White House tapes, September 30, 1962, JFKL.

15. White House tapes, September 30, 1962, JFKL; Brauer, *John F. Kennedy and the Second Reconstruction*, pp. 231–41, 295–97.

16. Robert L. Peabody, *The Ford-Halleck Minority Leadership Contest* (New York: McGraw-Hill, 1966); Henry Z. Scheele, *Charlie Halleck* (New York: Exposition Press, 1966).

17. Norbert Schlei, JFKL-OH; Wofford, *Of Kennedys and Kings*, p. 174.

18. White House tapes, July 30, 1962, to September 30, 1963, *passim*, JFKL; Arthur Okun succinctly informed James Tobin on June 1, 1962, "The President has been educated out of his previous thinking on fiscal policy": Box 4, Walter Heller Papers, JFKL. The Seymour Harris Papers are an excellent source on Kennedy's changing

economic thinking, JFKL; Michael Harrington, "A Reactionary Keynesianism," *Encounter*, Vol. 26 (March 1966), pp. 50–52.

19. Hobart Rowen, *The Free Enterprisers: Kennedy, Johnson and the Business Establishment* (New York: G. P. Putnam's, 1964).

20. Jim F. Heath mentions difficulties plaguing the steel industry in *John F. Kennedy and the Business Community* (Chicago: University of Chicago Press, 1969), pp. 68–83.

21. Theodore Sorensen, *The Kennedy Legacy* (New York: Macmillan, 1979), p. 211.

22. The asasssination literature seems endless. A recent interpretation denying the existence of a conspiracy is Jean Davison, *Oswald's Game* (New York: W. W. Norton, 1983). In support of the conspiracy interpretation is Michael L. Kurtz, *Crime of the Century: The Kennedy Assassination from a Historian's Perspective* (Knoxville: University of Tennessee Press, 1982); Kurtz relies to some extent on the work of Harold Weisberg.

23. Lasch, "The Life of Kennedy's Death," *Harper's*, Vol. 267 (October 1983), pp. 32–40; Lerner, *Ted and the Kennedy Legend* (New York: St. Martin's Press, 1980), p. 91.

24. FitzSimons, *The Kennedy Doctrine* (New York: Random House, 1982), p. 221; Vidal, "The Holy Family," *Esquire*, Vol. 67 (April 1977), pp. 99–103.

25. Wicker, *JFK and LBJ*, p. 78.

26. James MacGregor Burns, *The Deadlock of Democracy* (Englewood Cliffs: Prentice-Hall, 1963).

27. The left economist Robert Lekachman concludes, "Most reasonably impartial students of American tax history considered the reforms well conceived and well drawn. If enacted they promised to move the tax code measurably nearer justice and consistency": *The Age of Keynes* (New York: Vintage, 1968), pp. 277–78.

28. The Rovere article originally appeared in the November 30, 1963, *New Yorker* and is reprinted in Aïda DiPace Donald, ed., *John F. Kennedy and the New Frontier* (New York: Hill & Wang, 1966), pp. 247–54.

29. The oral histories of James K. Carr and of Clay Nunnerle are helpful on the environmental movement's beginnings under Kennedy, JFKL-OH. Secretary of the Interior Udall told Lewis Paper, "Kennedy was not terribly interested in natural resources and didn't really know much about the problems of conservation. . . . But I felt I had broad discretion to act, and he gave my efforts strong support": *The Promise and the Performance* (New York: Da Capo Press, 1975), p. 154.

Chapter 6
ROBERT KENNEDY: THE LEFTWARD JOURNEY

1. Though clearly overdefensive, Arthur Schlesinger, Jr., *Robert F. Kennedy and His Times* (Boston: Houghton Mifflin, 1978), is thorough and scholarly and by any measure a remarkably fine book.

2. Early biographical information on Robert Kennedy is available in Boxes 1 and 2 of the Robert F. Kennedy Papers, JFKL.

3. On Robert Kennedy's relationship with Senator Joe McCarthy, note particularly Edwin Guthman, *We Band of Brothers* (New York: Harper & Row, 1971), pp. 12–26. Schlesinger gives this and all other controversial RFK subjects detailed treatment: *Robert F. Kennedy*, pp. 103–25 and *passim*.

4. "RFK/Background," Box 47, National Files, Eugene J. McCarthy Papers, Georgetown University; Edwin R. Bayley, JFKL-OH.

5. Douglas, *Go East, Young Man* (New York: Random House, 1974); Douglas, JFKL-OH; RFK to Mrs. Henry Kelly, March 18, 1955, Box 3 and miscellaneous letters and diary, RFK Papers, JFKL; *NYT*, April 8, 1956.

6. Robert F. Kennedy, *The Enemy Within* (New York: Popular Library, 1960); John Bartlow Martin, *Jimmy Hoffa's Hot* (New York: Fawcett World, Crest, 1959); Pierre Salinger and John Seigenthaler, JFKL-OH.

7. Bickel, "Robert F. Kennedy: The Case Against Him for Attorney General," *New Republic*, Vol. 176 (January 9, 1961), pp. 17–20.

8. Hoffa, *The Trials of Jimmy Hoffa* (Chicago: H. Regnery, 1970), p. 108; Lisagor, JFKL-OH.

9. Some good sources on Robert Kennedy's role in 1960 are Paul B. Fay, *The Pleasure of His Company* (New York: Popular Library, 1966); Theodore C. Sorensen, *Kennedy* (New York: Harper & Row, 1965); Hubert Humphrey, *The Education of a Public Man* (Garden City: Doubleday, 1976); and Lawrence F. O'Brien, *No Final Victories* (Garden City: Doubleday, 1964).

10. Harold H. Martin, "The Amazing Kennedys," *Saturday Evening Post*, Vol. 230 (September 1, 1957), pp. 19–20, 40, 46–8.

11. Lonnie King, among other young civil rights workers, opposed Robert Kennedy's attempt to get more students to go to Mississippi to register blacks under the protection of marshals, and Jack

Newfield writes that as late as 1963 civil rights activists, he among them, thought as little of Robert Kennedy as southern governors did. Howell Raines, ed., *My Soul Is Rested* (New York: G. P. Putnam's, 1977), pp. 85–92, 228–29; Newfield, *Robert Kennedy: A Memoir* (New York: E. P. Dutton, 1969), p. 23; Guthman, *We Band of Brothers*, pp. 220–21. Victor Navasky's *Kennedy Justice* (New York: Atheneum, 1971) is the standard account.

12. Robert Kennedy gives his version of the Baldwin meeting in his oral history, JFKL-OH.

13. Gerald Gardner has written *Robert Kennedy in New York* (New York: Random House, 1965) on Kennedy's entrance into New York politics.

14. William Shannon explains Robert Kennedy's activities from 1964 to 1966 as simply a campaign for the presidency: *The Heir Apparent: Robert Kennedy and the Struggle for Power* (New York: Macmillan, 1967). Allard Lowenstein criticized a draft of Kennedy's South Africa speech, pushing the receptive senator leftward: David Halberstam, *The Unfinished Odyssey of Robert Kennedy* (New York: Random House, 1968), p. 7.

15. Arnold Weintraub, "The Public Statements and Speeches of Robert F. Kennedy on the Vietnam War Issue," unpublished doctoral dissertation, University of Nebraska, 1975; Craig W. Cutbirth, "A Strategic Perspective: Robert F. Kennedy's Dissent on the Vietnam War—1966 to 1968," unpublished doctoral dissertation, Bowling Green State University, 1976; Schlesinger, *Robert F. Kennedy*, pp. 721–33.

16. Newfield, *Robert Kennedy*, pp. 87–109.

17. David J. Garrow, *The FBI and Martin Luther King, Jr.* (New York: Penguin Books, 1983), pp. 91–8; Theodore C. Sorensen, *The Kennedy Legacy* (New York: Macmillan, 1969).

18. Ethel Kennedy's Marymount College is in Tarrytown, New York. Newfield gives the best account of this incident: *Robert Kennedy*, p. 140.

19. *Ibid.*, p. 82.

20. Robert F. Kennedy, JFKL-OH.

21. Jules Witcover gives the closest account of Robert Kennedy's last campaign: *85 Days* (New York: G. P. Putnam's, 1969).

22. Frederick C. Sanders, Jr., argues that McCarthy's cool, nonpolitical style came from a monastic interlude early in his life and from his Roman Catholicism. He conceived of the universe as governed by a moral order which it is the duty of an individual to obey. He understood that imposing a moral order takes time, and it was

easy for him to believe that his educative statement about the war was his duty, and his only duty, to that moral order: "The Rhetorical Strategies of Senator Robert Kennedy and Senator Eugene J. McCarthy in the 1968 Presidential Primaries," unpublished doctoral dissertation, University of Oregon, 1973, pp. 40–44.

23. In the primaries McCarthy would not seek help from established political leaders to the extent that Kennedy did, and by the account of student activists, decentralization in the ranks became disorganization. Among the many books on the McCarthy campaign are the senator's own *The Year of the People* (Garden City: Doubleday, 1969); his wife Abigail McCarthy, *Private Faces, Public Faces* (Philadelphia: Curtis reprint, 1972); Richard T. Stout, *People* (New York: Harper & Row, 1969); Penn Kimball, *Bobby Kennedy and the the New Politics* (Englewood Cliffs: Prentice-Hall, 1968); Arthur Herzog, *McCarthy for President* (New York: Viking, 1969). Ben Stavis comments on RFK's affinity for the pros on p. 66 of *We Were the Campaign: New Hampshire to Chicago for McCarthy* (Boston: Beacon Press, 1969).

24. Halberstam, *Unfinished Odyssey*, pp. 73–123.

25. George Plimpton has edited often beautifully spoken oral histories on RFK conducted by Jean Stein. *American Journey: The Times of Robert Kennedy* (New York: Harcourt Brace Jovanovich, 1970.

26. Ronald E. Lee, "The Rhetoric of the 'New Politics,'" unpublished doctoral dissertation, University of Iowa, 1981.

Chapter 7
EDWARD MOORE KENNEDY: THE HEIR

1. For materials on Edward Kennedy, scholars must direct themselves to two decades of the *Congressional Record* and the voluminous House and Senate *Hearings*. This chapter has relied heavily on James MacGregor Burns, *Edward Kennedy and the Camelot Legacy* (New York: W. W. Norton, 1976). Other interesting biographies of the surviving son include Murray B. Levin and T. A. Repak, *Edward Kennedy* (Boston: Houghton Mifflin, 1980); Theodore Lippman, Jr., *Senator Ted Kennedy* (New York: W. W. Norton, 1976); William Honan, *Ted Kennedy* (New York: Quadrangle Books, 1972); and Burton Hersh, *The Education of Edward Kennedy* (New York: William Morrow, 1972).

2. John F. Kennedy, ed., *As We Remember Joe* (Cambridge, Mass.: privately printed at the university press, 1945), p. 50.

3. Edward, with a candor that overcomes modesty, reports in *The Fruitful Bough* (privately printed, 1965) that Robert describes him as more congenial and gracious than Jack. Feldman's interesting remark is in *Time*, Vol. 98 (November 29, 1971), p. 18.

4. Burns seems to have telephoned for information the headmaster at every private school Edward ever attended: *Edward Kennedy, passim.*

5. Jack was to remark that WASPs disapproved strongly of cheating on exams, preferring to steal from banks: *NYT*, October 24, 1962.

6. Arthur Holcombe Papers, JFKL.

7. Nancy Gager Clinch makes much ado about the speeding offenses: *The Kennedy Neurosis* (New York: Grosset & Dunlap, 1973).

8. Theodore Lippman, Jr., portrays the Smith arrangement as less firm than it has usually been presented as being: *Senator Ted Kennedy*, p. 176ff.

9. The McCormack primary is the principal subject of Murray B. Levin, *Kennedy Campaigning* (Boston: Beacon Press, 1966).

10. There is an unpublished doctoral dissertation on Kennedy's 1970 campaign: Andrew M. McKenzie, "Senator Edward M. Kennedy and the 1970 Massachusetts Senatorial Campaign," Ohio University, 1971.

11. Lester David is a professional writer who probably has more information at his command about the Kennedys than anyone else. Among other books and articles, he has written *Joan: The Reluctant Kennedy* (New York: Funk & Wagnalls, 1974).

12. *Congressional Record*, May 11, 1965, p. 10081; May 13, 1965, pp. 7883–84.

13. *Ibid.*, September 4, 1968, pp. 25577–79; May 20, 1969, p. 13003.

14. *Washington Post*, January 4, 1969.

15. Jack Olsen, *The Bridge at Chappaquiddick* (Boston: Little, Brown, 1970). The famous essay by Robert Sherrill on Chappaquiddick, "Chappaquiddick + 5," appeared in the *New York Times* on August 25, 1975, and the author later published a nasty enlargement of the essay as a book: *The Last Kennedy* (New York: Dial, 1976). An even more vicious, as well as a more pretentious, piece is Lewis Lapham, "Edward Kennedy and the Romance of Death," *Harper's*, Vol. 259 (December 1979), pp. 33–41.

16. *Congressional Record*, February 4, 1969, pp. 1362–84, 2499–2500.

17. Murray B. Levin and T. A. Repak, *Edward Kennedy: The Myth of Leadership* (Boston: Houghton Mifflin, 1980); Edward Kennedy, *In Critical Condition: The Crisis in America's Health Care* (New York: Simon & Schuster, 1972).

18. *Congressional Record*, June 29, 1975, pp. 12563–64.

19. *Ibid.*, November 14, 1975, pp. 20058–60.

20. *Time*, Vol. 98 (November 29, 1971), p. 18.

21. See William Leuchtenburg on Edward Kennedy's moving to the left in 1980: *In the Shadow of FDR* (Ithaca: Cornell University Press, 1983), pp. 202–6.

22. Kempton's column appeared in *Newsday*, December 1, 1983.

EPILOGUE: A NOTE ON LIBERAL IDEOLOGY

1. Lowi, *The End of Liberalism: Ideology, Policy and the Crisis of Public Authority* (New York: W. W. Norton, 1969).

2. Trilling, *The Middle of the Journey* (New York: Viking, 1947).

3. Schlesinger, *The Vital Center: The Politics of Freedom* (Boston: Houghton Mifflin, 1949); *The Politics of Hope* (Boston: Houghton Mifflin, 1963).

4. Fairlie, *The Kennedy Promise: The Politics of Expectation* (Garden City: Doubleday, 1973).

5. Clinch, *The Kennedy Neurosis* (New York: Grosset & Dunlap, 1973).

6. Wills, *The Kennedy Imprisonment: A Meditation on Power* (Boston: Little, Brown, 1982).

7. Will, *Statecraft as Soulcraft: What Government Does* (New York: Simon & Schuster, 1983).

Index

isolationism, 43ff.
Israel, 103
Ives, Irving, 198, 200

Jackson, Henry M., 91
Jackson, Mississippi, 166
Javits, Jacob, 207
Jefferson, Thomas, 252
Jews, 29ff., 35, 212; *see also*
anti-Semitism
Joad family, 250
Johnson, Andrew, 57
Johnson, Gerald W., quoted 88
Johnson, Lyndon, 78, 102, 117,
174, 181, 202, 205, 210, 218,
235, 267; and Berlin, 123–24;
and civil rights, 167; and
memory of John Kennedy, 158;
at 1956 convention, 61; and
Robert Kennedy after 1963, 207;
selection as Vice-President,
85–88; and Vietnam War, 146
Joint Chiefs of Staff, 107, 113–14,
130ff., 142
Joseph, Peter, 158
Journalism, and liberals, chapter 3
passim; see also liberalism
Judiciary, and judges appointed by
John Kennedy, 166
Jupiter missiles, 129–37 *passim*
Justice Department, under Robert
Kennedy, 162–79, chapters 4
and 5 *passim*
Joseph P. Kennedy, Jr. (destroyer),
41, 194

Katanga, 117
Katzenbach, Nicholas, 165, 171,
211
Keating, Kenneth, 207, 219
Kefauver, Estes, 61, 78, 198
Kempton, Murray, quoted 246
Kennan, George F., 7, 107
Kennedy, Edward M., 3, 12, 44,
76, 202, 206, 265; busing, 180,
241–42; Chappaquiddick,

237–39; cheating at Harvard,
227–28; crime program, 242;
deregulation, 203; human rights,
240–41; law school at Virginia,
228–29; and liberals, 240;
medical program, 240; plane
crash, 233; in presidential
campaign of 1980, 244–45;
quoted, 226, 228, 230, 240; in
Senate, 230–37ff.; and Vietnam
War, 236–41; youth, 225–27
Kennedy, Ethel, 195
Kennedy, Eunice, 32, 55
Kennedy Family, The (Dineen),
23
Kennedy Imprisonment, The
(Wills), 265
Kennedy, Jacqueline, 53–54, 185
Kennedy, Joan, 229–30, 233–34
Kennedy, John F., 14, 224–25,
246, 247, 264, 265, 267, 269,
271; and Addison's disease,
50–51, 87, 96; at American
University, 139; assassination
and death of, 184–92; and
Berlin, 117–23; Berlin speech,
124, 139; and civil rights
movement, 151–86; and cold
war, 4, 6–8, 49, 50, chapters 1,
3, 4; at convention of 1956,
61–62; early reading, 33, 101–2;
and economic policy, 180–83;
in election of 1960, 81–95; *see
also* elections of 1956, 1958,
1960, 1962; and federal judiciary, 166; and foreign aid,
75, 117; foreign policy, 98–149,
see also cold war; and guerrilla
warfare, 98ff.; and Harvard,
chapter 2 *passim*, 47, 55; in
House of Representatives, 47–52;
Jewish vote, 53; and Lyndon
Johnson in 1960, 85–88;
journalism career, 46; and
Khrushchev, 139, *see also*
Khrushchev, Nikita; and labor

DAVID BURNER was born in upstate New York in 1937. He received his A.B. from Hamilton College and earned his Ph.D. in American history at Columbia University. He has taught at Colby College and Oakland University, and is presently professor of history at the State University of New York at Stony Brook. Mr. Burner, the recipient of fellowships from the Guggenheim Foundation and the National Endowment for the Humanities, is the author of *The Politics of Provincialism* and *Herbert Hoover*, as well as several textbooks. He and his family live in St. James, New York.

THOMAS R. WEST was born in Washington, D.C., in 1936. He earned his B.A. at Princeton University and his Ph.D. at Columbia University. Mr. West has taught at Michigan State University and Hunter College and is currently associate professor of history at The Catholic University of America. He is the author of *Flesh of Steel: Literature and the Machine in American Culture* and *Nature, Community, and Will: A Study in Literary and Social Thought*. He makes his home in Washington, D.C.